Psychotherapy Today

Other books by the same editor

Advances in educational psychology I
(Eds V. P. Varma and W. D. Wall)
Advances in educational psychology II
(Eds, V. P. Varma and M. L. Kellmer Pringle)
Stresses in children
(Ed V. P. Varma)
Published by The University of London Press

Psychotherapy Today

Edited by

Ved Varma

Constable London

First published in Great Britain 1974
by Constable and Company Ltd
10 Orange Street London WC2H 7EG
Introductory material copyright © 1974 by Ved Varma

ISBN 0 09 458910 0 hardback
0 09 459430 9 paperback

Set in Monotype Garamond
Printed in Great Britain by The Anchor Press Ltd,
and bound by Wm. Brendon & Son Ltd,
both of Tiptree, Essex

To my mother and father,
with all my affection and esteem

Ved Varma

Contents

Introduction

British psychotherapists have made a contribution second to none in handling and treating emotional sicknesses; as Malcolm Pines says elsewhere in the book: 'rising living standards in poor countries often precede and may eventually lead to revolution; similar conditions in more advanced western societies lead to a demand for psychotherapy; the hungry mind replaces the empty belly; the emotional sickness shows'. Despite this and all the other work that has been done by them, it is curious that there is no comprehensive survey available in book form which is not only practical but jargon free.

There are many useful accounts of psychotherapeutic help in relevant journals but these are usually inaccessible to intelligent lay readers; in addition, such literature and books do not usually make *rapprochements* among various disciplines and therefore do not cover the main kinds of therapies in common use. There are also admirable full-scale books by American authors; however, these present a somewhat different attitude to psychotherapy and its uses from that largely current here.

Therefore my colleagues and I have attempted to bridge this important gap. Briefly, the book recaptures the long history of psychotherapy and aims to testify our admiration of most men and women pioneers in this field. The articles, by leading and practising psychotherapists, build into a coherent statement of richness and variety; in our understanding of psychotherapy with pre-school children and adults, as well as Freudian, Jungian, Adlerian, Kleinian, behavioural, drug, social, religious, educational, group, short-term, and day psychotherapy; the fascinating interaction of psychotherapy outside the National Health Service with that under it – and the significance of training in dynamic aspects of psychotherapy. The various chapters follow an imaginative and harmonious course and discuss the whole range of psychotherapy past, present and, as far as possible, future. Concise and telling case histories, suitably disguised, illustrate themes wherever appropriate.

The authors themselves come from a wide spectrum of ages, disciplines and experience, and from many parts of the British Isles. Therefore the book is truly representative of psychotherapy today and should prove to have something enjoyable for every intelligent lay reader and important for the expert. In addition, the reader may also find it a subject of lively contention; however, it must be said that the views expressed in the book are personal to the authors and in no way represent any organization or employer.

I hope that every reader will take the book for what it is worth and compare it with the fruits of his own wisdom and experience; and that each contributor, in acknowledging the stimulus derived from its contents and acting upon this if possible, may conclude that all the authors have considered their significant issues with detached scrutiny. Finally, may those who read this book come to realize that the world belongs to those who work for the suffering.

The Editor would like to thank the reader for taking the trouble to read this book. As regards my colleagues and contributors, it is impossible to express my deep gratitude in words – it is implied in working in partnership with them in this context.

Ved Varma

Psychotherapy in the past, present and future

Lionel Kreeger

Psychotherapy in the past

The origins of modern dynamic psychotherapy may be traced back to primitive societies.[1] For example, there is evidence that the Shamans of certain Syberian tribes practised hypnotism. Primitive disease theories include such concepts as loss of the soul, sorcery, breach of taboo and spirit intrusion. As a result of very simple cause and effect reasoning, therapy included the finding and restoration of the soul, counter-magic, confession and propitiation, and exorcism. Parallels with modern psychotherapeutic techniques may be observed. The Greeks, whilst taking a basically physiological view of disease, were very much aware of psychological disturbances. Hippocrates, who lived in the fourth century BC was the first layman to become a professional doctor and was thus the father of medicine. One of his many contributions was to introduce psychiatric problems into medicine. Galen (130–200 AD) wrote a treatise entitled, *On the Passions of the Soul*. He taught that to master one's passions, the first step is to abstain from the crude expression of emotional outburst, and secondly to find a mentor, a wise and old counsellor who could point out your defects and dispense advice.

The Hindu culture also developed an elaborate medical system in which mental disorders remained largely the domain of priestly metaphysics. In other primitive societies, the technique of ceremonial healing was evolved in which re-enactment of the causative trauma occurred and with the aid of the gods of their society, cure ensued. Again one may acknowledge the similarity to the modern technique of psychodrama, a specialized form of psychotherapy involving the production of a drama based on the experiences of one patient, but enacted by a group, each person taking part in the reconstruction of the experience.

The emergence of dynamic psychiatry occurred towards the end of the eighteenth century, through the influence of, and rivalry between, Gassner and Mesmer. Johann Gassner (1727–1779) was an Austrian priest who obtained great notoriety for his spiritual healing. His main technique was that of exorcism, the removal of the effects of the devil.

Franz Anton Mesmer (1734–1815) was a German physician who initially studied theology but then turned to philosophy, later to law, and only finally to medicine. At the age of forty he treated one patient by making her swallow an iron preparation and then attaching magnets to her body. A remarkable cure ensued; and from this Mesmer developed his concept of 'Animal Magnetism'. Through extraordinary successes with patients, Mesmer concluded that he had some strange, mysterious power within himself which made healing possible. He believed that his own body contained certain magnetic streams which were the principal factor in obtaining these extraordinary cures. He had first to establish a rapport, a kind of 'tuning in' with his patient. Mesmer grouped his disciples into a society through which eventually it was realized that unknown psychological forces were at work. The scene was set for yet further developments.

In the early part of the nineteenth century, artificial somnambulism was the chief method of gaining access to the unconscious mind. This was a technique in which a state of altered consciousness similar to sleep was induced in the patient. In 1843, Braid introduced the term hypnotism for this method. Although used initially as a form of heightened suggestion, numerous observations were made during the use of this technique which led to an increasing interest in the unconscious mind, and to a reappraisal of certain psychiatric illnesses, such as hysteria (one type of neurosis in which repression and dissociation occur together, with a tendency to convert psychological stresses into physical symptoms.) New models of the mind were developed and with them an upsurge of dynamic psychiatric thinking.

In the year 1856, two men were born who were to have a profound effect upon psychiatry. One was Emil Kraepelin, who was destined to introduce a rational classification of mental illness, for example the division of the psychoses into two main groups: that of *dementia praecox* (today called schizophrenia, a form of mental illness characterized by loss of contact with reality, thought disorder, delusional ideas, and hallucinations) and manic depressive illness (in which periods of depression and elation follow each other in a cyclical form). The other was Sigmund Freud, the father of psychoanalysis. Pierre Janet was born three years later than Freud but in fact his contributions on dynamic psychology ante-date Freud's early papers. For example, the word 'subconscious' was coined by Janet.

Sigmund Freud (1856–1939)

He founded the school of psychoanalysis. In the early stages of his professional development he functioned mainly as a neurologist and employed hypnotic techniques in the treatment of his neurotic patients. He spent some months in Paris studying under Charcot, but became increasingly dissatisfied with the hypnotic method. His imagination was fired on learning of the experiences of his colleague, Josef Breuer with his patient Anna O, a young Viennese woman who developed a severe hysterical condition with numerous physical manifestations such as paralysis of her limbs. Breuer hypnotized her repeatedly, and in the hypnotic trances his patient was able to recall hitherto repressed memories, particularly concerning her relationship with her father whom she nursed through a severe illness until his death. Transient improvements occurred in her symptomatology with each new revelation. Eventually, however, she developed a phantom pregnancy and entered the throes of hysterical childbirth. At this point Breuer became overwhelmed with the emotional complexity of their relationship and terminated the treatment.

In 1895, Breuer and Freud published their book, *Studies in Hysteria* and from this Freud went on to make his monumental contributions to the understanding of the human mind.

Freud began with an attempt to build a new theory of the neuroses, and in 1897 embarked on the heroic task of his own self-analysis. In 1900 he published his book on *The Interpretation of Dreams*, regarded by some as his most important work. In 1905 he published his *Three Essays on The Theory of Sexuality*, tracing the origins of adult sexuality back into childhood. To quote from Ernest Jones' biography of Freud, 'It was this publication that brought the maximum of odium on his name; much of it still remains especially among the uneducated. The book was felt to be a calumny on the innocence of the nursery.' After many years of modifications to his theoretical formulations, in 1923 Freud published his essay *The Ego and The Id*. This structural theory of the mind represented the culmination of his creative thinking. He conceived the mind as having three main areas: the Id as the unorganized, unconscious source of all the drives or instincts; the Ego being that part of the mental structure mainly conscious, which is organized and rational; and the Super-Ego which is allied to conscience. Apart from the development of psychoanalysis as a form of treatment and its theoretical constructs, Freud also made many contributions to sociology, religion and literature.

In the early days of the psychoanalytic movement, Freud had many followers and associates. Two of the most eminent of these, Jung and Adler, eventually broke away from him to form their own independent schools.

Carl Gustav Jung (1875–1961)
Jung left the psychoanalytic movement. He no longer called himself a psychoanalyst, but instead founded the school of analytical psychology. Jung had an intense preoccupation with religion, symbols and myths. He was concerned with the concept of archetypes, the symbolic representatives of the collective unconscious. For example, the soul archetype he divided into the anima, and the animus. In man, the anima assumed the form of an ideal feminine figure and in a woman, the animus the form of a masculine one.

Alfred Adler (1870–1937)

Adler founded the school of individual psychology with the basic concepts of the inferiority complex and organ inferiority. Adler made significant contributions to education, and sociology, and some of his followers were among the earliest in this country to use group psychotherapy. The work of both Jung and Adler is discussed in greater detail later.

In the 1930s before the outbreak of the Second World War, and as a result of Nazi persecution, a large number of psychoanalysts left their countries to live in America or in England. In the United States many psychoanalysts developed their own particular theoretical concepts. Harry Stack Sullivan was concerned with a pragmatic approach with considerable flexibility in response on the part of the therapist. Erich Fromm focused on psychoanalysis in the perspective of the social sciences with individuation in the social context as an important principle. Karen Horney developed the holistic approach with the aim of regaining spontaneity and finding the courage to be oneself. She also published a book on self-analysis. Wilhelm Reich developed the technique of character analysis, but also deviated from the psychoanalytic movement by his application of orgone therapy, based on his belief that he had discovered a previously unknown form of 'Orgone Energy', allied to the feelings of tension and excitation which are discharged following orgasm.

Anna Freud

She accompanied her father to Britain in June 1938. She continued her work as a psychoanalyst making significant contributions particularly to child analysis and in the field of ego defences. One of her most important works, published in 1937, was *The Ego and The Mechanisms of Defence*, largely responsible for the development of the School of Ego-Psychology both here and in the United States. Ernest Jones dedicated his biography of Freud to her: 'To Anna Freud, true daughter of an immortal sire'.

Melanie Klein

Another important figure, Melanie Klein, also settled in Britain. She too, was mainly concerned with child analysis, but developed her own particular theoretical formulations concerning the experiences of the first six months of life. She attracted many followers and this led to the formation of the Kleinian group within the British Psychoanalytic Society.

Let us now turn away from the purely psychoanalytic movement to look briefly at other approaches. Adolf Meyer in the United States applied himself to the task of creating a science of man with the integration of both psychological and biological factors. His method was termed the psychobiological approach, in which longitudinal studies were made on the behaviour of an individual in his social setting. In the treatment situation combined methods were employed, utilizing both physical and psychological therapies concurrently, as indicated by the needs of the individual patient. Carl Rogers applied himself to the task of psychotherapeutic counselling, a technique he termed 'Client-centred Psychotherapy', in which the therapist remained non-directive and focused more on the reality of the relationship instead of attempting to analyse the transference (the process by which a patient displaces on to his therapist feelings and ideas deriving from previous figures in his life). Eric Berne was concerned with transactional analysis, a games theory which applies itself to the manipulative communications that occur between individuals, particularly in a family situation. Moreno worked mainly with groups, developing the technique of psychodrama. Lewis Wolberg employed hypnosis as a method of gaining rapid access to the unconscious, the technique of 'Hypnotherapy'.

In Switzerland, Ludwig Binswanger was an important figure in the development of the existential approach, based on the philosophical writings of the existential school of Kierkegaard and Heidegger. The method of dasein analysis is concerned with man being 'in the world' with the focus on the reality of his existence, and the attempt to help him realize his full potential. In Britain, Ronald Laing and David Cooper have continued working with the existential method.

Gestalt psychology

Gestalt psychology has been applied to psychotherapeutic treatment, particularly in the field of group work, one of its main proponents having been Kurt Lewin. Its basic theory is that the whole of an image is perceived, rather than its parts, and that the gestalt, or total perceptual experience, is greater than the sum of the parts. Cybernetics, the study of messages and communication in man, based on the functioning of electronic machines, has also made valuable contributions, particularly in the concept of feedback, a technique utilized particularly in training groups, to help the individual perceive himself as others see him.

Behaviour therapy was developed from the original studies of Pavlov on conditioning. It differs significantly from psychoanalytic theories in stressing that disordered behaviour is the result of learned responses, rather than arising from intra-psychic conflict. Specific techniques have been applied to a variety of conditions, for example desensitization in anxiety states, and aversion therapy in alcoholism and sexual deviations. Desensitization is a method of a gradual reduction in the intensity of emotional reaction to a particular stimulus, such as a fear of insects. This is usually obtained by relaxation together with a very gentle exposure to the stimulus increasing from one treatment session to the next. Aversion therapy, on the other hand, employs unpleasant stimuli such as an electric shock to condition the patient against his symptom.

Group psychotherapy

The development of group psychotherapy in the 1930s occurred both in America and Britain. Moreno introduced the term 'group psychotherapy' in 1931 and Kurt Lewin the term 'group dynamics' in 1939. Slavson, Wender and Schilder applied psychoanalytic concepts to small groups. In England, S. H. Foulkes was employing group methods before the Second World War, but it was particularly with the experiences of wartime that group psychotherapy came into its own. After the War, Maxwell Jones created the Social Rehabilitation Unit, later to be called the Henderson Hospital, organized as a therapeutic community for the treatment of personality disorders. Joshua Bierer founded the first day hospital. The utilization of the therapeutic community approach in mental hospitals and psychiatric units, together with discoveries and advances in drug therapy led to important changes and improvements in the psychiatric services. There has been increasing interest shown in family and marital relationships, and the application of psychotherapeutic techniques for the treatment of these social units has had an important influence on recent developments.

Psychotherapy in the present

Having surveyed the evolution of the psychotherapeutic method, let us now turn to the current situation. Without doubt psychotherapy has established itself as a valid and vital contribution to the treatment of psychological disorders. In the field of psychiatry each individual psychiatrist will have his own personal orientation with regard to the balance between a physical approach and a psychological one. Some will tend towards a more organic view of mental illness with a strong conviction of the physical aetiology (causation) and of the value of physical methods of treatment. Others will align themselves at the other end of the spectrum, favouring a more dynamic approach both in the understanding of causation in psychological illness and its treatment. The majority will, naturally, take up some central position between the extremes. The demand for psychotherapeutic facilities will vary from one unit to another, but in practical terms it is quite clear that there is a pressing need for the expansion of those facilities. In general medicine the awareness on the part of general practitioners of the psychological problems of their patients again increases the requirements for this particular form of treatment. There is an increasing emphasis on psychological factors in training of medical students and this will lead to a greater sophistication in their attitudes. The incidence of a neurotic disturbance amongst student populations is very high, as is the rate of suicide or suicidal attempt. Student health services are very much aware of the need to provide adequate psychotherapeutic facilities. Outside the realm of medicine, people may seek help through other organizations such as the Marriage Guidance Council, the Samaritans, and the Church. There has been a remarkable upsurge in the provision of encounter or sensitivity groups, again an indication of the desire for increasing self-awareness in society.

Most of the present trends in psychotherapy will be discussed in subsequent chapters of this book, and, therefore it would be unnecessarily repetitive to enter into a discussion of the current balance between the various schools at this point. What perhaps is more appropriate at this time is some brief account of the current applications of psychotherapy. Individual psychotherapy remains the solid foundation of the method. It continues to be applied in a variety of settings according to the need of the individual and the availability of the treatment. Within the National Health Service, unfortunately, the availability is inadequate in the majority of psychiatric units. Outside the hospital setting, in the private sphere, there is probably adequate provision of services, at least in major towns. To focus for a moment on one specific problem, that of adolescence, there is insufficient facility for helping this particular group. Adolescents seem constantly to fall between the services for adults and those for children. In recent years, the need for providing adequate care has been stressed but so far there has been a sadly limited realization of such facilities. For example, the provision of in-patient beds for adolescents has fallen well behind the target set. There are, of course, exceptions, such as the Brent Consultation Centre which provides an informal walk-in service, together with the possibility of intensive individual psychotherapy for certain selected adolescents, and the recently opened In-Patient Unit in Hertfordshire for the more disturbed or psychotic individuals.

The practice of group psychotherapy has expanded significantly in recent years. Its value as a method of treatment is becoming increasingly clear; no longer is it regarded as some inferior substitute method when individual psychotherapy is just not available. Apart from its therapeutic application, the group setting is one which particularly lends itself to training situations. One good example of this is the growth of the T-group technique (T stands for training, otherwise known as sensitivity groups). Individuals attend such groups in order to study the dynamics of group relationships and also to obtain greater self-awareness with the hope of increased personal and social growth.

The treatment of various social units again is receiving more attention today. In the fields of marital relationships, families, units in psychiatric hospitals, and even in industry, many workers in the field have been applying themselves to the specific problems related to such settings. It may, for example, prove to be of very limited value if one particular member of a family receives psychotherapeutic help without the family being considered as a whole. The illness of one individual may represent only the pinnacle of the iceberg. The dynamics of family interaction are being increasingly better understood, and treatment of the whole family can be most rewarding. In industry, valuable contributions have been made at the level of studying the dynamic interaction of the sub-units of an organization, such as the committee of managers and elected workers' representatives. Satisfactory social changes have been achieved which in turn have allowed for both increased efficiency and greater personal contentment.

In the mental hospital sphere, the concept of therapeutic community has been instrumental, along with advances in drug therapy, in allowing profound changes to occur in the care of patients residing in these institutions. Its main principles are: freeing of communications; analysis of all events; flattening of the authority pyramid; and the examination of roles of all those members of the community. It provides a setting in which the techniques of group psychotherapy can be applied in different ways and at different levels. The intensity with which these principles are applied varies from one unit to another, but the majority would nowadays at least pay lip service to the therapeutic community approach. With the changes in psychiatric hospital organization that are occurring at this time, it may become increasingly difficult to apply these techniques. The plans are for new, small (a-hundred-and-twenty-bedded) psychiatric units to be established in general hospitals to cope with all psychiatric problems of a local catchment area. Whilst there is much to commend in this reorganization, there are two areas of potential difficulty, firstly that the traditional medical model may be imposed upon the practice of psychiatry in such units, and secondly that there will be intense pressure necessitating very rapid turnover of cases. Under such circumstances, the difficulties of establishing and maintaining a therapeutic community atmosphere will be considerable. The hope must be that if the in-patient units are unable to utilize them, day hospitals and day centres will take over in this field.

Lastly, it should be emphasized that there has been an increasing eclecticism developing in recent years. The 'either/or' arguments that raged, for example, between the proponents of physical therapies and psychotherapy, appear to be diminishing. In spite of the differences in approach between the various schools it would seem now that efforts are being directed towards establishing a common language and recognizing those areas of similarity in basic theory. One example of this trend is the facility with which an individual may be treated by behavioural methods at one stage, later to receive more generalized psychotherapeutic help. Another is the increasingly commonly used method of combined treatment, in which the individual receives concurrently both group experience and individual treatment. The advantages of this method appear to outweigh any theoretical disadvantages that might be postulated.

Psychotherapy in the future

The future for psychotherapy, both in theoretical developments and technique, looks promising. Whatever the approach there is an increasing preoccupation with the need to improve technique and to evaluate the effects of treatment. The increase of service requirements is in itself a source of constant stimulation in this field. In spite of the intrinsic value of intensive, long-term individual psychotherapy, it is impossible to conceive that it could in itself be the answer to the service demands generally. The task must be to utilize the basic principles of the individual psychotherapeutic method, in the application to more economical

settings, such as group therapy, family therapy and brief psychotherapy.

At the present time, the term psychotherapist is virtually
meaningless. Anyone can call himself a psychotherapist irrespective of the quality of his training. The term may be applied
on the one hand to a medically-qualified psychiatrist who has
undertaken a full psychoanalytic training, but equally it is possible
for a person with little training, or experience, to claim the same
title. It is essential that some general agreement is reached with
regard to the basic training and minimum experience required of
those wishing to practise as psychotherapists. Ideally, there
should be some central register for psychotherapists in the same
way that they exist for psychoanalysts and other professional
workers. Membership of a recognized society or association
would go some way to the solution of this problem. The recent
Sir John Foster Report on the Enquiry into the Practice and
Effects of Scientology is concerned with the need to regularize
the profession of psychotherapy, and paragraph 258 of that report
states:

It is high time that the practice of psychotherapy for reward
should be restricted to members of a profession properly
qualified in its techniques, and trained – as all organized professions are trained – to use the patient's dependence which
flows from the inherent inequality of the relationship only for
the good of the patient himself, and never for the exploitation
of his weakness to the therapist's profit. Such legislation
already exists in a number of states in Europe, the Commonwealth and the United States.

Equally, it is necessary to re-examine the psychotherapy
training of those who do not necessarily wish to apply themselves entirely to this method. For example, the general psychiatrist who will have to acquire experience in a variety of techniques, amongst them that of psychotherapy. With the recent
creation of the Royal College of Psychiatry in Britain, one of its
aims is to lay down the basic requirements for the training of

future psychiatrists. In their recommendations psychotherapy assumes an important part. For the psychiatric nurse, an HMSO paper entitled *Psychiatric nursing, today and tomorrow*, recommends that all psychiatric nurses should have had experience of group work as part of their training programme.

Schools of psychotherapy continue to flourish and proliferate. For example, the writer Colin Wilson in the *Daily Telegraph Magazine*, 2 April 1971, discusses a new method from America called 'reality therapy', practised by attitude therapists. Little interest is shown in the probing of the subconscious, or of childhood experience; instead the question is put 'What do you intend to do?' Wilson ends his articles: 'Of one thing I am convinced: this spells the end of the Freudian era – a matter I have been personally looking forward to for a long time in the best possible sense. And no doubt attitude therapists will flourish and grow fat, like their Freudian forebears until it dawns on someone that the correct definition of a neurotic is: a man who is weak-minded enough to think he needs a psychiatrist. And what will happen then should be highly instructive–especially to the psychiatrists!' Even allowing for journalistic needs, this view seems to me to be typical of the dogmatic and intolerant approach, which should be abandoned.

There is a need for further research to be undertaken in a spirit of objective assessment. All psychotherapeutic methods should be subject to full assessment and re-assessment; controlled trials employing different techniques with statistical evaluation will help towards a rational and pragmatic application of the available methods.

In an attempt to anticipate the developments in the foreseeable future, I would offer the following speculations: firstly that in spite of the numerous different schools already in existence, and with the probability of many more to come, the psychoanalytic approach will continue largely to dominate the field. Whilst I consider it vital that psychoanalytic training as such develops and expands, I think it will be in the application of psychoanalytic principles that its main contribution will occur. It is for the teachers of psychotherapy, the trainers of the future generation of psychotherapists, for whom a psycho-analytic qualification will remain the best general grounding in the subject. Whatever the need for additional experience in other areas, a training analysis is invaluable. For those not wishing to become full-time psychotherapists, but requiring some personal treatment experience as part of their training, group psycho-therapy or a T-group experience lends itself admirably to this task.

In my view there will be a growing importance placed on the methods of family and marital treatments. The use of combined treatment, that is both individual and group psychotherapy em-ployed concurrently, will prove itself to be a most effective technique, both expedient and rewarding. Crisis-intervention techniques will need to be improved, again one aspect with im-mense possibilities. Increasing experience and sophistication will help towards the ability to offer 'instant psychotherapy', perhaps sufficient at least to alleviate the immediate crisis. Prophylaxis should concern us too, with the emphasis on attempting to pre-vent the emergence of psychological illness in our society. In the field of education much can be done to help avoid the pitfalls of development both in terms of the individual, his social unit, and society generally.

To end on a note of integration, I would quote the final para-graph of a paper read to the Psychotherapy and Social Psychiatry Section of the Royal-Medico Psychological Association (now transmuted to the Royal College of Psychiatry) and published in the *British Journal of Psychiatry* in January 1971. Dr Isaac Marks takes an eclectic view of the future of the psychotherapies, and states: 'A broadly based training will cultivate an open and flexible mind in trainee psychotherapists. A trainee needs more than a working knowledge of the psychiatric syndromes and the theory and practice of the school he happens to have selected, be it psychoanalytic, Adlerian, behaviourist or any other. An educated psychotherapist in the future will need to know about allied disciplines like ethology and clinical psychology. He will need to be familiar with all the many techniques now subsumed under the psychotherapies, even though there may only be time for him to become expert in a few of these. A psychotherapist who is sophisticated would know about individual and group interactional psychotherapy, about conjoint marital therapy, about crisis coping, meditational techniques, the concept of feedback control, desensitization, flooding, aversion, and the methods of operant shaping. Although there are moves in this direction, such training is hard to obtain at the moment. Its organization would be a major task, but an eminently rewarding one which would hasten the advance of psychotherapy towards an integrated and systematic discipline.'

Psychotherapy with the pre-school child: a psychoanalytic approach

Dina Rosenbluth

I shall deal in this chapter with the psychoanalytic approach to the treatment of emotionally disturbed children developed by Melanie Klein. There are of course almost as many approaches to the treatment of young children with psychological problems as there are to the treatment of adults. Even among psychoanalysts belonging to the British Psychoanalytical Society there are variations in theoretical emphasis, some laying more stress on environmental factors, others on internal factors within the child; and consequently the techniques used also vary. Although I shall discuss in particular some of the developments of Freudian theories and techniques stemming from the work of Melanie Klein, this account is necessarily coloured by my own understanding and experience.

I shall first give a very brief historical account, followed by a description of the kind of problems for which pre-school children may be referred for investigation and treatment, and some of the ways these may be dealt with in a psychiatric clinic. I shall then give in briefest outline some aspects of Klein's theories of early personality development before going on to the main theme of the chapter: the technique used in child analysis and child psychotherapy with particular emphasis on the interpretation of the child's transference relationship to the therapist (i.e. the patient's use of the therapist as a kind of screen in the treatment, where 'a whole series of psychological experiences are revived, not as belonging to the past but as applying to the physician at the present moment').[1]

Brief historical introduction

In the history of psychoanalysis the treatment of children lagged a long way behind that of adults. At one time it was thought that the lower age limit for undertaking analysis was about fifteen years. Later the lower age limit was thought to be around seven or eight years. Freud's own first child case, the famous 'Little Hans',[2] a five-year-old suffering from animal phobia, was in fact treated by Freud indirectly through his discussions with the father, who in turn conveyed the understanding he gained of the causes of the phobia to his little son. The arguments used in the past against the psychoanalytic treatment of all children are similar to the ones that are still at times voiced today against the treatment of the very young child: the relative immaturity of the ego, the fluidity of the personality, and particularly the fact that the child is still under the continuing influence of the parents with whom he lives and on whom he depends. It was held that the therapist can then not come to *represent* a parent to the child in treatment (transference) but will be regarded as an 'original second mother' in the life of the child.[3] This whole problem will constitute the main theme of this chapter.

Anna Freud and Melanie Klein, the two great pioneers in the field of psychoanalysis, differed in their approach to this problem of 'transference' in child treatment, particularly as regards the very young child. A. Freud and Klein both began publishing their findings and views on child treatment in the 'twenties. Whereas Anna Freud felt that the psychoanalytic technique had to be supplemented by educational measures,[3] Melanie Klein from the beginning of her work with young children held that purely psychoanalytic techniques should be used.[4,5] As I elaborate later on, she came to the conclusion that in contrast to parents, nursery school teachers, friends and relations, a psychoanalyst or therapist had a different, quite distinctive function, which even the very young child could appreciate and from which he could benefit; and that where, on the other hand, instruction, prohibitions, praise or reassurance were used this distinction was blurred, and the effectiveness of the treatment undermined.

Klein came to England in 1926 and for more than four decades worked and published her findings in this country and greatly influenced the work of other analysts, even those who do not count themselves as belonging to the Klein group of analysts within the British Psychoanalytical Society. So that what seemed new and startling in the 'twenties, the treatment of a young child by psychoanalytic technique, has now come to be widely accepted as a suitable treatment for disturbed young children. Candidates in child analysis at the British Institute of Psychoanalysis, as well as students in the two psychoanalytic training schools in child psychotherapy (at Anna Freud's Hampstead Child Therapy Clinic and at the Tavistock Clinic), all have to analyse a pre-school child as one of their three training cases in child analysis.

Referral for treatment

It is understandable that the treatment of children, and especially of the very young child, should give rise to controversy. Many difficult questions have to be considered in each case: to what extent does the problem reside predominantly within the child, and to what extent in the environment? It is naturally far more difficult to make a clear-cut diagnosis in the young child than in the case of an adult with psychological disturbance. Children are still developing and maturing and everything is relatively more labile and changeable than in adults; and one can always hope that even apparently major disturbances may be short lived and still within the range of normal development. This very factor, however, also makes for a better prognosis: changes can be expected more easily and quickly in a young child as a result of treatment.

The kinds of problem for which pre-school children may be referred for psychological investigation are many and varied: sleeping or eating disturbances; acute problems in toilet training, constipation or chronic soiling or wetting; mutism or speech defects; excessive clinging or demandingness or overt hostility towards the parents; excessive temper tantrums, destructiveness or jealousy; night terrors, fears and phobias of all kinds; excessive shyness or inability to play. Since all children go through phases of disturbance in some of these respects parents are often puzzled as to when a problem is really of a kind to warrant taking a child to a clinic. To determine this may then require the help of experts.

Although child guidance clinics and child psychiatric departments have long waiting lists, many have a policy of seeing a young child quickly, since the sooner a problem is tackled the less it is liable to become chronic and rigidly fixed and therefore difficult to treat. One often wishes a child had been taken to a clinic much sooner. In fact, however, in my experience the greatest number of referrals are in the eight-to-twelve-year-old group.

Take, for example, Timothy, aged eight years, who came to the clinic on the recommendation of his class teacher. He was an unhappy, timid, fearful child, unable to mix or play with other children. He had to be brought right into the classroom every morning by his mother and there was often a tearful scene when she left. Then he would cling to the teacher. In spite of good intelligence and an ability to learn easily, school was torture for him. Very frequently he stayed at home with minor illnesses. It became clear that this excessive clinging and acute separation anxiety had existed already from the age of two, and that both he and his family might have been spared much unhappiness and sense of failure had he been referred several years earlier.

Once the young child and his family have been investigated by a team of child guidance clinic experts (psychiatrist, child psychotherapist, education psychologist and psychiatric social worker), a choice of many psychotherapy treatment plans may be pursued, depending of course on the resources available. I shall mention just a few of these: the family may be seen for regular treatment conjointly: the child whose problems initially brought about the referral, the parents and maybe a sibling, by one or more members of the staff; the decision may be made that behind the child's problem there is in reality an acute parental marital problem, so that the child may not be treated at all but the parents only be seen on a regular basis by one or more members of the staff, jointly or separately; it may be felt that a crisis situation exists, and the parents or the mother and child be seen together for a few therapeutic consultations by one therapist;[6,7] the child may be seen on his own by a psychotherapist, while the parents are seen together or separately by one or two workers.

Some aspects of Klein's theories

I shall here limit myself to a description of the treatment of the young child, taking it as read that the parents, particularly the mother, will usually also need to receive some help concurrently from another worker. Before describing the method of treatment it is necessary to make brief mention of some of the findings and theories on which the technique is based. For naturally the methods employed in treating children do depend on the theory of personality development that the therapist holds, just as the methods employed will be influenced and modified by new findings.

There is only space to make very brief reference to a few basic findings and elements of Kleinian theory. The interested reader can refer to Melanie Klein's writings.[4,5,8]

Klein found evidence, from her experience of treating very young children, that from the beginning of life the child's instinctual drives seek not only pleasure but also an object. Taking Sigmund Freud's and Karl Abraham's findings of part object relations as a starting point, she found that the baby's earliest relationship is to parts or aspects of the mother or person caring for him, and that from this earliest relationship develops the later relation to whole people. This early object relation, at first to the feeding breast, implies that an image of this object gradually becomes firmly established in the infant's mind. This is not initially in conscious memory or thought but in unconscious phantasy.

The hypothesis is that phantasy is the mental expression of instinct, and that this is the first mental activity of the baby. It is unconscious, allied to feelings and bodily sensations. It is to be distinguished from later, conscious phantasies or daydreams. An unconscious phantasy of a feeding breast may be assumed, for instance, when a hungry baby is momentarily appeased by sucking his own thumb or blanket. This differs from a conscious phantasy such as a hungry adult might have when he daydreams about a meal. The older child can put his phantasies into words but behind this might be an unconscious phantasy akin to the baby's.

It is in unconscious phantasy that parts or aspects of the feeding mother are taken inside, introjected, as the mental counterpart of the actual feeding at the breast and taking in of food. All instinctual activity is thought to have a mental corollary, and the earliest, most primitive activity of the baby is the taking in and expelling of substances. The early introjection and projection in the oral stage of development had been stressed by Freud, as well as the earliest 'primary identification' with the breast: Klein added to this the continuing importance of unconscious phantasy which goes hand in hand with these early processes, and the importance of these early mechanisms in establishing an inner world of objects, which form the basis of the later more integrated ego and super-ego. (For meaning see p. 34.)

The early relationship is a two-way process from the start. The picture of the mother, or initially of parts or aspects of the mother, that is taken inside the baby is coloured and distorted by his own impulses and feelings; by the projection on to his objects of his own libidinal and destructive drives. In other words the baby attributes to the mother the same friendly or angry feelings and impulses which he experiences within himself. The earliest relationship to the mother tends to be split into a wholly good and a wholly bad one. This results from the 'all or none' quality of the baby's emotions as well as from the lack of cohesion of the ego.

There is a need to split off in particular the destructive impulses and project them outside 'for the young infant's self-preservation depends on his trust in a good mother. By splitting the two aspects and clinging on to the good one he preserves his belief in a good object and his capacity to love it; and this is an essential condition for keeping alive.'[9]

This split into the idealized and the persecuting figures are evidenced in all children's fairy tales, the witch-like figures and the fairy godmother, the demons and devils on the one hand and the good magicians on the other. The earliest anxieties of the

baby seem to be then of a persecutory nature; all babies can at
times be observed to behave as if the breast were a 'big bad
wolf' that will gobble him up.

As the baby grows into a more integrated person and becomes
able to differentiate between an inner and an outer world, he
develops an increased feeling of responsibility for his own impulses. He becomes, at first only dimly, aware that in fact it is he
himself who wants to gobble up his mother's breast. In his relation to the mother and to the father, each seen now as a whole
and separate person, a new anxiety then appears. He realizes that
in one person there are both good and bad, loved and hated
aspects. This marks the beginning of the true conflict of ambivalence, and the resulting anxiety Klein called the 'depressive
anxiety'. This new anxiety, which involves a concern for the
object, is very different from the persecutory anxiety, where the
fear is one of annihilation of the self. The central conflict, once
the baby is sufficiently integrated to become aware of a distinction
between self and other, once he comes to perceive the mother
who is loved to be the same that at other moments is hated, is
now the fear that hate may prove stronger than love, and the
fearful consequences of this; that harm might come to the loved
mother on whom the baby utterly depends. There are now long-
ings for the mother, sadness in her absences, and feelings of guilt
arise because of the concurrent hatred. (Winnicott suggested
calling this the beginning of the stage of 'concern'.[10]) Depressive
anxieties are thought to be originally linked to oral sadistic
impulses and phantasies, so that weaning might be felt as a loss
resulting from the greedy attacks on the feeding mother or
breast. The loss of the close, intimate contact with the feeding,
holding, comforting mother, results in the illusion of 'oneness'
with her being shattered. This is succeeded by many other further
separations from her, possibly through the birth of siblings and
certainly through the growing awareness of father in the triangular
oedipal relationships, when he begins to be aware of the fact
that the parents have a special relationship with one another
from which he is excluded, and feelings of jealousy and rivalry
set in. The fear will therefore constantly arise again that the good

objects might be lost, internally and externally, as a result of the child's ambivalent attitudes. Depending on the child's inner security he will react with greater or lesser 'depressive anxiety' to all these situations of separation in later stages of libidinal development. A differentiation between persecutory and depressive anxieties has become a tremendous help and of great importance both in diagnosis and treatment. To illustrate this we might take the example of Anne, aged three years, and her reaction to spilling a lot of water from the basin on to the therapy room floor: at one stage she would whimper, cower in the opposite corner of the room, gradually become more and more anxious and frightened of me and the room, and finally demand to go back to her mother in the waiting room. At the next treatment session she came into the room only very reluctantly, still frightened of me and fearfully looking at the part of the room which had previously been flooded, avoiding going anywhere near the basin. At a later stage in the treatment she reacted to the same kind of situation very differently: instead of behaving as if she feared retaliation from me, and as if the damage were an overwhelming persecution, she felt concern, could acknowledge that it was her own carelessness or even hostile intent which had led to the flooding. She looked sad, said: 'Poor Rosenbluth, poor Rosenbluth', as she attempted to wipe up the water from the floor, and 'Me clean, me wipe, bad Anne! Me good now!', all the while appearing anxious whether my room and my feelings could be repaired.

To summarize some of the aspects of Klein's theories which have profoundly affected our attitude to the treatment of young children: the theory of instinct being object seeking, of early object relations; the hypothesis of early primitive mental activity in the baby, with the gradual building up of an inner world of objects in the child's mind, compounded of the baby's impulses and external experiences; together with the finding of early anxiety situations, and the differentiation between persecutory and depressive anxieties, with varying ways in which a baby defends against these, or becomes able gradually to 'work through' anxiety situations in healthy development; all these have convinced us that even a two- or three-year-old child already has a personality structure (an ego which has to deal with and defend itself against inner dangers from the super-ego phantasy parental figures which come into conflict with his instinctual drives), to make psychoanalytic therapy in his own right the appropriate treatment in cases of emotional disturbance.

Aspects of Klein's technique of child analysis

Having found that even the young child brings to the treatment situation, and transfers to the new person, the therapist, a host of expectations, feelings, conflicts and anxieties which date back to his earlier babyhood relations with his parents, as well as his own individual methods of defending against these, Klein found she was justified in developing a technique of child analysis which retained the essentials of psychoanalysis: the interpretation of the unconscious and the consistent interpretation of the transference nature of the child's feelings to the therapist as the main tool for achieving this.

Just as in the analysis of adults a setting has been evolved which aims to facilitate such a transfer of feelings and conflicts from earlier situations (the analyst remaining a non-directive figure, the patient being encouraged to free associate, reclining on a couch, with the analyst sitting out of view of the patient, the regularity of both appointment times and duration of the treatment sessions), so Klein evolved a setting for the treatment of the child with the same aim in view: to enable him to project on to the therapist whatever phantasies and feelings or anxieties are active at the moment. She provided play and drawing materials in order to enable the child to communicate by means of play where he could not yet communicate sufficiently easily in words. The toys were provided merely to facilitate communication, not so that play should become an end in itself. The play is carefully observed and the main anxieties and conflicts, as they become clear, are put into words and interpreted to the child in simple language. In other words, the child's play activity is regarded as an equivalent to the adult's dreams and free associations.

The toys Klein originally provided are still commonly used by psychotherapists today: she provided small toys, people, animals, cars, fences and bricks, endeavouring to keep everything very simple so that the child could use them in different situations and roles; also painting materials, scissors, string, plasticine. Each child patient has his individual toys, and we endeavour not to have any toys in the room which a number of children share. The playroom itself is also kept as simple as possible. Many therapists have come to discard the formerly traditional sandtrays, although most do have water available. The aim is to arrange a setting where there will be a minimum need to make prohibitions. Each patient is provided with his own lockable box or drawer where his own toys and drawing materials can be kept, so that he can do what he likes with them, keeping his own drawings safe or add toys from home when he feels like it. The total setting is designed so as to enable the therapist to avoid as much as possible acting the 'good' gratifying or the 'bad' forbidding parent. The lockable drawers become part of the private relation between the analyst and the child patient, an essential prerequisite for the transference relationship.

Student therapists and parents are often at first afraid that the permissive atmosphere of the therapy room will make the child patient unruly at home but are usually amazed how soon the child realizes that the treatment setting is something quite different from his everyday life outside, at home or at nursery school. Although children are restricted as little as possible, can make a mess or destroy their own toys, some limits will inevitably have to be set. Phases occur in the treatment of almost all children where they will test out how far they can go. Even with the most foolproof playroom there will be times when the therapist has to restrict certain activities, for the patient cannot be allowed to endanger himself, the therapist or the room. At times one will then have to act as an authority figure but then we try to interpret at the same time why the child is trying to make us into the forbidding parental figure at that moment. For instance, the child's feelings of guilt may at times be so unbearable, or the anxieties about his own destructiveness so great that he attempts to provoke situations where he wants to be punished, or forcibly prevented from carrying out certain actions, and hopes the therapist will be a kind of policeman. All such situations we attempt to interpret to the child.

Similarly, the child will at other times attempt to force the therapist to become a gratifying figure, to give him food or presents. However, we avoid giving any such actual gratifications, just as we do not send birthday or Christmas cards, since this could be acting the 'good' therapist/parent to the child, when in fact our aim is to enable him to transfer his own picture of good or bad internal parents on to us.

In such a setting we find that even a very young child, who is only beginning to be able to talk, but provided he understands verbal communication of a simple kind, can show us his anxieties and conflicts, and can benefit from psychoanalytic therapy. We use simple language and endeavour to interpret in such a way as to incorporate as much as possible his own idiosyncratic manner of expressing himself (having if necessary found out from the parents what his own words are for various familiar objects, people, bodily functions and feelings). The child's play can then become the equivalent of the adult's dreams and will symbolically represent his current preoccupations, as well as their unconscious significance. We do not, of course, automatically translate symbols but observe carefully the child's mood, emotions and general behaviour in the therapy room, his reaction to the therapist and to what the therapist says to him. In other words, it is the sequences and context of play and behaviour which are significant and take on meaning, not a single action alone.

In our experience it is most helpful, then, if the central focus of the treatment technique lies in a consistent interpretation of the child's relationship to the therapist and on the transference nature of this relationship. We attempt to make transference interpretations which are emotionally immediate, that is, in touch with the feelings and anxieties which are active at the moment, and attempt to keep them specific, detailed and concrete. James Strachey[11] called such interpretations 'mutative', which really can effect a change and shift in the patient's attitudes, and stressed that they should include two phases: the first should enable the patient to become aware of the feelings and impulses towards the therapist, and the second should make him aware that this impulse is directed towards 'a phantasy object and not a real one', i.e. that the child is acting in accordance with feelings that are not evoked in fact by the reality of the person of the therapist so much as through reliving earlier experiences and projecting his internal phantasy figures on to the analyst.

Before some experience in psychotherapeutic work with children has been gained, therapists often fear that by interpreting the transference relationship they may alienate the child from his parents, that the child might become too attached to the therapist and have less good relationships at home. However, if one is careful to interpret all the child's reactions as they appear in the treatment, the negative as well as the positive ones, their interaction as well as their transference nature, one soon becomes convinced that such an alienation from the parents is not at all the result. On the contrary, the relationships at home usually become less strained as the conflicts originating in babyhood are brought more and more into the treatment situation instead. We become less afraid of interpreting all the child's feelings towards us once we become fully convinced that they are in fact transferred, do not belong to us in our own right. If we were to interpret the positive feelings too exclusively, or if we were to grant all kinds of gratifications during the treatment, then indeed the child might become encouraged to split off his negative feelings and direct them with renewed force against his parents at home.

Small children often have phases of difficulty in separating from their mother and remaining alone with the therapist in the consulting room. This may be a difficult time for the inexperienced therapist. Often some splitting has taken place where either the mother or the therapist has momentarily come to represent a fearful or damaged object, and the other is idealized and clung to. Sometimes it may then be necessary for the mother to stay with the child for a little while in the playroom while the situation is interpreted and worked through. In my experience there has only been one case where the mother needed to remain in the consulting room for a lengthy period. With this child, where the separation anxiety was acute and had been a chronic problem, the mother proved to be very understanding, and was able gradually to withdraw into reading a book in the corner of the room, until finally she was allowed to leave altogether. The usual fifty-minute sessions never needed to be curtailed. In other cases, however, where there were brief phases of extreme anxiety, I have at times had to shorten the session and take the child back to the mother in the waiting room after fifteen or twenty minutes.

Sometimes a therapist is afraid of interpreting the child's negative, angry feelings for fear that this might only increase his aggression in the treatment. But we find that it is in fact often only after anxiety has been relieved as a result of interpreting the negative transference that the more genuinely positive feelings can emerge.

Here is a brief example: Johnny, four years old, was suffering from severe nightmares and sleeping disturbances, food fads, as well as very great jealousy of his baby sister. He showed me some of the contents of his nightmares immediately on starting treatment: the toy tiger was picked out of his drawer and threatened to bite and eat up the tame animals. At the same time he kept at some distance from me. He took particular notice of the small pig, calling him a 'good boy!' It was plain that he felt he had been sent to me because he did not feel he was such a good boy, and feared punishment from me. I said that it seemed he felt I was the wild tiger and he was afraid of me, and maybe he was the little pig? He said he was not afraid, but confirmed how frightened he was by looking fearfully at the door as if wishing to escape, then erecting two chairs between himself and me, then fencing in the tiger so as 'not to hurt the piggies'. After some silence he pointed out that there were two baby pigs, a bigger and a smaller one. He said he was the bigger one, the little one was his baby sister. Then he brightened, moved nearer to me and told me the tiger was going to eat up his little sister.

For a long while the tiger and the baby pigs figured large in the treatment sessions. It could often be shown to him that he was feeling that I was the very terrifying tiger-treatment-mummy who had to be kept at bay, and at other times when he himself acted the growling, biting tiger threatening to eat me up if I did not comply with some request for more toys or drawing materials one could show him the whole situation of his greed, biting attacks and fear of retaliation in relation to me, as well as how these were phantasies accompanying his early relation to his feeding mother. The interpretation of the link between this and the content of his nightmares resulted in a speedy clearing up of the latter. However the nightmare situation became transferred for a long while to the treatment situation, with much destructiveness in the play-room and angry attacks on me, and consequent anxieties and reluctance about returning to the treatment the subsequent time. His aggressiveness towards me, representing in this phase pre-dominantly the feeding mother whom he envied and wished to control, had to be shown to him, interpreted and worked through over and over again, before his more affectionate, loving relationship to the mother could come to the fore.

Even the very young child's co-operation in treatment can be fostered effectively only when he gains conviction that he is understood; that the therapist is not afraid to put into words even the most violently hostile impulses and phantasies, can understand and interpret and thus make such feelings more manageable for him. This is usually in contrast to the parents, and always in contrast to that part of the patient that wants to deny or gloss over his aggressive feelings.

Kleinian analysts attempt to stress, then, both the positive as well as the negative feelings as they arise and try to link them both with the current transference relation and situation in the playroom, as well as with the past babyhood relationship to the parents, or initially to the feeding mother. Actual historical events, possibly past real deprivations, such as a mother's difficulty in feeding her baby, or separations from the mother, or being in fact supplanted in the mother's or father's affection by a new baby in the family, often no doubt play a part in the origin of the child's emotional problems. We do not deny such external difficulties in the way we interpret, however, we do not feel that it is particularly helpful to interpret in such a way as to encourage the child to fasten on to them so as to justify his aggression. If one did, then indeed one might again encourage the child to act out his hostile baby feelings at home, whereas our aim is not only to keep the baby transference in the treatment but to focus it there increasingly.

It is in fact only internal reality which can be influenced in the treatment, past external reality can no longer be changed, and it is the internal reality we stress. We emphasize then the child's impulses and phantasies and try to show how these distort reality in the current transference situation. Gradually, then, more and more of the child's unconscious phantasies and impulses become centred around the treatment, and the baby-relationship becomes fully transferred to the therapist. The situation at home then usually becomes easier as the babyhood relationships need no longer interfere so much with the present-day relationship between the child and his parents. But a deepening of the transference depends on the technique used, that is, on a consistent interpretation of all transference phenomena, negative as well as positive, from the beginning of treatment. For, as Klein wrote:[12] 'Transference originates in the same processes which in the earliest stages determine object relations. Therefore, we have to go back again and again in analysis to the fluctuations between objects, loved and hated, external and internal, which dominate early infancy.'

Only when the child's earlier relationships and anxieties are fully re-experienced in the transference can they be worked through and a real change take place. The hard work of the treatment, for patient and therapist, consists of a struggle and working over again and again of the conflicts and anxieties, persecutory as well as depressive, in the consulting room. The aim of child treatment, as that of adults, is an integrative one, to take back and re-integrate parts of the self. The unacceptable impulses which had been split off and projected, which had led to distortions of the pictures of the parents, both externally and internally, and of the self, must be acknowledged. Every step towards integration is an achievement; if there is a lessening of projective mechanisms, a lessening of phantasies of omnipotence and a diminution of persecutory anxiety, this is clearly a great gain, and will make for a better, healthier development of the child, once treatment is terminated.

Psychotherapy for the school-aged child: a Margaret Lowenfeld approach

Phyllis Traill

Methods of psychotherapy differ. In writing about psychotherapy with the school-age child, I will be discussing the methods of psychotherapy devised by Dr Margaret Lowenfeld, which are practised and taught at the Institute of Child Psychology.

Origins of this technique

Dr Margaret Lowenfeld was born and educated in England. She qualified in medicine in 1918. After experience of relief work in Poland she became interested in paediatrics. She obtained a scholarship from the Medical Research Council and the Muirhead Research Scholarship and joined a research team at the Royal Hospital for Sick Children, Glasgow, working on 'social conditions and acute rheumatism'. She also did research work on lactation. During this time, she noticed the different reactions of children to their illnesses and also the different interactions of mother and baby during breast feeding.

Working as a children's physician, she became interested in the psychological aspect of children's illnesses. At the time, work with disturbed children was based on experience of work with disturbed adults. Dr Lowenfeld decided to find out what the children themselves thought and felt. She wanted to find a way to make direct contact with the thoughts, feelings, and desires of children as communicated by the children themselves. Play seemed to her the obvious way of making such contact. She decided to see what children produced when allowed to play freely with an interested adult as playmate, adding to the play material as the children called for it.[1]

In 1928 she extended her work to children whose parents could not afford private fees. She set up a children's clinic with voluntary helpers in North Kensington. The clinic met two afternoons a week in a room used for other purposes the rest of the time. In 1929, the work was recognized by the local education authority. Gradually, enough money was found to start a permanent clinic. It was called The Children's Centre, The Institute of Child Psychology. In 1933, a training course for non-medical child psychotherapists was begun in Warwick Avenue. In 1938, the Institute was given the present house where the clinical work and the training still continue.

In her work with children, Dr Lowenfeld found that the findings of psychoanalysis were often seen in children's play, but she came to the conclusion that this material produced by the children was not unconscious in the usually accepted sense of the term. The child was aware of its problems, but unable to understand them. The child had never been able to put into words what he was experiencing and thus, was unable to communicate it to anyone. These experiences were often difficult for the child to deal with, to sort out and to come to terms with, having no one to 'talk' to about it. In addition to the emotional conflicts described by the psychoanalysts, Dr Lowenfeld found that children 'thought' from an early age and tried to make sense of their experiences, but that the conclusions they came to were often false and harmful to their development. They formed concepts which became the bases of their thoughts, actions and emotions and it was necessary to help the children to understand these concepts, explain their origin and then to correct them. She found that emotional difficulties were often based on a false concept formed before words became the main medium of thought and communication. The age at which this happens varied enormously with different children.

Play, as many have found,[2] is the way to make direct contact with children. Dr Lowenfeld gradually worked out play techniques[3] which helped the child to 'say' what he wanted. One of the principal techniques being the 'world' technique.[4] This consists of a shallow tray with sand to which water can be added, and a cabinet full of different kinds of objects. There are ordinary people, historical, entertainers, soldiers, cowboys, indians, etc., wild and tame animals, transport of all kinds, road furniture, trees and fences, houses, farm furniture, house furniture, and all kinds of odds and ends. With these, the child makes his own world.

The bases or reasons for these children's difficulties differed widely and were based on the individual's own experience, his bodily experience, the happenings to himself, the family relationships, type of mother and father, and so on. It was no good guessing or deciding beforehand what had affected this particular child with this particular temperament from a particular environment, one had to wait to see what the child himself had presented.

Principles

The principles, therefore, on which this technique is based are simple but complex to work out in practice. Small children 'think' entirely in a non-verbal manner.[5] Later, much thinking is of this type. Indeed, new ideas are probably formed in this way, the main mental work having been done before they can be put into words. The child, in trying to make sense of the world around him and of his own experiences and reactions, forms a complex network of sensations, feelings and ideas. These networks, or 'clusters' as we call them, which cause difficulties, must be undone, sorted out and corrected.

Verbal thinking is linear. One idea follows another, but non-verbal thinking is not linear. It is global, there altogether and has to be stated as a whole first. Early non-verbal thinking has no space and time; in and out are the same. Two events which are alike coalesce and become one. This 'language' has to be re-learned by the therapist. Here is an example of a very muddled child aged seven who not only had some terrifying personal experiences in infancy, but also has a terrifying home environment.

World: D. went straight to the damp sand tray in the front playroom. He put a large stick into the top left-hand corner and took it out again, saying that it was a hole for a bomb at the end of the road. He later replaced the stick and it was the post-office tower for seeing if anything attacks the world. He then put in a house to the left, people are going there and they blow the house up. Two planes, for attacking things that come were put beside this, and below these, stinging plants. To the right was the pig house and in it was a man whose car was parked to the left. To the right of the pig house was another house with a fenced-in area, in front, an old man was leaving this with his bags. Beside this was a guard house and a palm-tree, and below, an ambulance. D. did not know what for. D. then made a circular space in the sand towards the bottom and said it was a river. He put a lion in the bottom left hand corner and put a low wall of sand round it. This lion is doing what he wants to be doing and what he should be doing; he is invisible to humans and is watching from his cage. A bridge was then added in the centre and cars passed under it in different directions. D. then made holes all over the sand with one finger, saying that it is snowing. It is Christmas. He then put a bee-hive at the bottom of the tray and grimaced, so W. remarked that he did not like bees, did he? D. said, 'Bees tease me, they buzz in my head.' W. said, 'What happens then?' So he said, 'They do it when I'm in bed and sometimes my head's like a merry-go-round.' He then put a large shed at the bottom left of the tray; this had two fire-engines coming out of it. A man with a camera was on top of the shed making a movie. It was only a rubber movie made of 'plasticums'. It was probably a 'gangster movie'. Monsters now arrived from a different planet, nobody can see these creatures, they are 'un-noised'. The rhino pecks at the apple tree and the beautiful monster does not know where he is going. An elephant eats the honey from the bees who are 'scrumbled and squashed'. Two women were put up by the pig house, one was a mother who was a different one to the other one who was playing (?). The monsters are trying to talk to the humans but they are 'un-noised'. The monsters are trying to talk to the humans, but they are invisible, so they are ignored. The fire engines are about to go to the house which is blowing up.

In this 'world' the boy has presented everything at once in a complicated network of feelings, and ideas. These will take time to disentangle, sort out, and realign – so that he can understand and then deal with his feelings and the world around him.

The findings of all serious work with children are relevant to helping the therapist to understand his productions, but care has to be taken that the therapist does not jump to a conclusion and decide on the child's problem before he has clearly stated it as the therapist may be wrong. The problem may be very individual to that particular child. A very careful history is necessary as so many problems are related to the child's own experiences, as well as to his own temperament and reaction to the environment, the parents' own mistakes with this particular child and so on.

The relationship of a therapist to the child is one of helper. Together with the child, the therapist examines what the child does, draws his attention to the different aspects, and to the recurrence of certain features, and thus helps him to work it out. It is only when the child's meaning has become quite clear that interpretation is given. Interpretation is only given at a point when it is possible for the child really to understand it.

Psychotherapy with the school age child is very rewarding. I am taking the age range from five up to eleven. During this period the child is eager to grow up, eager to be well, and to be released from handicaps of anxiety, fears, bed-wetting, explosive anger and so on. He is naturally changing all the time, growing, developing, finding new interests and learning new things. The normal difficulties of adolescence, both physical and emotional have not yet added to his troubles. He has not yet to think of the future or worry about girl-friends. He is able to understand the help that is being offered, and to accept and to respond to any positive change of attitude on the part of the parents.

Types of difficulties

Children are referred to the Institute by head teachers, the social services, school medical officers, and general practitioners for the following types of difficulty which can be divided into four main categories.

1. *Behaviour difficulties.* This category includes delinquency, aggression, violence, unmanageable behaviour at school or at home.
2. *Fears.* Many kinds, including nightmares, phobias, timid and withdrawn behaviour, depression and so on.
3. *Educational failure.* When a child is of average or above average ability, but is failing in school work; this may be because he cannot concentrate, or for some other psychological reason, he fails to read or do arithmetic, and remedial teaching does not help.
4. *Physical difficulties.* Which either have no physical cause, or where the illness is exaggerated by psychological factors. Examples of these are abdominal pains, headaches, bed-wetting, soiling, asthma, eating and sleeping disturbances, speech disorders, nail biting, tics and so on. There is also the so-called 'delicate' child who is pale, has dark rings under his eyes and has a poor appetite. After psychotherapy, these children often become lively and robust. The relief of anxiety, produces release of energy, which goes towards physical growth and development.

The origins of difficulties

The origins of these children's difficulties generally stem from their early years before school age, which then become aggravated by the disapproval, anger and frustration their parents and teachers show towards these difficulties. The longer a child wets the bed, the more hopeless everyone feels and the more of a settled habit it becomes. The longer a child is unable to concentrate at school, the more backward his school work becomes. The longer a child remains timid and unable to make friends, the more difficult will it be for him to change, and so on. Therefore, the sooner a child with difficulties can have psychotherapy, the better.

As we have said, the origins of most difficulties go back to an early age. Therefore, we must consider infants and toddlers and the way they think and build their concept of themselves and the world around, as this technique is based on the non-verbal thinking of infants and small children as well as the non-verbal aspects of older children's thinking. Small children are only learning to talk and cannot think in words, yet it is obvious they are noticing, exploring, finding out, coming to conclusions of one sort or another.[6] It is quite a long time before words become the main medium for thought and expression. The age varies according to the verbal ability of the child, but it is comparatively late before a child can really describe clearly an event or write an essay. It is even more difficult to describe or express in words feelings or attitudes. This is even difficult for adults unless they are poets or great writers. These latter have put into words for us feelings, emotions and attitudes, and are extensively quoted to convey what we want to say. Adults in attempting to convey feelings often use a picture language, such as – 'I am going off the deep end', 'I'm walking on air', 'He's sitting on the fence.' Children's thinking is largely non-verbal, entirely so to begin with, yet they come to simple conclusions, they develop attitudes, they work things out for themselves. Their thinking is not done in words, but in images, sensation, emotion and feelings, all at once, forming a network of happenings and impressions. An infant is bombarded with experiences, with things happening to him both from within and from without. These he does not understand as we understand; there are sensations, emotions, movements. Gradually, he begins to sort out these happenings, to discover his body and his separateness from other happenings. During this early time, he is recording these happenings, images are formed, visual, auditory, sensory, kinaesthetic, all involved with strong emotions. These can be anything from pleasurable and comforting, to terrifying and painful. If the child has many or prolonged painful and terrifying experiences, these colour his expectations and his conclusions about life in a negative and harmful manner. A child has a tremendous drive to make sense of and to understand himself and the world around him. He must come to some sort of conclusions which, owing to lack of experience, are often wrong. He has, after all, only his experience to go by. He cannot yet compare other experiences, of his own or those of other people. His conclusions are absolute, axiomatic, so taken for granted that they become the basis of his actions and are never questioned. They colour his attitude and affect his behaviour according to his temperament. Thus, everyone's outlooks, ambitions, likes and dislikes are due, not only to differing temperaments, abilities, physical aptitudes and so on, but also to early experiences, and what is made of them. To take an example from ordinary life, where something is taken completely for granted. A child in a large town in Great Britain must take food completely for granted, because it is always there and never fails. If something he wants to eat is not in the shops, then this must be due to people not bothering to get it, or his mother stopping him from having it. He has no idea of the hard work, the experiments, and the difficulties that are associated with the production of food; disasters that can overtake food crops, leaving people with nothing to eat, as does a child in a rural setting. To him, food will always automatically appear and he need do nothing about it. Only later he realizes that it has something to do with money. Water is also something that appears out of a tap, the supply of which is unlimited. Everyone has come across the town child who is convinced that his milk comes originally from the dairy, and that seeds come from a factory.

The child has come to perfectly good conclusions about the above facts from his own experience and he never questions them. Thus a child who has had a series of bad and painful experiences will take it for granted that life is painful and unpredictable and will react according to his temperament. He may withdraw into himself or he may fight and defend himself and become very 'difficult' – attempting to ward off what may happen. One boy of ten came to the following wrong conclusion. His mother had been pregnant, but had to have an abortion. The children were told she was to have her appendix out. A boy of that age knows or senses when his mother is pregnant, and she comes back from hospital obviously not pregnant any more. A little while later the boy had an appendix operation himself after which he was very upset. Finally it was discovered that he thought 'they' must have taken a little man out of him.

These happenings are experienced as a totality, a network of sensations, feelings, with rudimentary ideas and some attempt to make sense of it all. An adult has learnt to discriminate, to realize which pieces of his actual experience are interrelated, and which are not. The infant and small child do not know this. Thus an infant with colic, suffering from painful spasm of the intestinal tract, may experience fear and anger, movement, pain, food and the noise of a buzzing fly at the same time and the whole experience is one – so that food or a buzzing fly or a certain type of movement will reproduce anger and fear. He may refuse food, or certain types of food. He may become afraid of the noise of a buzzing fly to everyone's mystification. The whole experience remains in the form of images, which cannot later be expressed in words, and have to be expressed in images. They form what at the Institute of Child Psychotherapy we call a 'cluster'.

In later life, much of the individual flavour of each person's experience, as described above, is given by these early 'clusters' formed by the pre-school child. Most of us have known pleasant experiences such as supper by a warm fire, followed by our mother telling a story, the scene is always the same, the same chair is used, the same picture on the wall, a certain cushion, the same object is cuddled and so on. To the child, this experience is a whole, nothing must be changed, if a different chair is used the child will protest and feel that something is missing. In adult life, any one of the ingredients present in the scene will bring back the warm well-being of childhood. The same applies to terrifying or painful experiences. The first type of experience does not lead to difficulties, the latter often does.

The early images that the infant or toddler forms are vague and ill-defined. They are later given shape by the pictures or scenes we present to him in the form of pictures or stories, or objects in the world around and he can use these to express the vague images he had formed. Thus, breast-shaped mountains can mean motherness, and the story around the mountain can express feelings of long ago. Volcanoes which explode and have lava pouring from them can be a way of expressing explosive anger either on his part or on the part of someone else, as where the explosion comes from is difficult to define. They can also express a bad experience of prolonged diarrhoea.

Monsters which attack are used to express some terrible happening in which the child felt attacked by some monster, the mother sometimes seeming like this. The recent interest in prehistoric monsters has given the child a way of saying that he is concerned with happenings of a long time ago. The images of beings from outer space express the infant's experience of adults coming and going.

During infancy he gradually gains some knowledge that his body is separate from other things, and he begins to sort out the happenings around him. He learns about space and gains a rudimentary idea of time; he has learnt that mother is mother, is always the same whether she is associated with pleasurable or painful experiences, and is separate from other people; that there is also father, and people you know and do not know. After this he begins to assert himself as an individual in his own right, to have strong feelings of anger and love, and to have likes and dislikes. We all know the stage when a child says 'No' continually. He feels jealousy and possessiveness, feelings sweep over him like a wave and possess him entirely, so that at one moment all is calm and peace, and at the next he is the rage, he is the demand and nothing else exists for him. All these emotions have to be realized and dealt with, separated out and linked with other experiences; frustrations must be borne and ways round them discovered. This he does with the firm understanding help of the adult, and through playing it out. He also tests the adult to see what happens. In addition, there is conflict between himself and the environment, and between his own feelings and desires. Life is not easy and a great deal has to be learnt. In addition, the child may have a difficult home situation, where parents are not understanding to each other, who quarrel and cannot co-operate over the handling of the child. The parents themselves may not be able to understand children and help them. In such a case, a feeling of insecurity develops and of life not being pleasant.

A girl of normal intelligence was sent to us for stealing food and money from home and for occasionally wetting herself in the day. She was a girl who felt she was worthless. She was the second of four girls. She had always been overweight and was smacked daily for wetting the bed at eighteen months, until her mother found it was her sister upsetting a pot in the bed to cause her trouble. She developed normally, but at the age of one year was in hospital for a week with 'tummy upset' and she screamed the whole time; she had diarrhoea and vomited. Then at eighteen months she had measles with bronchitis and ear trouble with discharge and a lot of pain, which was recurrent. One day she did a picture in the sand which seemed to be a real cluster about her early body experiences and enquiries about bodies in general. (Rounded mounds with holes, caves and tunnels, we have found to be concerned with feelings and ideas about the body.) She made a mound in the centre and smaller ones in each corner, a few trees on the surface of the valleys which had been formed by earthquakes. It is prehistoric times. A snake is emerging from a hole in the centre mound—another hole goes right down from the top. Holes in the sides of two corner mounds with a crocodile going in one, and holes down from the top in the other two. Prehistoric animals are coming out. Cavemen live in one cave which has a tunnel leading right down. A grotesque animal is on top of this hill and the cavemen do not know it is there. Some animals are looking down the holes to see what is there. There is lava inside the earth, bubbling and boiling, causing earthquakes, and it will come erupting out of the holes.

A little girl of five, highly intelligent, was mother-tied and unhappy. She had an older brother. The parents had separated when the little girl was about two years old. She saw her father occasionally. Her mother was thinking of getting a divorce, possibly remarrying, but she herself was very dependent on her husband's parents. Towards the beginning of treatment, the little girl made a picture in the sand in which she has expressed a 'cluster' about family relationships, and what might happen to over-demanding children. She is obviously thinking about it and all its possibilities. She used animals, and there was a family of elephants, consisting of father, mother and baby, and a similar one of ducks and one of bears with two babies. The babies were told to be good or they would get no food. There was a father giraffe with a baby – the mother had gone away. A small lamb was alone as it had lost its mother because it wanted more and more. There was a mother monkey with a baby, then two lambs together who would look after each other, a crocodile who could eat you up, it had lost its two children and the father.

Therapeutic play

The child expresses himself in action and play. Play to the adult is recreation, to a child it is life itself. By play, he learns, finds out, experiments, acts like fathers and mothers in order to understand and work out what it is all about. Also through play he develops his muscles, body control, physical co-ordination and manual skills; work and play are one. He learns social living and control of emotion and impulses by playing with others, by listening to or inventing stories which he acts out.

When children come to us, we therefore play with them, but it is not play in the adult recreation sense, but play with a purpose. It is explained to the child what the Institute is trying to do, to help him with whatever difficulties he has. He agrees he does not know why he has to disrupt the class at school, why he is unable to make friends, or why he wets the bed. The therapist does not know either, and he is told, 'We have to be like detectives and find out.' The reasons for his behaviour are somewhere in his head. The child always agrees emphatically that he has a lot of pictures in his head that he cannot talk about, and understands when the therapist tells him that we are going to make the pictures in his head and we will together find out how his difficulties came so that he can get rid of them. He knows how you can tell from people's actions what they are feeling; for example from the way they bang the door, or the way they dance into a room with shiny eyes, and so on. They also know that comic strips tell a story, and that cartoons and certain advertisements say things through pictures, like the advertisement 'There is a tiger in your tank'.

He is then ready to produce his pictures and have them dis-

cussed with him. At the same time he is told that what he does in
the playroom is private and known only to the therapist. He is
told that someone (usually a psychiatric social worker) will see
mother upstairs to find out about things at home and to help her
to understand; that what mother says specifically about him will
be told to him, but what he does and says will not be told to
mother without his permission. He is also told that it is his point
of view that interests the therapist. The child will then be shown
round the playrooms and be asked to do a picture in the sand.
What they do their first day is often very revealing.

Play in the Institute has three aspects:

1. It is a means of expression for thoughts and feelings the child
   does not understand and cannot manage.
2. Through play he can gain satisfaction in doing things he has
   never been able to do for one reason or another, and he can
   find out what he can do.
3. The energy released from trying to cope with his difficulties
   is put into constructive channels.

First aspect of play

What he has to express is very varied. The therapist does not
know until he tells her through his play. Every child is different,
his needs and experiences are different. This form of psychotherapy is geared to the differing needs of the individual children,
and their own personal experiences, and the therapist attempts to
give each child what he needs in the way of understanding and
help. We have, therefore, a great deal of play material of various
kinds. As children express themselves in different ways, we need
a large 'vocabulary' for them to 'talk' with. We have material
with which they can make pictures, a sand tray which can hold
water, and a cabinet full of miniature objects. With these, the
child can make his world of feelings and ideas. There is also
painting and drawing, plasticine and water. Some children,
however, express themselves more readily through drama, with
puppets, a doll's house with miniature figures, house play, shop
play, school play, dressing up and dramatizing.

Some examples of what these children have to express might

give some idea of how a child's basic concepts can be formed. First I will give examples of wrong feeling-concepts. These examples are necessarily simplified. The whole process whereby the child gradually clarifies the pictures in his head until he can state his ideas in a way in which both he and the therapist can understand, takes time and skill on the part of the therapist. Here we can only give the end process, the final crystallizing out of the basic concept. Children attend for treatment for a year to eighteen months as a rule, though some difficult cases take longer, and some take less time.

A little girl of nine was sent for bed wetting, and for depressed and lethargic behaviour. She was the second child of seven, with a rough but large-hearted mother who did a great deal for her children. For some time, she expressed little in the playroom, until one day she went to the doll's house where she staged the following scene: there was a mother and a baby and a little girl crying in a corner because mother no longer loved her – which in this girl's case was not true. When this little girl was around two-and-a-half years the next baby was born. The mother of course carried it about, fed it, made a fuss of it. The little girl, however, had come to the age when the mother would expect her to begin to feed herself, be able to dress herself, etc. To this girl, that meant her mother no longer loved her and led to the conclusion that love was rationed; mother had only so much to give. When all this had been uncovered, she could now realize that her feeling-idea was not correct. She said this one day when playing again in the doll's house; the therapist reminded her of her former play where she thought her mother no longer loved her. She replied that she used to think this, but now she knew this was not true. She was able then to come out of her lethargy and depression and to give up desperately hanging on to babyhood by wetting the bed. This attitude-feeling-idea on the part of children is very common.

A boy of ten was sent for sudden violent attacks on children at school; he had to be held firmly until he calmed down. Children and teachers co-operated in running after and holding him when this happened. Everyone, however, agreed he was a nice boy.

He could sit and read quietly, go fishing and so on, without violence, but when other people were involved, violence seemed part of his very nature; he could not run about, kick a ball, play with anyone without banging into everyone and everything – banging, hurting, etc. He also was continually hurting himself, doing things so clumsily that he fell in awkward ways, etc. The case was a long and complicated one – he had to be made to look at the fact of his violence which he hardly realized. Also he had to look at the fact that he was continually hurting himself. In other words, relationships either hurt others or himself. His pictures in the sand were violent fights, and bombings. One of the decisive days in his treatment was when he produced a picture in the sand where small soldiers with guns and tanks were continually attacked by enormous aeroplanes and tanks which were ten times larger than the toys usually used in the sand tray. These came from outer space, and kept appearing and disappearing. Now this child was an only boy. His father was quite a good father, though he had a bad temper. His mother was a very disturbed person. She had a loud, shouting voice, had very aggressive attitudes in general and always arrived at the Institute furious about something – a shopkeeper or a teacher, or the Institute. It was obvious that this was not recent, she had always been like that; she must often have gone to pick up her baby when she felt angry about something. Her movements were jerky and sharp. The baby must have been snatched at and surrounded by an aura of fury and aggression – till it became part of himself. He would also as an infant find it impossible to distinguish whether the anger was inside him or outside. This muddle is fairly common, and lasts into adult life if not corrected. When this picture he had made was explained in terms of his infancy experience of the mother, coming so to speak, from outer space, being cross and snatchy at him – it was an illumination and he visibly relaxed and he was able to throw off the innate feeling of violence being life. He knew all about the violence at home and suffered from it as the house was too small for him to get away from his parents' tempers. Recognition helped him to make friends and to go ahead normally in his grammar school, and the violence of his attitude lessened enormously.

A boy of eleven was very effeminate – he wanted to be a girl, and played like a girl, doing cooking, playing with dolls and so on. He never played with boys at school or joined in with friends. At last, his mother confessed that the father was a violent drunkard, and they lived in surroundings where many were like this. This boy had come to the conclusion that men were horrid, violent creatures and women were nice. He wanted therefore to be like a woman. When this was found out, he was able, with help, to realize most men were not like that, and that many were very nice, kind people. He was able then to accept his maleness and to become a proper boy. To a child, what father or mother are like can be what men and women are like and these early conclusions are never questioned until someone does it for them.

Another boy of nine, whose father disappeared when he was born, lived alone with his mother. She was not a very warm person and unable to give him a great deal. She also worked full-time and used to go out dressed up in the evening, often taking the boy with her on Saturdays to cabarets. She did not want to re-marry, just to have a good time. As she worked full-time, the boy was looked after by other families after school. The boy continually dressed up as a woman, often being a housewife, but generally doing dances and cabaret turns very well indeed. He was also said to dress up in his mother's clothes. It was obvious he was being like his mother. It took a long time for him to produce angry feelings about his mother. One day, he said that his mother had once told him what his name would have been if he had been a girl. He concluded that mother was disappointed he was not a girl, and he was doing his best to oblige. This was the turning point where he was able to begin to accept himself as a boy.

An adopted boy aged ten, of average intelligence, was referred for help because he had terrible temper outbursts. He seemed to have something on his mind. He threatened to leave home and accused his parents of not loving him, but he insisted on sleeping in his parents' room. Recently he was refusing to go to school. Most of these difficulties seemed to start after he had been to a Cubs' camp.

His adoptive parents were warm and cheerful with a good extended family living in the district. They tended to spoil the boy, but lacked understanding and insight. They adopted the boy when he was three months old. When he was three years old, they told him that they had gone to a home and chosen him from a lot of other babies and he had never asked any further questions. A few months after the Cub camp he suddenly accused his parents of never telling him he had been adopted; he had to find out for himself when he was away at camp. Obviously, the other boys had thrown at him that he was adopted and he had taken this to mean something dreadful.

In the playroom he remained huddled up in a duffle coat with the hood up, and hardly said a word. He did, however, make pictures in the sand tray in which one end of the tray was shut off by thick sand walls reinforced by several rows of high fences. Behind the walls was a secret place with secret ways in. People try to find out these secrets which are being kept from them, no amount of attack on their part was successful.

The secret was taken to be the fact of his adoption. He did not understand what this meant. After we had discussed the difference between an adopted son and a son who was not adopted – he removed his coat, he looked more cheerful and he became quite talkative. He could then produce his strong feelings of rivalry with father for mother's attention, and therapy could continue. This is a good example of how difficult it is for a child to ask the right questions and how they jump to conclusions from other people's attitudes as well as from what they say.

Terrifying or horrifying ideas about sex can also cause some of a child's difficulties. One boy of nine was very aggressive and abusive to his mother. His father was away a great deal in the army. One of the reasons for his aggression was that he thought women could have babies just whenever they liked, without consulting anyone, and that men were only there to make money for these women.

One girl had suddenly become afraid, hated to go to school and would not go out and meet her friends. This was quite different behaviour. The whole difficulty in this case stemmed from her idea that when babies were born, the mothers were ripped open and the baby burst out, and she had now arrived at the age when she could have babies. When she understood the true facts, there were no more difficulties.

A boy of about ten, a very complex case from a difficult and unhappy home situation, was one day painting on the wall pictures of dogs and puppies in a muddy brown colour. When asked how puppies came out he said that the dog ate 'business' which made the puppies. He had seen dogs eating 'business' in the streets. This became connected with human beings as well, so that the whole idea of birth and babies was disgusting for him. He could of course have found out by asking questions, but children rarely ask these difficult questions; very often they get no answer if they do, though it may never occur to them to ask, or the question may never have been clearly formulated. This has to be done by the therapist.

In addition to such harmful feeling-ideas which the child may develop there is the whole field of conflict with the parents, the child's wishes in conflict with each other, wanting what he cannot have. Here, work with the parents is essential – as the child lets us know through his play what are his needs, then we must see that parents modify their attitudes to supply these needs.

For example, one little boy of four was shy, subdued and full of fears. When he came to the playroom, he was a sturdy little boy and in the atmosphere of the playroom he began letting himself go, running around, riding a horse, messing with sand and water and paint and so on. It was found that the nice young parents were anxious that their child should behave properly and thought this meant being clean and quiet. When they realized that normal little boys were not like this, they allowed him to behave differently, to their own relief. As he let go, he became very active at school, letting off all his pent-up energy. He had an understanding teacher who every now and then sent him out to run so many times round the playground. Needless to say, his fear disappeared and he soon settled to being a normal rumbustious small boy.

Two little girls, one of seven, and another of nine, from very different backgrounds at different dates, were leading their families a real dance. The younger girl had one older sister. She had had an accident when she was five, falling off a swing. Naturally, a great fuss was made of this and of her resultant fears at night. Gradually, this passed, but her fears began to increase and she disturbed her parents at all hours. She also continually behaved in the most trying manner, making a noise on the piano when her parents wanted to be quiet, making a fuss at meal times, then screaming and rushing off to lock herself in the lavatory. She was making no friends at school. Her parents were very worried and frightened. When she first came to the playroom, she kicked and screamed and wanted to run off. The therapist held her firmly and told her she would stay for an hour and then go home. It was obvious from her attitude and behaviour that what she was expressing was temper and not fear. The next time she came to the clinic, she greeted the therapist with a smile and ran into the playroom. It then seemed she had become afraid of her temper and could not get out of the pattern she had set herself. Firmness on the part of the therapist had reassured her. It soon became obvious that she wanted attention, as we all do, and through her experience after the accident, had decided that her trying behaviour was the way to get this. The parents were advised to pay no attention to negative behaviour, but to welcome quietly, more positive behaviour. This they bravely did, putting up with terrible behaviour and taking no notice. During this time, her problems were discussed with her in the playroom. She soon gave up her infuriating behaviour. Then one day, her father came in tired from the farm and sat down. To his surprise and delight, he found the little girl shyly bringing him a cup of tea she had made. She now began to behave in a more positive manner, was able to go out and play and make friends and to behave normally at home.

The other little girl behaved in much the same way. She was

the middle child of five brothers and sisters. She wanted to be mother's baby for ever. This wish was portrayed in her drawings and sand pictures of idyllic family scenes, always with lots of water around in bowls and basins. The parents were given the same advice, and were able to carry this out and to get the older siblings to co-operate. The unreality of her wishes were discussed in the playroom. Her behaviour no longer produced the desired effect at home and with help, she was able gradually to accept her position as a little girl of nine, and to deal with this in a normal manner, thus becoming very much happier.

Another example is of a boy of eleven with a twin brother. His twin was always just a little better at everything than he was. He also had a brother of two-and-a-half. The crisis came to a head when the twins were put into different classes in their new school. This boy then refused to attend school. One day he did a picture in the sand. There was a castle in which was King Richard and his knights. Approaching the castle is Prince John with his knights, who will attack the castle. The two are brothers and Prince John wants his brother's throne. The conflict between brothers is one problem here.

A boy of seven came to us because of his screaming tantrums and uncontrolled behaviour at school. He played out with puppets a very usual boys' conflict, that of rivalry with his father and his fear of the consequences. He took the boy puppet and gave the king puppet to the therapist. The boy then proceeded to knock out the king, saying that he wanted to be king. When the king was completely knocked out, the therapist was given the crocodile and the boy puppet put his head in the crocodile's mouth.

Second aspect of play
We now come to the second aspect of play at the Institute. Through play, a child can gain satisfaction, doing things he has never been able to do for one reason or another. He is also able to find out what he can do, or that he is capable of doing things he always thought he could not do.

Many children who come to us have a horror of anything

dirty, dare not make a noise, or have never run about freely or dared to climb. Such inhibitions may be due to a variety of underlying feelings or ideas. When these have been expressed or discussed, the child will tentatively at first, touch wet sand, spill paint, make a noise, or rush about and begin to climb. He thus finds out that he can really do such things and nothing dreadful happens. He can also get satisfaction from really being very messy and so on, in the clinic, and not outside, so that this phase can disappear in its exaggerated form without causing trouble in the family.

Some children long to be babies. They do not want to grow older. They want the time when they had their mother's whole attention and she ran after them bringing them all they needed. Some such children will play at being a baby, even to lying in a cot, sucking a bottle, with the therapist being mother. This is a tremendous experience for them. The therapist soon points out that as he is a baby, he cannot just get up and go and play and so on, and he comes to realize that being a baby is not all that he imagined, and can put this false longing behind him.

One boy of ten was sent to us because he had asthma and was over-attached to his mother. She was a highly nervous woman and over-protective, but one who was willing to do all she could for her son. Towards the end of treatment, the boy played out most graphically being attached to his mother, and wanting to leave her. He filled the baby's bottle and sucked it leaning against the therapist. He then pointed to the rail of the open sliding doors between the two rooms and said that if he crossed that line, the war would start; if he crossed back again, he would be the therapist's prisoner. He then left the bottle, crossed over the line and the therapist had to throw things at him; then he crossed back again and once more sucked at the bottle leaning against the therapist. This was played out for some time while the therapist talked about the baby becoming independent and feeling that his mother did not like this. Gradually, instead of the therapist throwing things at the baby, the baby began attacking the therapist and finally going off on his own. This clearly shows the boy's conflict about growing up, as a baby he is a prisoner, but when he leaves his mother she does not like it. By playing this out he was able to get free.

Some children who come have never succeeded in anything and are in despair. In the playroom they can gradually find out that they can do things, and can therefore gain gradually more confidence to express their underlying difficulties. We have a good deal of construction material for this purpose, and also so that a child who has been aggressive and destructive can sit down and put things together, thus so to speak, putting himself together. Some children have been told that they are no good with their hands, or have never been given play material and are sure they cannot make anything, they feel they are no good. This affects their school-work and their social life, in our experience this particularly applies to West Indian children. Starting with very simple material, these children gain confidence, then want to try something more difficult. They acquire a sense of achievement for the first time, which helps considerably in their treatment.

There was one boy who was very depressed and very inarticulate, from an Educationally Sub-Normal school. Very quickly he found construction material with which he built very imaginative structures. Soon he began decorating the doll's house; he quickly grasped how to cut out 'Contact' to stick on the walls and round the doors. He did this meticulously and very accurately. He painted the woodwork well, made new doors and attached them with hinges. From this he moved to carpentry, and with our primitive tools and scrappy wood made several toys for his sister. No one before had realized he was capable in this practical manner. He became more alert and more talkative at home. He was then given help with his reading. Unfortunately, his school had no woodwork, and we could not get him transferred, so his real skill was not consolidated and followed up.

Many West Indian children who come to us are at first only able to run around in a rather aimless manner. They will not try to do anything else. It is with difficulty that they can be persuaded that they have ideas and can do things. Gradually, they make tentative efforts at making a picture in the sand tray or a drawing, setting up a railway, or making a simple construction.

When they find that after all they have ideas and can do things, they are delighted; much of our work with these children is giving them the kind of education that most English families give to their small children before they go to school. Some West Indian parents, however, consider that as long as they feed and clothe them well, that is all they need do. It never occurs to them to play with their children, read to them or take them out. Often the children are given no worthwhile toys. These children are then precipitated into our schools with none of the basic education that English children have had. They start, therefore, at a disadvantage and find the only way to make some impression is to disrupt the school. At the clinic, we try to fill that gap and make them realize they are as adept as English children.

Third aspect of play

We now come to the third aspect of the playroom. When the various difficulties for which the children come begin to be resolved, a great deal of energy is released. They are now able to co-operate and to have a positive attitude to life. Their play will change, and they become responsive and constructive. Reports from school frequently confirm the changed attitude. They show greater concentration, make friends and go ahead with their school-work.

During the period when the child attends, wherever possible the parents are seen regularly or at varying intervals. Reports from the parents are obtained which can be discussed with the child. The parents are also helped to understand their child and to change their attitude to him. Often their own difficulties are discussed so they too reach a better understanding of themselves and their family relationship.

Psychotherapy with adolescents

William Allchin

Introduction

Present-day psychiatry provides no unified theoretical base from which to work, nor does it give a coherent account of practical, pragmatic measures. Thus it would be almost impossible to state briefly a definition of psychotherapy which would be accepted by many as satisfactory. Such a definition would be taken as referring to therapeutic work with adult patients and from that position, the special variations necessary for dealing with children and adolescents might become clear, along with the reasons for them.

Psychotherapy entails a special kind of relationship, sometimes involving two people only, sometimes including a number. It may give rise to an extraordinary intimacy, combined with a strange remoteness. It is a deep relationship, yet on a very narrow base. There is an element of mutuality in it, yet in other respects it is hopelessly lop-sided. It is rarely freely chosen. And patients seeking psychotherapy within a state health service may have no choice when it comes to the actual therapist.

The meeting of these persons, two or more, will be profoundly affected by many other people. There will be those who, over historical time, have established the general cultural and religious framework of thought and feeling. There will be those who contributed more directly to the body of 'professional' or technical knowledge which informs the particular therapist or clinic. Then there will be a whole set of economic and political factors which determine the kind of place the therapy takes place in, the frequency of it (through the pressure of numbers on the therapist), and how the money aspect of the relationship is expressed, and experienced.

A good working definition is provided by R. F. Hobson, who writes: 'Psychotherapy is regarded as a process of creative problem-solving occurring in a dialogue between two or more persons.'[1]

Such a process is set under way for particular reasons, and it comes to an end when the problems are resolved, or those particular people find they can produce no resolution. The limits of psychotherapy have been clearly stated by Karl Jaspers in the following passage:

> Therapy cannot be a substitute for something that only life itself can bring. For instance, we can only become transparently ourselves through a lifetime of loving communication in the course of a destiny shared with others. On the other hand such clarification as is brought about by psychotherapeutic means always remains something limited, objective, theoretical and restricted by authority. A professional performance constantly repeated on behalf of many never reaches the goal which only engagement in mutuality can attain. Further life brings responsible tasks, perforce, and there are the real demands of work which no therapy however artful can contrive.[2]

Two basic modes of psychotherapy can be described. Both are founded on the hypothesis of the unconscious mind and its reciprocal and compensatory relationship to consciousness. The first mode is 'analytical' or uncovering, and includes, of course, what is usually referred to as psychoanalysis. R. F. Hobson sums it up thus:

> By analysis I mean the modification of conscious attitudes by the assimilation of hitherto unconscious elements, achieved by experience and understanding of a relationship with one or more people. The main feature of analysis is the recognition, elucidation and solution of resistances, resulting in more complete relationships, correction of defects in the apprehension of the external and social environment, and the release of healing (wholing) processes in the psyche.[3]

Under the same heading comes analytically oriented psycho-therapy. The second mode is the supportive one, where although objectives sound more limited, and the therapy less demanding, yet this is not so. The same skills are required of the therapist including understanding of the transference and countertrans-ference aspects of the relationship, although these are not to be analysed or brought into awareness.

Either type of therapy may involve the therapist in a deep and prolonged commitment. As Karl Jaspers puts it: 'In psycho-therapy the demand for the personal involvement of the doctor is so heavy that complete gratification only occurs in isolated cases, if at all. V. Weizsäcker formulated the demand as follows: "only when the doctor has been deeply touched by the illness, infected by it, excited, frightened, shaken, only when it has been transferred to him, continues in him, and is referred to himself by his own consciousness – only then and to that extent can he deal with it successfully!" '[4]

These general considerations apply to the work with adoles-cents, and it was necessary to state them so as to have a context in which to set the special characteristics to be discussed. In this endeavour the term adolescent is used to refer to people coming within the age range of twelve to twenty years. The London Borough of Brent Consultation Centre for the Study of Adoles-cence usually see adolescents ranging from fourteen to twenty-three years. Varma[5] says: 'There is no universally accepted definition of adolescence.' Rogers[6] writes that adolescence may be defined in a number of ways – for example, as a period of physical development, as a chronological age span, or as a socio-logical phenomenon. To this certainly should be added, as a fourth way, the psychological approach which views adoles-cence as a period of distinct changes.

The term adolescence comes from the Latin verb *adolescere* meaning to grow into maturity. In this sense Rogers thinks ado-lescence is a process rather than a period, a process of achieving the attitudes and beliefs needed for effective participation in society.

Physical development is taken into consideration in the definition of adolescence given by English.[7] This period lasts from the beginning of puberty to the attainment of maturity: the transitional stage during which the youth is becoming an adult man or woman.

In a chronological approach we find that in her book *Child Development*, Hurlock[8] distinguishes pre-adolescence, age ten through twelve; early adolescence, age thirteen through sixteen; and late adolescence, age seventeen through twenty-one . . . For further details in this connection, the reader should consult these and other references.

The state of being between these ages has its own features and these will determine the forms and functioning of the appropriate psychotherapy. Its characteristics have been so much studied and discussed in recent years[9, 10] that a brief capitulation will be sufficient.

Any organism in a state of rapid change is vulnerable, and the adolescent is especially so. The physical expression of his being is changing, producing disfigurements such as bulges or spots and, even more, producing a whole series of phantasies and excitations which seem to have their own meaning and momentum. Emotionally there is marked instability of mood. Rapid changes lead to uncertainty as to how the feeling state will be from one minute to another. And the swings of mood sound extreme when viewed from the relative stability of later experience. Intellectually the development of conceptual and abstract thought has a kind of intoxication all its own. And the failure to reach this stage also has significant repercussions. In Western culture the organism in this state is subject to massive social demands, requiring decisions and choices which can affect the person's subsequent life pattern in an almost irreversible manner.

The very fluidity of the psychic state, leading as it does to bewildering and profuse symptomatology, is also hopeful. At this stage with powerful inner drives towards development and integration, these may be a significant chance to resolve some of the earlier emotional tangles, and to heal some of the wounds already sustained.

All these factors will point to the need for the therapist to be especially flexible, sensitive, and alert. The steady, plodding sessions of adult analysis faced with a relatively stable ego and years of defensive manoeuvres to deal with, must give place to a capacity to deal with wide and rapid fluctuations of depth, tempo, intensity and degree of disturbance of the adolescent state.

It seems an obvious requirement that therapists working in this field must have some first-hand experience of the analytical and therapeutic process from the standpoint of the 'patient', and some chance to look again at the vulnerable areas of their own adolescence. The adolescent patient may be particularly skilful in tempting, seducing or luring the 'adult' therapist into situations of surprising unawareness and weakness.

In the neurotic problems of the adolescent an analytical type of therapy may be indicated. This implies working with a patient who has experienced basic care in the early years and whose levels of development have been activated by the relationships in the home with both parents, and very likely siblings as well. The therapy can proceed on the basis of a transference neurosis and the 'as if' of symbolic elements in the relationship can be experienced as such by both parties, and do their healing work. In border-line or frankly psychotic states the symbolic process itself is out of balance, with the unconscious processes predominating. Here analysis is hardly yet possible but the therapist's skill will be put to establishing a relationship within which the patient's ego can be strengthened and enlarged. Analytical work might then be called for at a later stage.

States of emotional deprivation with consequent failure of personality development, particularly in areas dealing with impulse control and self-awareness seem to require something different. The relationship cannot be intellectually satisfying, nor experienced on an 'as if' level. Needs to be met are concrete, realistic and immediate. Hence the psychotherapist has to exercise a different skill. The forming of the relationship itself may be the keystone. It may be limited, yet it may also be for the deprived person, a relationship which is emotionally nutritious, without persecuting ideas or interpretations being offered. It may be one in which trust can be discovered or rediscovered, and later, generalized out to others. But the psychotherapy alone cannot play more than a part in the attempted healing of the deprivation. All other staff members along with the therapist will bear a heavy share of the day-to-day 'treatment' or 'living together' process. Here the therapist must try to act as an interpreter, on the basis of his knowledge of the dynamics of the condition, and with the actual authority and insight springing from his own relationship with the patient. Again, he must give genuine understanding and emotional support to those others involved with the patient. Clever explanations and interpretations may be felt by them also as persecution, and render them less able to try to sustain the emotional burden of the prolonged care which is involved.

Therapy with out-patients

It is sometimes possible to attempt the resolution of a neurotic disorder by means of out-patient sessions. Such a situation might be the treatment of school refusal based on a high level of separation anxiety. A small number of well-motivated adolescents can be helped by regular sessions once a week. Two sessions a week gives the possibility of more consecutive work, and greater containment of anxiety. Such therapy may aim at uncovering, at making conscious and may involve some analysis of the transference.

Sessions or visits spaced out at one every two weeks, or the monthly visit, allow for no more than a friendly supportive relationship to develop. But such an intervention may lead to change, i.e. as the balance of affective intake improves, behaviour such as stealing may, 'unexpectedly', stop.

In general, the setting for this work needs to be different from the usual consulting room used for work with children, with its drawing and painting equipment, dolls and toys, and sand trays. There needs to be a friendliness and informality about the reception on arrival, and about the telephone persona of the clinic. Hesitant adolescents may so easily be put off. The adolescent clinic should make psychotherapy sessions available after working hours. There will need to be ready availability for extra sessions, if patients cannot contain the anxiety and tension in between weekly or fortnightly sessions.

Effective psychotherapeutic work can be done in groups, either of an analytic or supportive kind.

Because the disturbed adolescent becomes disorganized socially, the psychotherapist is often involved in trying to mobilize other forms of help. Related supportive measures include:

a) Day centres
b) Hostels, with psychiatric support and supervision
c) Attention to work problems

Psychotherapy should be one of the facilities available at a day centre. For the older adolescent, who is struggling to establish himself in a working role while living in a hostel, any kind of explorative psychotherapy is likely to be contra-indicated. The demands of the full working day are likely to be exhausting. However, supportive interviews may be helpful, not only supplementing the help given by the hostel staff, but also enabling the therapist to guide the staff in their approach. The placing of an adolescent boy or girl in a hostel where a work capacity is assumed often leads to a great deal of suffering. And this is not only for the boy or girl. If the adolescent is still so immature both emotionally and socially, then the hostel itself is set an impossible task. This is to establish normal work, social and recreational activities, where the psychological foundation for them does not yet exist. Ideally, a proper therapeutic placement may be somewhere where work is available on the premises, and where its demands can be regulated and graded according to the adolescent's actual state of development and ability to function.

Therapy with in-patients

Where out-patient measures have failed the in-patient setting offers another chance of resolving the adolescent's difficulties. Ideally it should be one specially created to meet the needs of the patient who may be living away from home for the first time, and even if not for the first time, yet the move itself should be one which may confer a therapeutic advantage. Within an environment which itself ought to be therapeutic, facilities should be available for individual psychotherapy, group therapy, and both of these, supported by educational, recreational and other facilities.

It is now recognized that institutions are not, *per se*, as Dr Meyer shows elsewhere in this book, therapeutic. Continuous work is necessary to ensure that an institution at least does not add to a patient's difficulties, let alone make a positive contribution in helping him to solve them. Gathering together groups of young people with various difficulties, however described, makes for a potentially explosive situation. It is dangerous and futile to set up such a group unless there is a serious intention to provide adequate facilities. If the unit is designated as psychiatric, then there must be adequate time for the provision of psychotherapy. The necessity for such provision is underlined by the experience that the use of drugs makes only a small contribution to the overall therapeutic plan for young people.

Individual psychotherapy in the in-patient setting presents special opportunities and difficulties.

The milieu itself must be working harmoniously with the consulting room. That is to say, the ideology of treatment must be consistent throughout the environment. The value system that governs the interaction of the two-group within the office or consulting room, must be consonant with that animating the unit as a whole. Thus therapy needs to be founded on a sound theoretical base which provides a coherent account of psychopathological phenomena, and also of treatment procedures. The in-patient setting should then make provision for intensive contact, daily if necessary, between therapist and patient for a prolonged period. It should provide adequate 'holding power' in order that the therapist can take the patient safely through stages of disintegration of ego function, the capacity to distinguish between reality and phantasy, or marked regression. Such psychotherapy will need to be 'analytical' in the sense already described. Modifications on classical techniques described in work with adult patients will be necessary. The therapist may need to be more active in every way, and more flexible, in line with the rapidly changing state of the patient's psyche. There will inevitably be discussion of confidential material outside the actual sessions, and distorted views and irrational feelings may spread from one person to another. The therapist both knows more about, and is held responsible for many other things which the patient experiences each twenty-four hours in the unit, than he would know or deal with as a result of the out-patient session, with the patient living at home or elsewhere. The relationship of patient and therapist in a particular room forms one inner container. The unit itself provides an overall container which must contain and sustain both therapist and patient. This will call for a high degree of intimate working together of doctor or therapist, nursing or house staff and of other staff members who make up the living tissue of the unit container. Such a system will be put to a high degree of test when the adolescent requires nursing in bed in a state of marked regression, when primitive states of dependence, fear and rage may mark the treatment situation.

Such intensive therapy may be likened to the journey which goes through distinct phases. These have often been described. The initial phase after admission is when defences hold up, and the patient assesses the unit, and the people in it. If he feels safe, then can begin an unwinding or disintegration, with increasing anxiety, depression or acting out. Much reliance is now placed on the therapist, who must guide himself and his patient and the supporting staff through these dangerous periods. Later comes a new integration and finally an emphasis on preparation for taking the next step, usually away from the unit to home or to lodgings or to a hostel. During this process which may last for up to two or three years, therapeutic ends may be assisted by drawing, painting, modelling, playing football or writing poetry, as well as other activities.

Such a major operation, opening the patient to serious risks, is a constant hazard if facilities are inadequate. Shortage of nursing staff can undermine the whole proceeding. But in this sense, it differs in no way from medical or surgical procedures elsewhere, except that the intensity is variable and the duration may be long.

However, such prolonged and intensive psychotherapy is

neither indicated nor available for all patients. Some may be more suitable for group psychotherapy, but how far such groups can be successfully conducted, alongside intensive individual sessions is not certain. If the unit as a whole has unresolved tensions and conflicts, then these may well force their way out through the groups and have a disruptive effect. For other patients the main therapeutic effect will be mediated through the milieu as a whole, and the psychotherapist's task will be directed to the measures needed to maintain the therapeutic milieu. These include community meetings, staff meetings and conferences and other special planned or *ad hoc* staff/patient confrontations.

Thus the psychotherapist will need to be a robust and versatile person, able to be sensitive and disciplined for the strict interchanges of the individual session, but also able and willing to play a full part in the work of creating the total milieu in which his office or consulting room finds itself.

After prolonged and intensive in-patient treatment, the therapist or the unit will continue to function as a special kind of support, particularly where the residues of the dependent relationships are gradually dissolving. It is rarely possible for the home clinic or referring psychiatrist to carry on this task. If hostel placement is indicated, then again it is clear that the therapeutic approach of the hostel must be at least generally sympathetic to and understanding of the kind of struggle which the young person has been through in the adolescent unit itself, whilst undergoing psychotherapy.

Problems of treatment and security

With the strong basic drives which operate during the period of adolescence and the relatively weak ego-function which is also characteristic, the question of 'acting out' and of ensuring the physical safety of the adolescent patient undergoing treatment is of paramount importance. Possibilities of suicidal behaviour, self-mutilation, damage to other patients and to the safety of the physical environment make naturally for a high level of anxiety for the psychotherapist.

Security, or safety for the patient in this sense, is seen as the function of the container. This comprises both the physical buildings, the people in them and intangible psychological atmosphere which has a containing, restraining, or supporting effect. At the present time, a generalization could, perhaps, be made, that where there are possibilities of active and even intensive psychotherapy, there tends to be less physical security; where the physical security exists, there tends to be less emphasis on the personal and psychological provision. For example, the open adolescent unit, with barely adequate staff members may fail as a container for a patient who becomes acutely and determinedly suicidal, or psychotic to a degree requiring definite physical boundaries, such as a closed ward. Yet the safer setting of the closed ward in an adult psychiatric unit will rarely be able to provide the facility for regular psychotherapy. Again, the community home (ex-approved school) or Borstal institution may provide a high degree of physical security, and control, but not have the possibilities of regular psychotherapy. How far these requirements may be able to be brought together, either in establishments designed and run by the Home Office, or in hospital-type units within the Health Service, remains to be seen. For the motivated and willing patient, going through an intense adolescent crisis, or a psychotic episode, or in the throes of untangling a severe neurosis of long standing, the hospital type of unit seems indicated.

For the emotionally deprived adolescent still immature in every way, and functioning on a level of primitive and paranoid anxieties, there exist at the moment quite inadequate facilities. It is possible, by means of external routine and control to help some such youngsters develop at least a measure of control and social behaviour. But such a limited objective still leaves them partially handicapped and exceedingly vulnerable. Their continuing social maladjustment is likely to prove costly to the community over the long term, and destines them to a life pattern of continuing sadness, frustration and isolation.

Ultimately, security for them, as for ourselves, is based on stable and satisfying human relationships within a context of adequate material provisions, shared with justice.

Conclusion

Psychotherapy, whether analytical or supportive is an effective treatment method in cases of adolescent neuroses, borderline or acute psychosis and in some personality disorders. In some cases drugs may be needed as adjuvants.

The in-patient setting offers an important 'last chance' when other attempts have failed. The techniques, disciplines and methods of psychoanalysis, using that term broadly, supply a basic treatment model to which suitable adaptation can be made to meet the specific needs of this age group. There is now a large body of knowledge, clinical observation and worked out theory, to supply something which will go towards a rational basis for psychotherapy, firmly grounded in developmental and dynamic concepts. But such therapy is not practised in a vacuum and experience soon shows how rudimentary and inadequate facilities are, and how in practice, psychotherapy is rarely possible, except on a small scale.

There are those who believe that such a personal and rational method of treatment such as psychoanalysis or psychotherapy has never been shown to be effective, or been proved, in what they would call a scientific sense. And there are those who hail the psycho-pharmacological revolution as the greatest therapeutic advance in recent times. Enthusiasts for drug treatment rarely talk of its failures. And the medical journals abound in advertisements for the use of drugs. Underlying this whole situation are factors beyond the clinical field itself, factors which are essentially economic and political. The current vogue for drug therapy of psychiatric disorders is convenient economically and politically, for it is economical of medical and therapeutic manpower, and profitable to the makers of drugs. Psychotherapy, although humane, rational and personal as a treatment method, is expensive in terms of people and time, and money.

These political and economic factors are what may be implied by the term 'State', used by Jaspers, when he writes as follows:

All therapy, psychotherapy and attitudes to patients depend upon the State, religion, social conditions, the dominant cultural tendencies of the age, and finally but never solely on accepted scientific views.

The State lays down, or moulds by its policies the basic human relationships, the organization of help and security, the utilization of resources, the giving or withholding of rights.[11]

One of the striking features of an overall view of present-day psychiatry is its amazing impoverishment, and one aspect of this is how small are the possibilities for psychotherapeutic treatment for adolescents. But not only for them. Over the whole field the dearth of facilities means not only inadequate treatment now, but continuing ignorance of psychopathology and its appropriate therapy in the future.

Psychotherapy with adults

Lionel Kreeger

Rycroft[1] in his *Critical Dictionary of Psychoanalysis*, offers the following definition of psychotherapy: 'any form of "talking cure" (in all forms of psychotherapy one or other party talks and in most forms, both). Psychotherapy may be either individual or group, superficial or deep, interpretive, supportive, or suggestive, the latter three differing in the intention underlying the therapist's utterances. Intensive refers either to the frequency of the patient's attendances or to the zeal displayed by the therapist. The term always differentiates from physical treatment but, according to context, either includes or excludes psychoanalysis despite the fact that psychoanalysis can correctly be described as long-term, intensive, interpretive psychotherapy.'

Let us take this definition as the basis for exploring this field.

The talking cure

Psychotherapy is primarily concerned with communication, usually verbal, but it must be accepted that non-verbal communications can be of the greatest importance in this form of treatment. It is common knowledge that talking about one's problems can be helpful; to unload on somebody else, to get things off one's chest brings a certain degree of relief. In its most dramatic form catharsis, which means literally purging, occurs when hitherto repressed memories flood into consciousness accompanied by the discharge of the emotion attached to the repressed memory or experience. At a non-verbal level, 'acting-out' may occur, in which activity substitutes for memory. Instead of giving a conscious verbal expression to some area of conflict within him, he demonstrates that conflict by some action on his part. For example, one patient was unable to consciously acknowledge the degree of frustration that she experienced within the psychotherapeutic relationship. However, at the end of a session, she would call in at the local baker's shop and buy half a dozen doughnuts, which she would devour voraciously in the street on the way to her car. Eventually she obtained insight into this repetition-compulsion and its significance in terms of her deprived childhood. Although sometimes regarded as being anti-therapeutic, acting-out is an invariable aspect to some extent within the psychotherapeutic relationships and, so long as it does not become an end in itself, should be acknowledged and worked with.

Individual or group psychotherapy

Whilst it is quite possible to draw up lists of the indications for, and value of, both individual and group treatments, frequently the decision as to which is required is based on expediency, that is the availability of treatment. So often within the National Health Service setting of psychiatric practice in this country, the availability of individual staff time is extremely limited. On the whole, individual psychotherapy is more freely available at particular centres which specialize in training and therefore have greater facilities. In ordinary mental hospitals or psychiatric clinics, however, because of short staffing it may just be impossible to provide the individual attention that would be demanded by the number of patients requiring that particular form of treatment. It is here that group psychotherapy presents itself as the treatment of choice in terms of its economy in time. In a recent piece of research, Wing[2] working in Camberwell assessing the need for psychotherapeutic help amongst the patient population, concluded that for the country as a whole there would be a need to appoint a total of some four hundred and eighty full-time consultant psychotherapists in order to cope with the demand for psychotherapy. It is clearly hopeless in these days of governmental economies to expect that any solution will be found at this level. The question of who should do psychotherapy is one which is receiving much attention and is being discussed widely at this present time. One alternative to the appointment of consultant psychotherapists to undertake the actual psychotherapeutic work itself is to use the psychotherapist in the training of ancillary staff; that is nurses, psychiatric social workers, occupational therapists, social therapists, who can then take over the direct treatment of patients under supervision.

Types of psychotherapy

1. *Supportive psychotherapy* – essentially this consists of a therapist listening attentively with understanding and concern to the utterances of the patient. Encouragement may be given to the patient to explore his own thoughts and to express problems, conflicts and anxiety. The therapist may give reassurance, may help with advice dependent upon his own understanding of the situation and may try to help by offering his own personal experiences as a model for the patient to identify with or reject as he feels appropriate.

2. *Suggestive* – In this type of psychotherapy more reliance is placed upon direct suggestion to the patient as an attempt to resolve the underlying difficulties. The most intense and dramatic of the suggestive therapies is hypnosis, or hypnotherapy in which an altered state of consciousness is imposed upon the patient with his co-operation, following which active directions are given. Some hypnotherapists may employ the technique in order to obtain repressed memories, the belief being that it is possible in the hypnotic state to get into closer contact with the deeper areas of the mind. But on the whole hypnosis is used more as a form of suggestion, with post-hypnotic suggestion as the basic tool of the technique.

3. *Interpretive* – With interpretive psychotherapy, the main attempt is to help the understanding of the patient in terms of the meaning of his symptomatology or personal difficulty. The task of the psychotherapist is to try to understand what has happened in the patient's life both externally and internally and thereby to give

meaning to symptoms. Interpretations may be given at the level of the pure understanding of the patient's difficulties as they occurred in his ordinary life, but frequently a special type of interpretive work is employed, that is, the interpretations of the transference relationships between patient and therapist. The term transference means, loosely, the patient's emotional relationship towards the therapist but more specifically, it is the process by which the patient displaces on to the therapist feelings and ideas which derive from previous figures and relationships in his life. He relates to the therapist as if he were in fact some former object or person with whom he has had a relationship. He endows the analyst with the emotional significance of another person or object with which contact has been maintained at some earlier stage of development. For example, a patient might appear to be in a state of great anxiety at the beginning of treatment, conducting himself subserviently in an effort to ingratiate himself with the therapist. This could indicate an uneasy relationship with his father throughout childhood, who may have had a violent and explosive disposition. Essentially, it is the working with the transference that distinguishes analytic psychotherapy from other forms of psychotherapeutic treatment. In intensive, on-going psychotherapy (also of course with psychoanalysis) there is the development of the transference neurosis in which the patient's basic sickness is brought into the therapeutic relationship, which in turn allows it to be worked through in detail during the course of the treatment.

Intensity – Intensive psychotherapy usually refers to a treatment situation in which the patient is seen, say, two or three times a week over a period of perhaps a year or several years. It may be difficult to say where intensive psychotherapy leaves off and psychoanalysis, as such, begins. On the whole, most Freudian analysts consider that psychoanalysis entails the attendance by the patient on five days a week over a period of about four years, though many would agree that four times a week also constitutes psychoanalysis. Below that it is more usual to refer to intensive, psychoanalytically-orientated psychotherapy. With lesser intensity of treatment in which the patient attends perhaps once a week over a period of six months or so, this is termed brief psychotherapy, although the term focal therapy may be used, which would imply that the short-term psychotherapeutic technique is to focus essentially on a specific area of conflict in the patient's emotional make-up.

Physical treatments

The purpose of physical methods of treatment is to remove or counteract the organic cause of the condition, or to modify the symptoms arising from it, usually without any consideration of the meaning of the illness. There is, therefore, a fundamental difference in the theoretical approaches, and it would seem logical in each individual to determine which is the appropriate method. There can, however, be a combination employing both techniques, for example with a person experiencing severe depression it may be reasonable to give him anti-depressant drugs initially whilst undertaking psychotherapeutic exploration of the problems. With intense anxiety, perhaps small doses of a tranquillizing drug may facilitate the ability of the patient to endure the experience of psychotherapy in the initial stages. On the whole, it would seem that ECT (electro-convulsive therapy) contra-indicates psychotherapy in conjunction with this particular form of treatment. Perhaps at the end of a course of ECT it may be appropriate at that time to initiate psychotherapy in order to attempt to understand the causation of the depressive illness, but the physiological and psychological changes connected with ECT usually makes psychotherapy at that time extremely difficult. One way of looking at the effect of ECT is to consider it in psychological terms, that is that the application of ECT supports the manic defences. Basically this entails denial of depression and the psychological factors leading to it, with a flight into a happier state of mind, sometimes to the point of gaiety, which may be inappropriate to the situation. An attempt at this time to go into the underlying conflicts would appear to be antagonistic to the effects of the treatment.

Technique

The technique employed in psychotherapy will depend upon the theoretical structures underlying the method. There are, therefore, as many different techniques, as there are different schools of individual psychotherapeutic thought. Basically one can divide the techniques into two groups: those based upon psychoanalytic principles, and the others. In analytic psychotherapy, the priority will be the examination of the transference and interpretations will tend to be made at the level of the transference relationship. Attention will be directed towards the end of understanding all communications from the patient in terms of the here-and-now relationship with the therapist. Links will be made between remembered childhood experiences and the present experience of the relationship with the therapist. The detailed quality of the interpretations will depend upon the particular school of analytic thinking: for example the classical, Freudian approach will be centred on Oedipal conflict, the manifestations of the Oedipus complex. Briefly this consists of the child's love for and wish to possess the parent of the opposite sex, and his hatred for, and resentment of, the parent of the same sex. Thus the male child will resent the intrusion of his father in his wish to possess his mother. It is a triadic (threesome) situation. In classical psychoanalytic thinking the manifestations of the Oedipus complex will begin in a child of about the age of eighteen months, and will progress in intensity through to the age of five or six years at which time repressive mechanisms come into play with some degree of resolution of the earlier conflict. It is at this time that the latency period is said to begin. Kleinians, on the other hand, believe that the most significant developments occur much earlier, in the first six months of life, and will see the manifestations of Oedipus complex at this early stage. They will be concerned too with the pre-Oedipal developments, the dyadic (one-to-one) relationship of the infant to its mother. At this level of development, the emphasis will be upon part-object relationships (that is the infant's relationship to parts of the mother such as the breast). Certain differences in the quality of interpretation will also result from a Jungian approach to psychotherapy, for example involving the delineation of the collective unconscious from the personal unconscious, and in terms of archetypal symbolism. These concepts will be considered more fully in the later chapter on the work of Jung.

There are many other approaches to psychotherapy. For example, the technique of Rogers which is termed client-centred therapy. In this, the relationship is central to therapy and the reality of the relationship is felt to be the essential aspect. Transference interpretations will be avoided and it is claimed that the dependent relationship on the therapist does not occur with the same intensity as with a transference-interpretive technique. The application of games theory in psychotherapy, as typified by Eric Berne, again will focus more on the manipulative transactions that occur between people rather than concern itself with the analytic aspects. The existentialists focus more on the validation of the individual, of his 'being in the world', and attempt to understand the confusion that results from family conflicts and social pressures. Behavioural psychotherapy employs a quite different technique dependent upon conditioning methods and the basic belief that symptoms are without meaning and purely learned responses. The influence of the transference upon the treatment situation is denied by many behavioural therapists, but some would admit that, although not dealt with during the course of treatment, it plays some part in the therapeutic result.

Analytic psychotherapy

Having considered the background, let us now turn to a more detailed account of psychotherapy with adults based on psychoanalytic principles. We can exclude group psychotherapy, at this point, as it will be dealt with in another chapter. Analytic psychotherapy can be of two main types: intensive, psychoanalytically-orientated psychotherapy, and brief or focal psychotherapy. Although having much in common, these two techniques do have basic differences. The decision as to which type of analytic therapy to apply to an individual will be determined firstly by the attitude of the therapist, secondly by the needs of the patient, and thirdly as a matter of expediency, that is the availability of a psychotherapist's time.

Intensive, psychoanalytically-orientated psychotherapy

The border between this technique and full psychoanalysis is blurred; the one merges into the other. Therefore, the consideration of this method is virtually the same as for psychoanalysis.

Timing – The treatment plan will be mutually agreed between patient and therapist on a basis of perhaps two or three sessions per week with the anticipation that treatment will continue for a year or two or perhaps more. The analytic hour usually consists of a 50-minute session, thus allowing the therapist a 10-minute break between patients. Although attempts have been made to reduce the length of time of individual psychotherapeutic sessions, in one case to 20-minute periods, the majority of psychotherapists find that it is just too short a time in which to allow any real contact, involvement, and working through of problems. Longer sessions than the traditional 50-minute period might well be of value with certain patients, but this would involve a further diminution in the number of patients that could be seen by each therapist in a working day.

Punctuality is important on the parts of both patient and therapist and it is usual to keep very strictly to time. Although somewhat rigid in arrangement, it is necessary for the therapist to order his working day and patients develop an increased security within the relationship as a result. Not infrequently, patients may act out by being late or by missing sessions altogether and although this can be useful material in terms of understanding what is happening in the psychotherapeutic situation, the strict arrangements about time will tend to deter against this particular way of resentment or hostility. With regard to holidays, patients are usually expected to fit in with the plans of the therapist.

Analytic setting – It is desirable for the consulting room to be reasonably quiet without the likelihood of interruption. It should be comfortable and warm. Ideally, there should be both a couch and a chair available for the patient so that he can choose whether to adopt the standard, classical, psychoanalytic position, or to sit face to face. Therapists differ in their approach to the question of position; some perhaps insisting on the patient lying on the couch and sitting out of visual range, others may give no clear direction but deal with the choice of the patient in terms of trying to understand the psychopathology of the patient. The supine position probably encourages regression on the part of the patient, that is a tendency to revert to some earlier stage of development. It may also allow easier access to the phantasies surrounding the therapist. A face to face confrontation on the other hand will allow for more reality testing in relationship to the therapist.

Role of therapist – The essential function of the therapist is to be in touch with the mental life of the patient both conscious and unconscious. He must endeavour to set aside his own personal preoccupations and listen with attention, interest, and sympathy to what is being said or demonstrated. His task is to offer deeper meaning to the communications he receives and also to afford greater insight, that is self-awareness, to the patient – to put it in analytic terms, to increase the conscious part of the mind through the investigation of its unconscious area. In Freud's terms, 'where id was there shall ego be'. (Id – the primitive, unorganized, instinctual part of the mind; ego – the rational, reality-based, and organized part of the psychic apparatus.) Another aim of the treatment process is to modify super-ego function. (Super-ego – that part of the ego concerned with self-observation and self-criticism, allied to conscience.)

Originally, the analyst was encouraged to function as a mirror, passively reflecting back to the patient his own image. In recent years, the analyst has assumed a more active role, for example, his own self-awareness of internal reactions to the patient, that is, his counter-transference.

Free association – In the early days of psychoanalysis patients would be instructed in the method of free association, that is to say that they would be told to allow their minds to wander freely and to say anything and everything that comes to mind without conscious withholding. The analyst would insist that they obey the basic rule, that they should report their thoughts without reservation. In this way it was hoped that resistance to communicating thoughts or ideas would be minimized. Today it is probable that few therapists would bother to give this instruction, preferring to deal with resistance as it arises. They will know from their own experience and that of others that even with the most co-operative of patients, there will be withholding and blocking of certain ideas and feelings and that one of the tasks of psychotherapy is to provide a safe situation in which eventually it will be possible for these to be expressed.

Dream work – Freud described dreams as the 'Royal road to the unconscious', and certainly the reporting of dreams during psychotherapy can be of profound significance on the development of the treatment situation. For example, after the first session of psychotherapy a patient reported a dream in which he was in a motor car driving along a winding road with many hazards. He found himself not in the driving seat but in the back of the car and had to lean over the front seats in order to control the steering wheel. He could not get his feet to the accelerator or brake pedals and was therefore unable to control the speed of the vehicle. This dream clearly symbolized his intense anxiety on entering psychotherapy with the threat of losing emotional control.

From a psychoanalytic point of view, dreams have firstly a manifest content which is the consciously remembered detail of the dream, and secondly a latent content which is arrived at by association to the dream material by the patient and the working together of patient and therapist at an interpretive level. Originally the symbolic content of a dream received primary consideration but today, whilst acknowledging the potential importance of dream symbols, priority may be given to the context of the dream as it relates to the transference relationship. For example, the patient who floods the therapist with dreams may be doing so as a defensive manoeuvre. Fascinating dream content and impressive, associative work may be obscuring some other important area of conflict. One patient went through a period in which he would bring to his sessions several dreams from the previous night. They were long, complicated, full of interesting material. He appeared to be working hard in associating to the dreams and all would seem to be going well. It eventually transpired, however, that throughout this period he was experiencing considerable marital difficulties and was planning to leave his wife, none of this being reported at that time.

Transference – The importance of transference in analytic therapy has already been stressed. Transference elements may be apparent in the first contact, but it is with the development of the transference neurosis that the main psychotherapeutic work is done. This term implies the introduction into the psychotherapeutic relationship of the neurotic conflicts that have pre-existed. Within the transference neurosis, re-constructions can be made of earlier conflicts and experiences. This is of particular importance in Kleinian psychotherapy in which an attempt is made to work with the events of the first six months of life. At this pre-verbal stage of development there are no words to specify the experiences and one can only attempt to make the necessary verbal re-constructions in the course of therapy. The hope is that with the working through and resolution of the transference neurosis there will be significant changes in symptomatology or basic character structure in the patient.

In the early days of psychoanalysis, the term counter-transference used to be applied in the sense of the analyst's transference to his patient. In other words, that the analyst's own neurotic conflicts will be involved in his perception of the individual. Naturally this would be a source of disturbance to the analyst's objective assessment. In current analytic thinking, counter-transference is also understood in terms of the analyst's spontaneous emotional response to his patient which is valued as a subjective indication of what the patient is doing to him. Another way of putting it is that he is on the receiving end of the process known as projective identification in which the patient psychologically pushes into the therapist his own emotional activity. It is at this level of working that perhaps the value of personal analysis for the therapist is so vital so that he may more readily be able to distinguish between his own emotional responses as an expression of his own personal neurosis as against a more valid response to the patient.

Termination – The decision to end a course of psychotherapy may be taken by both patient and therapist together or unilaterally. The patient may feel content with the progress made during psychotherapy or may decide to stop for other reasons. The therapist may conclude that it is unlikely that further progress will occur or that it is in the best interests of the patient to work through termination at this time. However the decision is taken it is desirable that sufficient time be allowed to complete the work of terminating. Mixed emotional responses are common with loving feelings and gratitude on the one hand but also resentment and anger at having to end the relationship. Frequently, a sense of being able to make a 'new beginning' (to use Balint's phrase), emerges as a result of having dealt with disabling neurotic tendencies.

Brief psychotherapy
This is also known as short-term psychotherapy or focal therapy. Whilst psychoanalytic principles may be applied to this method, the sense of timelessness inherent in psychoanalysis or in intensive psychoanalytic psychotherapy is absent. From the beginning of psychoanalysis, many attempts have been made to shorten treatment; for example, Ferenczi applied active techniques such as playing a definite role in relationship to a patient, and encouraging forced phantasies on chosen themes. Stekel again worked in an active way, employing his personality and intuition in the furtherance of therapeutic change. The most recent and comprehensive assessment of the value and technique of brief psycho-

therapy is that by Malan[3] in his book *A Study of Brief Psychotherapy*. His findings were based on the work of a team of psychoanalytically orientated psychotherapists at the Tavistock Clinic in London. A detailed assessment of patients by the application of standard interviews and specialized psychological tests allowed a focus on the central neurotic conflict. A thorough and early interpretation of the transference surrounding the conflict was then possible and indeed those therapists who were most successful were the ones who made transference interpretations at a very early stage of treatment. The essence of their findings was as follows: 'Prognosis seems to be most favourable when the following conditions apply: the patient has a high motivation; the therapist has a high enthusiasm; transference arises early and becomes a major feature of therapy; and grief and anger at termination are important issues.' Their final conclusion was 'that the prognosis is best when there is a willingness on the part of both patient and therapist to become deeply involved, and (in Balint's words), to bear the tension that inevitably ensues'. The importance of this work is that it has shown that good results can be obtained with this technique in patients with moderately severe and long-standing illnesses, and that the results were subject to a careful statistical evaluation.

In undertaking brief psychotherapy, the therapist must make it quite clear at the outset that the number of sessions will be limited. The decision as to the exact number of sessions will depend upon the attitude of the therapist together with the time available to be devoted to this treatment. Usually some twelve to twenty-four sessions in all are offered, that is over a period of three to six months, meeting once a week. On the whole I think it best for therapist and patient to sit face to face, which encourages a more immediate and intense interaction between them. Whilst it is desirable that the therapist allows and indeed encourages the patient to free-associate, some degree of selective attention is necessary. The therapist must be capable at times of setting aside communications which do not appear to focus on the central area of conflict. This is best achieved by an intense preoccupation with the transference manifestations of the relationship.

Perhaps a short clinical example would be helpful in indicating the potential of this technique. A young American woman was referred by her general practitioner because of increasing depression since her engagement a year previously. She had been subject to episodes of depression throughout her life but this had become constant and intense since the engagement. She expressed numerous anxieties about her forthcoming marriage, particularly her fear that the marriage would repeat the pattern of her parents' relationship. From an early age she had been aware of their unhappiness together, of the lack of love between them, and the constant rowing that went on. She had never felt secure in her family situation and was clearly aware of her greedy desire to be loved. She spoke about her rich phantasy life in which she would experience the gratifications denied to her in reality. Her philosophy of life was that it is better to travel hopefully than to arrive. Finalization of any situation or relationship filled her with despair. At her lowest ebb, she would experience the intense desire to stand in the street and scream 'love me, care for me'. She was fearful of having children as she felt incapable of giving them the loving care that she herself had been denied. She was also concerned about her sexual frigidity, enjoying just being held and caressed but being totally unable to allow any genital contact.

She was seen for a total of thirteen sessions over a period of three months. The first few sessions of psychotherapy were concerned with the expression of her despair, and of her deep conviction that she was incapable of committing herself permanently to a relationship, but interspersed with these depressive themes were the indications of her phantasy expectations of me, that in some magical way I could omnipotently provide all the emotional gratifications hitherto denied her. Through working with the transference, and relating her perception of me to her contact with other figures in her life, it became clear that her mother was experienced as a person who had always spoilt things; for example she remembered how she had decorated her room one Christmas, but that when mother saw what she had done her comment was 'what a mess'. Her father was seen as withdrawn, taking little responsibility for what went on in the family. She recalled with surprise that in childhood the only way she could obtain love or concern was by being ill or upset.

At the beginning of the fifth session she reported a sudden and marked improvement in her symptoms. She was less depressed and had been able to experience some sexual pleasure with her fiancé. She related these changes to seeing me in a new light. She thought of me now as 'an impartial judge', and felt that she could begin to trust me. Over the next few sessions, she became aware that part of herself wanted to make some sort of reparation to her parents. She expressed feelings of guilt about receiving help herself whereas her mother was too old to change. She would like to be able to help her parents gain a new and better relationship with each other. At the same time she could begin to look forward to the idea of marriage and of having children. However, these developments were short-lived and by the eighth session she was once again feeling depressed and hopeless. She was very much aware that her treatment was coming to the end and she was 'counting the days'. She was in tears through most of the last two sessions, and complained bitterly that I was failing her in not continuing with the treatment. The thirteenth and final session was taken up with her ambivalence concerning me; on the one hand feeling a certain degree of gratitude and a wish to leave me in a good state, but on the other her anger and resentment at having to accept termination. I left it open for her to contact me again in the future if things were not going well, when we could consider the possibility of alternative treatment. (I had in mind the possibility of placing her in a psychotherapeutic group.) She responded to this, however, by saying that she would prefer to keep me as a phantasy figure so as to continue the relationship in her daydreams. She also dreaded the thought of contacting me again in case I refused to see her which would be a terrible rejection. The session ended and she left in tears. A year later I received a letter from her saying that she was well, that she had married, that sexual relationships were established and enjoyable to her, and that she was expecting a baby.

This abbreviated account illustrates some aspects of the quality of brief psychotherapy, and indeed its therapeutic potential. Not all cases are as dramatically successful as this, and some will undoubtedly need further treatment. Within the National Health Service perhaps the most expedient technique of psychotherapy is a period of brief individual treatment followed by group psychotherapy.

Freud and psychotherapy

Edward Glover

One of the supreme merits of an omnibus volume dealing with methods of treating mental disorder is that it affords the student an opportunity not only of distinguishing between different methods but of comparing the principles on which these techniques are grounded, if indeed the readers happen to be clear that there are principles governing mental function. Per contra, one of the outstanding demerits of the omnibus approach is that the unfortunate student is plunged helplessly into a state of confusion at the very time when he needs to have dependable principles by which to orientate himself about a confused and confusing subject. I fear therefore that it will be necessary from time to time to present views which may be regarded as unjustifiably polemical. I regret this necessity but see no way of avoiding the dilemma.

The protean difficulties, massed misunderstandings and passionate controversies that bedevil those authors who make bold to write on the subject of psychotherapy can best be envisaged if we reflect that *everything* that happens to or is inflicted on a 'patient' (or as our dictionaries wisely suggest – a 'sufferer') whether originating from without or within the 'mental apparatus' constitutes a form of 'treatment'. To be sure 'treatment' and 'therapy' are by no means synonymous, the latter term being almost redolent of prognostic optimism which ultimately leads to abuse of that most ambiguous word 'cure'. To take a simple example: to inflict a prison 'sentence' on an 'offender' is a form of 'treatment', although in fairness it must be admitted that our modern criminologists prefer to use that grimmer and more fatalistic term 'disposal'. The crucial question, however, is whether this 'treatment' lives up to therapeutic standards, in other words, is beneficial at the same time to the needs of the individual and those of the society against whose mandatory standards he has 'offended'. I have indugled in this somewhat tedious exordium for a number of reasons: first and foremost because it is impossible to furnish an intelligible account of the principles and practices of 'Freudian therapy' within the space limitations imposed by multi-disciplined treatises; and second, because the ancillary problems of diagnosis, classification and methodology cannot be rendered adequate justice thereby.

As our more idealistic poets remind us: 'It was not always thus'! Some twenty-five or so years after Freud finally devoted himself to exclusive study of the 'mental apparatus', a distinguished English psychologist (T. W. Mitchell) laid down the standard that whosoever believed in the existence of an 'unconscious mind' (including thereby the existence of an 'unconscious Ego', of repression, of infantile sexuality, of 'conflict' and of 'transference' phenomena) could claim the status of psychoanalyst. A somewhat generous sanction no doubt, since intellectual convictions are no measure of 'belief'; but not far off the mark both then and now. For intellectual conviction may play only a decorative role in scientific understanding.

Should, however, the budding student agree that the concept of unconscious mental function be based on incontrovertible clinical evidence, he thereby commits himself to conceptions that distinguish his systems from those of neurologists, laboratory psychologists, behaviourists, Buddhists (or other supernaturalists) not excluding voo-doists, faith healers or those who believe in the virtues of horoscopy. He may in his more sceptical moments maintain that psychoanalytic theories are as full of lacunae as a Gruyère cheese is distinguished by its empty spaces, but at least he would be prepared to agree that *caseus ipsissimus* is more nutritive than its rind. And again he would not be far wrong; for psychoanalytic theory is notoriously fissile and has just barely escaped the fate of fissile sciences which end in nothingness. So when, as now, I may appear to speak about psychoanalytic therapy, I mean the psychoanalysis of Freud, not of those multifarious ideologies which since his death have been unthinkingly regarded as additions, corrections or emendation of Freudian thinking.

Here, no doubt, the earnest student will naturally say to himself: 'I don't want to be submerged by the factors common to different systems of treatment: all I ask is to be orientated regarding the fundamental differences between various systems.' So be it. But let him again reflect: Once upon a time Ptolemaic astrologers of the period maintained that the sun goes round the earth, a view incidentally that was enthusiastically endorsed by those shepherds who pay attention to the optimum time for milking cows. 'No,' said those revolutionary Copernicans who were prepared to brave the penitential furies of the Inquisition, 'the earth goes round the sun.' Faced with this dilemma many astrological eclectics followed the principle of being all things to all men and Janus-like voted for a compromise. Both propositions, they averred, were true. And to this day the eclectic has basked in the joys of resolving opposites.[1] There are, of course, many ways of distinguishing (Freudian) psychoanalysis from other forms of therapy (treatment). Perhaps one of the most effective of these lies in the tendency of the non-analyst, whether organically or psychologically orientated to assume that 'mind' and 'consciousness' are co-terminous. The psychoanalyst maintains that perceptual consciousness is a 'surface' system exploited by the ego to cope with instinctual stress of whatever form. Granting, as he does, that the first step in the investigation of mind is to study the content of consciousness whether introspected or reported, his concern is to pursue these studies with a view to establishing the nature of the energies that activate mental function, the modes of ego-formation, the laws, principles or mechanisms which regulate the activities of this for the most part unconscious ego-system and ultimately to locate psychically their position in a series which, starting from somatic sources, ends ultimately in action whether adapted or not. When he has reason to believe that the end result is ill-adapted to the patient's needs, or runs contrary to the controls imposed by society or by what he calls the patient's 'super-ego' (unconscious conscience), he is prepared to venture a 'diagnosis' and even to treat the condition *secundam artem*. It is this type of thinking, speculation and formulation that goes by the name of *metapsychology*, and it is this approach that however inadequate or incomplete ultimately dictates the form and rationale of Freudian technique.

Just one more precautionary tag. *Caveat emptor*. Let the neophyte beware of confusing metapsychology with metaphysics (or moral philosophy) or any other form of supernaturalism, for these are no more than exercises in logic-chopping, the authority for which is confined to the more superficial (adult) layers of the mind. But, of course, even the neophyte must start from scratch: and so, fortified by his general scientific reading, he may well consider the proposition that what, for lack of a more illuminating term, we call psychic activities operate somewhere, or rather somewhen, between the phenomena of stimulation and those of discharge (or, in pathological cases, inhibition). This step, however, will involve him in the further concession that the sequence excitation-discharge presupposes some form of energy (power, force, potential and probably instinctual, which by the way should be distinguished from 'instinct'). He need not worry himself too much about the *location* of these forces but he should worry about their sequence in time, their source and development during maturation.

Should he follow this course our neophyte could fairly claim that ideologically speaking he is a 'dynamic psychologist'; the observer in any reputable restaurant who recognizes the energy expended by those who are in process of satisfying their appetites and concludes that the process of satisfying hunger involves the expenditure of mental as well as physical energy is clearly a dynamic psychologist; for the matter of that, the country holiday-maker who has occasion to observe the nuptial flight of the Queen Bee is wittingly, or unwittingly, a dynamic naturalist; although whether this isolated interest in apiarian bio-dynamics would qualify him for membership of the Bee Research Association, or even of the Bee-keepers Association, is quite a different matter. The dynamic psychologist we shall always have with us;

what really matters in this present context is whether the professional dynamic psychologist or general psychiatrist, observing some of the thousand and one mental disorders to which mankind is heir, or which they themselves develop, is prepared in the first place to diagnose the flaws which derive from inadequacy in the mental apparatus, whether these take the form of distortion or inhibition of what are nowadays described somewhat journalistically as 'drives'.

It is at this point that we can come to grips with the problems posed in the present chapter – although under strictly limited conditions. For desirable as it undoubtedly is to follow the steps leading to psychoanalytic formulations this is neither the time nor the place to do so. All we can hope to achieve is a brief reference to the considerations that led Freud to set up his famous 'model' of psychoneurotic symptom-formation.[2] Condensing the transitional boundary between neurology and psychology Freud's ideology was based on the view that, having classified various types of mental disorder – (no mean feat, by the way) there was only one valid approach to their investigation, namely, to observe in what manner the products of conscious introspection shed light on their origins. Hence what has come to be regarded as the *technique of free association*. The logical sequence was incontrovertible, since whatever blocks or inhibits the process of uncensored thinking is a pointer to the nature of 'conflict' ('defence') and, therefore, to the existence of unconscious mentation.

Here we encounter one of the risks of condensed presentation. It would be a profound misapprehension to assume that the study of uncensored, waking or sleeping, introspections constitutes of itself the technique of psychoanalysis. Consider, for example, what is implicit in the phrase 'a model of psychoneurotic symptom-formation'. Expressed in the barest psychoanalytical terms this implies that owing to frustration of (conscious or unconscious) 'drives' (instinctual relations with 'objects' of the 'drives') a process of regression is initiated (aversion) leading to 'inversion' of object libido, already prone constitutionally to traumatic reaction. The retrogression of this quantum of loosened (unbound) energy reaches back and is concentrated on the 'fixation point' whether this be traumatic in nature or the consequence of earlier instinctual gratification (in the case of psychotic, prepsychotic or extensive character disorders, there is reason to believe that these fixation points are multiple). At this point (or points) the regressing charges are reinforced by charges of unconscious energies which owing to inadequate repression seek to obtain (pre)conscious expression and ultimately action. The resultant commingling of energies gives rise to a state of tension that exceeds the limits of psychic tolerance. The result is 'compromise formation', the establishment of what one might call a *tertium quid* which goes by the name of symptom formation. And so . . .? And so there is no question of confining psycho-analytical therapy to the study of uncensored introspections or reports of dream-life. To begin with the candidate for psycho-analytical status must have (or acquire) a thorough clinical grounding in psychiatric diagnosis.[3] He must be able to distinguish between (a) constitutional factors, (b) endopsychic (developmental) factors in mental disorder, and (c) the impact of environmental (object-relation) stimulation. He must not only be familiar with the classification of instinctual forces, but be able to recognize the characteristic layers of ego-development, and the psychic mechanisms characteristic of archaic ego-function. Above all he must comprehend the fundamental difference between 'primary' (dynamically unconscious) processes and the 'secondary' (preconscious) processes that reduce perceptual experiences to a verbal level. In short, he must be able to dis-tinguish prognostically between an insoluble and a resoluble symptomatic expression. Such stipulations are hard to accept. Nevertheless they bear vitally on the problem of psychotherapy. Many years ago it was the habit of that Welsh psychoanalytical pioneer, Ernest Jones, to maintain that there are only two forms of psychotherapy, namely, *rapport therapy* (including hypnosis, suggestion *et alia*) and psychoanalysis. A hard, uncompromising standard no doubt but one that few experienced analysts would venture to contravert. No doubt it would have been wiser had he said that even should psychoanalysis prove yet another form of rapport therapy, nevertheless the analyst having first exploited it, does his best to eliminate the 'transference' factor in psycho-analysis. Hence the generally accepted regulation that psycho-analytical candidates should undergo a personal experience of analysis – or 'training analysis' as it has optimistically come to be designated. Not a very convincing argument, to be sure, since unquestionably the most brilliant discoveries in psychoanalysis were made by a first generation whose training consisted of self-analysis. (I exclude here the instance of Freud himself, for there can be no question but that his case was *sui generis*) or at least of an abbreviated month or two of intellectual exchange such as would make our present training personnel guffaw with ambiva-lent indulgence and condescension.[4]

Here I think it is justifiable to introduce some apparently polemical considerations. In the first place no sooner does one mention the phrase 'training analysis', than a covey of neurologic-ally trained (or indeed untrained) behaviourists are heard to say 'Aha: indoctrination' forgetting the days when they were taught that two by two make four. Otherwise we shall suffer from an infinity of error. A burnt child they say dreads the fire. No doubt. *Experientia docet*; but there is a world of sapient indoctrination in the part of parents which goes far to support this conclusion. And, in this case, the parents happen to be right. Only an arsonist would seek to deny the fact.

But perhaps a simpler example would serve our purposes better. An essential part of the analyst's approach is not simply to interpret his data in terms of developmental level, but to provide a glossary of those ideational and ultimately verbal expressions that are comprised under the heading of 'symbolism'. This archaic origin of imaginal and verbal communication (whether occurring in dreams or in a waking state) provides, he asserts, a neglected approach to the deepest unconscious forerunners of thought, including here most of the most primitive levels of pre-conscious activities. Here again he lays himself open to the charge of indoctrination. To this charge the psychoanalyst is happy to plead guilty, since he does agree with the etymologists that the meaning of a word or image depends ultimately on its relation to those perceptual experiences which, duly elaborated, constitute the basis of adult communication systems between the ego and its multifarious objects. So what between analysis and common sense there exists a gulf which is unlikely ever to be completely bridged; there is obviously little room for a gentleman's agreement.[5]

I have introduced these polemical ripostes here in order to emphasize the fact that there is no psychoanalyst having any pretensions to scientific integrity but would admit that the sources of error in psychoanalytic thinking and methodology are manifold. All he maintains is that these sources cannot be eluded by substituting systems of thought of a positively infantile naïveté. He does so in order to underscore precisely the difficulty of explaining the seemingly inexplicable. The 'psychoanalytic situation' which he postulates (including interpretation, transference *et hoc genus*) is merely a step towards understanding what differentiates man from the rest of the animal kingdom. He agrees that at every step of the process he is at his wits' end to eliminate his own private mythology; but he refuses to accept the rationalizations of those who would seek to explain the inexplicable by the relatively naïve processes of common sense thinking. Stirred to repartee, he is prepared to say that the ancillary sciences of neurology and behaviourism are merely fairy tales of an order that is used by five-year-olds to prove the existence of Father Christmas.

Let us, therefore, review some of the other animadversions on psychoanalytic therapy that pass muster in current psychological polemics. Perhaps the simplest case takes the form of saying that psychoanalysis as practised nowadays is interminable, that instead of 'curing' patients after a three-day interview, it may last up to fifteen or twenty years. Now a general practitioner of unexampled skill and experience may treat (or supervise the treatment of) a chronic 'rheumatoid arthritis' for twenty years without any notable success, without a qualm of conscience. Indeed, he may regard it as a sign of professional skill that he has at least reinforced the unfortunate patient's morale in the face of recurring disappointments. But should he be faced with a monosymptomatic anxiety phobia which he cannot resolve, he is inclined to lay the 'onus' for this on the corpus of the analyst (or psychiatrist) to whom in despair he has referred the case. Having embarked on this 'projective' technique of self-justification, our organic physician is frequently emboldened to add that in any case he has not encountered a case of psychoanalytical 'cure', that psychoanalysts produce no reliable statistics of 'results' and that they neglect the most elementary statistical precautions, in particular the use of 'controls' such as are a routine precaution in the natural sciences.

Here it would seem our critic scores a solitary point, but one that is not peculiar to the after-histories of psychoanalysis. I do not hold in high esteem the efforts of any psychiatric institution, department or clinic that does not apply the strictest controls to such data as *can* be 'controlled'. The fact is, however, that psychological investigations and treatment comprise a number of variables and imponderables that do not lend themselves to the rough and ready methods of 'control' that apparently satisfy the practitioner of organic medicine. To this argument the obvious counter is that the striking variability of diagnostic, prognostic and therapeutic standards is no justification for despondency, and a consequent retreat to methods of investigation suitable for organic or even psychosomatic explanation. I believe it was Ernest Jones who pointed out that the discovery of histologically observed blue dots in neuro-cellular structures would not provide a satisfactory explanation of a four-year-old nephew's dislike of his Uncle Willie. To be sure Freud anticipated a time when, for example, bio-chemical discoveries might render psychological theories superfluous. This I venture to say was to gild the lily of material explanation. To deal with a problem that by common consent is psychological in nature with the remedies prescribed by a materialistic science is to confess defeat.

To take one simple instance, namely, that of the 'after-history' of analytically treated cases (or indeed of any case treated by psychological techniques), *viz*: the optimum range of an 'after-history', the barest necessities would call for an after-history of at least five years (in the case of child analysis, ten to fifteen years during which period the analyst himself may have perished). No such data are available. Nor are they available in the case of conventional psychiatric therapy.[6] No great misfortune perhaps, since in the last resort a sound clinical opinion on one case may be more dependable than the statistical analysis of two thousand cases, superficially observed and chronologically unchecked. For my part I would go so far as to say that, given appropriate skill, the interpretation of an isolated dream fragment may exceed in value the combined efforts of a variety of multi-disciplined observers following the apparently common-sense precautions suitable for superficial observations of multitudinous controlled 'researches'. Clearly there is a dilemma here, but I venture to say that the deficiencies in reliability (or even plausibility) of 'controlled' methods cannot be overcome by neglecting the fact that the major part of mental activity, structure and dynamics is either totally unconscious, or recognizable only by interpretation of such derivatives as, despite the numerous and delicate fallibilities of the methods employed, are the only psychic measures we possess to evaluate psychic phenomena.[7] Man may render lip service to the shakiest logic of reality thinking but this does not warrant neglect of his obvious duty to penetrate the unknown, if not indeed the unknowable. To be sure there are two groups whose members have endeavoured to resolve this dilemma, the schizophrenics and the artists. And it may be said without undue pessimism that where the schizophrenic has failed it is not likely that the artist will succeed. In fact if the schizophrenic is not too guarded he may find himself incarcerated in a mental institution for his pains. The novelist, the painter and the poet have done their best, but they have never been able to obliterate the distinction between 'primary' and 'secondary' (preconscious) processes that constitutes the breaking point of human function. It is to my mind extremely unlikely that they ever will do so. But should they determine to follow this *ignis fatuus*, it would perhaps be well for them to learn something of the archaic development of man's mind. Should they nevertheless fail in their ameliorative designs, at least their failures – like the not infrequent failures of psychiatrists of any colour – are, in the scientific sense, honourable failures from which indeed much may be learned. In any case we must accept the fact that they will continue to indulge their psychological curiosity unabashed.

As I have indicated in the introduction to this essay, I am well aware that this inadequate survey will not satisfy even the most dedicated student of clinical psychology. I have deliberately abstained from attempting to produce a condensed *vade mecum* of psychoanalytical theory and practice, and have restricted myself to a general commentary on psychotherapy and psychoanalytical theory. At the risk of being considered unduly cantankerous I have emphasized some of the points at which Freudian theory and practice can be distinguished from other forms of psychotherapy. I have I trust indicated also some of the difficulties and sources of error confronting a developing science. To this I would like to add a personal assessment of the importance of Freudian theory and practice.

Here I find myself faced with some terminological difficulties: for although it is natural that 'psychoanalysis' should be regarded simply as a form of 'treatment' of mental disorder, this estimate runs far short of the actuality. Although built on the strength of observations on dream life and on the waking manifestations of psychoneurotics, Freud's ultimate aim was the development of a *system of psychology*: and the methods he evolved were primarily *instruments of research*. Therapeutically speaking Freud was by far the most acute of his own critics and was frequently embarrassed by the over-enthusiasms of his original followers, both clinical and theoretical, whom from time to time he reluctantly disavowed. Here I think he was unduly pessimistic, for despite frequent discouragements, there seems to be no doubt that conditions which far exceed the limits of the psychoneuroses, can, given sufficient assiduity in the application of psychoanalytic technique, be made to respond to situations of chronic 'conflict' with a surprising degree of adaptability. Failures? Yes. Interminable treatments? Yes. But so what? Life itself takes (a variable) time. 'Conflict' tends to endure. Indeed civilization itself depends on this endurance factor. And it ill becomes 'psychic healers' who, dwelling on the hither side of the repression barrier and pinning their faith on the therapeutic effect of a logical approach, criticize any attempt however forlorn to penetrate this protective frontier in the hope of assuaging mental suffering. To take one last instance, namely, the treatment of conflict by the analysis of 'transferences'. This was no 'Freudian discovery'. Man, the animal, discovered in the remote past that should his medicine men refuse to treat his difficulties by transference therapy (magic), his patient would insist on treating himself by precisely this technique. Nowadays this simple fact is varnished over by the use of such terms as 'communication therapy' or 'interpersonal relations therapy' and leads to an abundance of platitudes regarding 'identity formation' or 'the divided self'.

Well, perhaps no great matter this nosological mania. 'A rose by any other name', etc., etc. Nevertheless, it is incumbent on observers of integrity to distinguish between an invisible rose and a blade of grass. But should he decide to concentrate on the blade of grass, by all means let him do so. It may take fifty to a thousand years to correct his error in policy. But after all, what is time or truth?

Contributions of Melanie Klein to psychoanalytic technique

Athol Hughes

Introduction

Kleinian psychoanalysis was developed by Melanie Klein from the work of Sigmund Freud and Karl Abraham. It is a branch of Freudian psychoanalysis. Klein used Freud's theories to develop a play technique with which she psychoanalysed very young children, from two years of age. From this work she gained insight into the emotional life of infancy in much the way that Freud gained insight into the mental life of childhood through the psychoanalyses of adults. Her theories have influenced large numbers of psychoanalysts, many of whom are working in London, as well as in other psychoanalytic centres throughout the world.

Melanie Klein was born in 1882, the youngest child in the family of a Viennese Jewish doctor. Although she had wanted to study medicine, her marriage when she was twenty-one years of age precluded that, and it was not until she was in her thirties and after her three children were born that she became involved in the new science of psychoanalysis. Her interest was motivated by a strong wish to understand and help others, as well as by personal need. She was psychoanalysed first by Ferenczi who encouraged her work with children, and then by Abraham, whose particular interest in very early phases of psychological development stimulated her to turn her attention to the mind of the infant. Abraham[1] was particularly interested in the oral phase of infant development, that in which the mouth is the principal source of pleasure, and he attached great significance to the ways in which infants take in and make part of themselves, not only food, but also impressions and experiences in relation to others.

Klein began to describe the technique she developed for child analysis in 1921, the same year that she published her first paper *The development of a child.*[2] She found that in undirected play children demonstrate for the analyst the content of their unconscious phantasy life. The analyst can interpret this to the child, in terms the latter understands, in the same way that the content of dreams and other associations are interpreted to the adult. Ernest Jones, who had been instrumental in introducing psychoanalysis to England, recognized Melanie Klein's great gifts, and invited her to come and work in London. This she did in 1926. She continued to work there, developing her theories on the psychology of infancy, practising, writing and teaching right up to the time of her death in 1960.

The Kleinian psychoanalytic technique

Klein enlarged and elaborated Freud's and Abraham's theories concerning the infant's very early relationships to people. From her psychoanalytic work with very young children, she became convinced of the importance of the infant's own feelings and unconscious phantasies in affecting the ways he perceived himself and others. In her view, infants have unconscious phantasies from birth. These are thoughts of a rudimentary nature, shaped by impulses and feelings that have their origins within the individual and of which he is not aware.

The importance placed by Kleinian psychoanalysts on the role of unconscious phantasy in the mental life of child and adult profoundly influences the Kleinian psychoanalytic approach. As it will be explained in the chapter, since the psychoanalysis centres on the elucidation of the patient's unconscious perceptions of himself and of others, the transference is of utmost importance. The transference is the process first noted by Freud: the patient feels towards the analyst emotions that were first experienced and expressed in relation to parental and other figures of great importance in the individual's early years. Within the Kleinian framework, the analyst considers that the transference is present from the very beginning of the analysis. He uses it to investigate not only positive feelings directed towards him by the patient, but negative feelings as well. In general, the analyst takes a comparatively active part in interpreting and in fostering the interchange between himself and the patient. However, in ways that are comparable to other techniques, he keeps expressions of his own personality and points of view out of the analytic situation, so that the patient is provided with opportunities to see that he has expectations of others that may bear more connection to his own emotions and impulses than they do to any external relationship.

Kleinian technique requires that all aspects of the psychoanalytical setting be kept as constant and as regular as possible; this includes the physical setting of the consulting room, the times and frequencies of the sessions, as well as the analyst's manner and approach to his work. So that the personality of the analyst intrudes as little as possible, the patient usually lies on the couch. Since the emphasis is on the investigation of character rather than on cure of symptoms, psychoanalyses extend over long periods, usually years. The analyst sees the patient in fifty-minute sessions, as often as possible, usually five times a week.

The symptoms that bring the patient for Kleinian analysis are of the usual nature: the patient may be concerned about his dealings with others in sexual, social, or occupational spheres. He may suffer from phobias, perversions, or anxiety states, or he may complain of a sense of unreality or an inability to love. Whatever the symptom, be the individual child or adult, it will be investigated within the psychoanalytic setting in terms of deeper conflicts, conflicts that will have their origins not only in terms of childhood impressions, but in terms of earlier emotional development, that of the first year of life.

Since, according to Kleinian theory, unconscious phantasies have their origins in infancy, a patient, although an adult, and quite aware of his adult capabilities, and responsibilities, may find it very disconcerting and painful to become aware of infantile aspects of his personality and infantile feelings directed towards the analyst. These he may experience as quite alien to his adult self and attempt to deny them. In order that the patient accept them, the analyst has to show considerable tact and understanding, over a very long period in his dealings with the patient.

I shall give in this chapter a brief résumé of some of the principal Kleinian theories and relate them to the ways that the analyst uses them in his observations and to interpret to the patient. Interpretations are explanations given to the patient of the conscious and unconscious meanings of what he tells the psychoanalyst. Although the theories behind the interpretations relate to psychic processes that have their origins in infancy, the analyst uses words and concepts in giving interpretations that are appropriate to the patient's present situation and stage of development.

This résumé is, of necessity, brief, but a list of books on page 324 will be helpful for further reference.

Résumé of principal Kleinian theories

Like Freud, Klein considers that mental processes derive from instinctual needs. However, in her view, not only are people driven towards the satisfaction of their basic instincts, but, in addition, they are motivated from the beginning of life by the need to relate to others. All behaviour is object related; infants have from birth some rudimentary awareness of 'objects'. The object that the infant first needs is a breast, that is a 'part'-object, and only later does his need encompass the idea of a person, the mother, a 'whole object'. Consistent with his impulses, the infant builds up phantasies about the objects he needs. For instance, if he is extremely hungry and has to wait even a short time, the feelings he will have about the object, breast or bottle, he wants, will be quite different from the feelings he will have at another time, when he is not so hungry and does not have to wait. In the latter situation his feelings about the object he wants may be quite benign, and he will feel 'good' towards it, while in the former situation he may see the breast as responsible for his hunger and feel in general 'bad' towards it. It is difficult to use words to describe such primitive feelings, but it is important to understand that, in Kleinian theory, the infant's, and later the adult's perceptions of objects, or people, he needs, are shaped not only by the external reality of what the objects do and have done to him, but by the inner reality of his own phantasies about the objects he needs.

Freud emphasizes the manner in which individuals are driven by instinctual need, but considers that only gradually do they become aware of the people who satisfy the need. Klein agrees with that, but considers, furthermore, that basic instinctual needs drive people towards objects, consciously or unconsciously perceived and shaped according to their need. The addition of the concept of an inherent awareness of an object plays a major part in the use of the transference in the therapeutic alliance between patient and analyst. If the individual is seen as relating to people according to his phantasies about them, then his relationship to the analyst in the transference is of a different order than if the analysis is conceived of as dealing with the individual's struggle with his impulse alone, or with impulses directed to actual people in the external world.

In addition to accepting Freud's theory of the life instincts, Klein considers Freud's theory of the death instinct to be extremely important. She uses it to explain the struggle she observed in the analyses of children and adults between an urge to destroy and an urge to preserve objects. Freud describes the drive towards death within the organism as a death instinct against which the organism defends itself. Klein thinks that the death instinct expresses itself as a fear of annihilation, that is, a fear of destruction of life within the self. She sees it as closely related to primitive aggression. She considers that the threat of death within the self is dealt with partly by projection; some aspects of the feelings of self-destructiveness are disowned and invested in objects considered to be outside the self. This process results in feelings of intense persecution. Other aspects of the destructiveness, not projected, are turned into aggression which is then used by the individual in his struggle against the persecutors.

Although many analysts do not accept either Freud's or Klein's conceptions of the death instinct, the idea of a primary aggressive drive is now widely accepted. Some analysts, however, think of aggression as a response to situations imposed by the external world, such as the frustration of a need, rather than as an expression of an inherent impulse. Kleinian analysts agree that aggression may be roused by frustration, but they emphasize that the conflicts that the individual has in struggling with hating and loving impulses give rise to more difficulty in relationships to others than do actual external situations. As he recognizes and tolerates something of his own hostile reactions, so the infant, and later the adult, is able to experience good feelings for those who care for and about him, and to invest them with loving feelings.

Klein gives a brief description of the infant's early struggle with his hostile and loving impulses in a paper called *Our adult world and its roots in infancy* (1960).[3] She says: 'the newborn baby experiences, both in the process of birth and in the adjustment to the post-natal situation, anxiety of a persecutory nature. This can be explained by the fact that the young infant, without being able to grasp it intellectually, feels unconsciously every discomfort as though it were inflicted on him by hostile forces. If comfort is given to him soon – in particular warmth, the loving way he is held, and the gratification of being fed – this gives rise to happier emotions. Such comfort is felt to come from good forces and, I believe, makes possible the infant's first loving relation to a person, or as the psychoanalyst would put it, to an object.'

Klein describes in that paper, and in other publications[4, 5] the ways in which the infant deals with anxieties of a persecutory nature, accentuated by resentment over frustration, and hatred of dependency combined with feelings of envy for the all powerful mother. She elaborates further how he comes to integrate these negative emotions with feelings of love for the mother who satisfies and comforts him. In his phantasy, the infant splits his idea of a good, satisfying mother and keeps it quite separate from his idea or phantasy of a bad, frustrating one. He disowns and keeps separate the part of himself and of his object that he considers contains bad destructive impulses from the part of himself and his object, that he considers contains good, life-giving qualities. He can then take in and receive help from the good aspects of a good mother, by keeping her and his good feelings separate in his mind from his hostile impulses, which he, at that point, disowns and sees only outside himself in what could be termed the phantasy of a 'bad mother'. Moreover, to deal with his conflict, the infant may accentuate the good aspect of his relationship to the mother to such an extent that she becomes idealized and represents for him all aspects of security, hope and fulfilment; while the bad aspects of the relationship become the embodiment of all evil: an infantile conception of heaven and hell. As the individual perceives people and their function in infancy, so throughout his life in modified form, he perceives others as he feels them to be, in general, satisfying, or in general, frustrating, to him.

Use of transference in the analysis

In the analytic situation the patient perceives the analyst in much the same way and attributes to him impulses and emotions that he had attributed to those important to him from birth. He can look at his perceptions in the light of his more mature personality and examine their applicability in his present circumstances. I have said that the personality of the analyst should intrude as little as possible; but this is not to say that the analyst is not receptive to the feelings that are being stirred in him by the patient's communications. The analyst uses his intuition and sensitivity, fostered by his own analysis, to express to the patient what the latter is feeling but is unable to express himself.

An example of this process may help to illustrate it. A man patient was speaking in the analysis in a rather envious way of how his sister had been chatting on the telephone to a woman friend, talking of matters of mutual interest. The patient spoke of this incident in such a way that the sense of isolation of his rather 'cut-off' personality was apparent to the analyst. Although it was not made explicit, it was inferred as well, and known from previous communications, that the patient thought that women could chat in this informal friendly manner but that men could not. As a consequence, the analyst said that she thought that the patient was expressing some feelings of loneliness of which he was not aware, although he was aware of feeling that, in being a man, he was deprived of a relationship shared by women. This interpretation gave access in succeeding sessions to the patient's unconscious envy of women's maternal functions, from which he felt isolated. He came to recognize, as well, the manner in which he isolated himself from what was available in the analysis, because to partake of it would mean that he would have to admire it, as belonging to someone else. This his envy prevented him from doing.

Thus the patient is provided, in the transference, with opportunities to examine his expectations and reactions with a person who, although sensitive to them, is not involved in them. He can then see for himself that he is attracted to ways of perceiving others that interfere with his relationships to them. Reasons for the inappropriate ways of functioning have to be understood repeatedly in many contexts, as the patient sees them operating in different areas of his life. In the example just given the patient came to see over a period of time that resentment of his sister's relationship to the mother was one facet of his envy of the mother herself, of her capacity to bear and to feed children; and that he was envious of the analyst for having analytic training and insight, just as he was of his father and his colleagues for their professional skills and abilities.

As the patient is helped to distinguish good experiences, he can identify with the analyst as a person who cares for his own insight and mental well-being, and the way is open for the patient to do the same. As his envy lessens he can appreciate positive qualities in himself and in others, acknowledged along with destructive qualities. Integration of split-off parts of himself is comparable to a process in the development of the normal infant who begins, at about three months of age, to tolerate loving and hating the same object, with less splitting and projection. On the basis of repeated satisfying experiences, he is able to introject, that is, to take into his own personality, ideas and feelings of a good mother with less hostility and idealization. He is then in a position to tolerate feelings of concern and responsibility towards his mother, in a way that is not available to infants in whom the capacity to introject is crippled.

Destructiveness in the personality

The process of introjection may have been crippled either because of actual bad or confusing early situations or because of a more than usual amount of destructiveness in the personality, or by a combination of these two factors. If the infant is unable to maintain what Hanna Segal[6] in *Introduction to the work of Melanie Klein* calls a 'tidy split' between good and bad impulses, he becomes confused and disturbed and fears the implications of taking from a source that he considers to be contaminated by bad feelings. He denies his needs and resorts to magic omnipotent phantasy to satisfy them. He then lives in the phantasy that he can feed himself and look after himself in a delusional way. This process has been described by Rosenfeld[7] in relation to severe disturbances in patients with psychoses, perversions and addictions. Rosenfeld attributes the narcissistic overvaluation of self to the death instinct aroused by anything that stirs envy. Insight and understanding gained in the analysis threatens the individual's omnipotence and self-sufficiency and leads to the nullification of the analyst's work. This may be done in a variety of ways designed to allow the patient to continue in the phantasy that he provides for himself by himself. He may forget, for instance, what the analyst has said, and then repeat it later as though he had thought of it himself. He may reverse his dependent position in the analysis, and consider that rather than he being the one who is helped, he helps the analyst with his practice and profession by giving interesting case material. He may give himself interpretations or find insight in books; and in general, he denies his dependency and takes all life out of the analytic situation, deadening it and making it impotent and sterile. Rosenfeld considers that from the infant's point of view, life in the mother, and from the patient's point of view, life in the mind of the analyst, not only stirs envious destructiveness, but emphasizes the separateness of people and the fear of loneliness. A separate object is not under the domination and control of the one who would otherwise see himself as dependent.

Envious destructiveness is illustrated by a patient who after a session in which he has felt and expressed appreciation to the analyst for the understanding he has gained, returns the next day oblivious to what happened the day before, and showing by his attitude that he wants to provoke an angry or rejecting response in the analyst. In other words, he seems happier when he sees signs of disharmony than when there are signs of satisfaction and well-being. The rationale for behaviour that leads to the destruction of life itself lies in its relationship to the infantile ego. Some infants are unable to tolerate feelings related to need of an object, and concern over what happened to the needed object. These infants show that feelings of concern, depression and guilt are intolerably painful. Situations that might arouse these feelings are avoided at any cost. This is true of adults as well; any situation that might lead to painful feelings is attacked before the painful feelings come into consciousness.

Attacks on situations that might evoke depression and guilt take many forms. In an actual event such as the death of a person close to an individual, some people show that they can go through a period of mourning in which depressive feelings are experienced and expressed, while others show by excessive activity or by withdrawal, that they cannot bear the feelings aroused by their loss and they show that they anticipate being overwhelmed by emotions whose effects they fear might be catastrophic.

When patients show that they fear having to bear feelings of guilt and depression roused by the acknowledgement of their destructiveness, they frequently act like recently bereaved individuals who cannot mourn. Methods used to avoid depressive pain may vary in sophistication from a subtle change of subject, to attacks on the whole analytic setting, as shown in the analysis of a severely disturbed adolescent boy. At a point in his analysis he became aware for the first time how sad he felt about the attacks he made in denigrating and belittling whatever the analyst said.

Tears came to his eyes, but he showed that he could not stand these feelings; he distracted his own attention and that of the analyst, who had been talking about his distress, by shouting, banging his fists on the table, and his heels on the floor, so that he could hear nothing of what the analyst was saying. The depressive feelings had to be ejected as soon as they were experienced.

Thus depression and guilt are frequently met with defensive manoeuvres that deny the feelings as well as the implications of them. However, the analytic situation provides an opportunity for the patient to re-experience feelings that his infantile self found unbearable, but which his more mature self may eventually come to tolerate. The patient then enters another phase of his analysis, one that is comparable to the 'depressive position' described by Klein.[4]

Tolerance of depressive feelings

Klein sees the capacity to tolerate depression as the sequel to the early months of psychic splitting and projection. At about six months of life the normal infant's relationship to people changes, he becomes more consistently aware of his mother as a 'whole' person, that is, the sees her as an entity in herself, and not merely as an amalgam of parts that satisfy his needs. She is seen as separate from himself and less under his domination and control; he is aware too that he is dependent on her, and that he loves, but also hates and attacks her. He becomes anxious and depressed and tries to deal with his ambivalence by making reparation. To overcome the guilt he feels, he tries to please his mother and others. As he discovers the limits of his hate and of his love, he gives up some of the strength of his idealization and of his beliefs that he can put things right on his own. As he identifies with his mother as a person who cares for him and about him, he sees his world as a more benign place. This process in the adult world has been well described by Salzberger-Wittenberg[8] with reference to the use of Kleinian concepts in social casework.

As the patient in analysis acknowledges his ambivalence, he also acknowledges his need of help and abandons to some degree his omnipotent ways of providing for himself in the analytic situation. He begins to tolerate depression related to his regret that things are not as they could have been if he had not wasted time and talent. In tolerating the capacity of the analyst to help him, he tolerates his own insight, too, even if it includes insight into some unpleasant aspects of his own personality. As the conditions around which they have been structured are changed he can give up his inconsistencies and provocations. He learns that constructive aspects of his personality exist side by side with destructive aspects, and so his envy of the analyst's constructive work is modified.

As long as envy is a predominant emotion, any two-party relationship, such as the patient and analyst co-operating in the analysis, is nullified in the envious person's mind. However, as envy lessens, jealousy, a more sophisticated emotion, makes its appearance. Jealousy presupposes a three-party relationship, that is, a relationship of two people from which the third is excluded, and who, as a consequence, responds with jealous reactions towards one of the other two people, who has what he has not, that is, the loved object. As positive loving aspects of the patient's personality are reinforced, Oedipal reactions may come into the analytic situation. As the child is jealous of the parent of the same sex who has the love of the parent of the opposite sex, so the patient may be jealous of the analyst's commitments and relationships to people other than himself. The patient's jealousy includes the analyst's relationship to analysis, from which he feels excluded, in a way analogous to the child's exclusion from the parental sexual relationship.

Prior to tolerating depressive feelings over any length of time, the patient will continue to attack the meanings provided by the analyst's interpretations that might lead him once more to painful feelings. The attacks on meaningful connections are comparable to the child's phantasy attacks on his parents' intercourse, of which he has only a dim awareness, but which, he feels, threatens his omnipotent phantasies that he can control and dominate his parents.

A dream of a woman patient who had had several years of

analysis for severe emotional problems illustrates the way she attacked connections that had for her symbolic significance of good parental intercourse. The woman dreamed that she and her husband were going out for the evening. One of her children, a girl of eight years of age, told the patient, her mother, that she did not want her to go out. As a consequence, the patient stayed at home.

The patient attempts, in the dream, to hide from herself the way she attacks the parental activity of the analysis, by projecting the attack into her child, with whom she then colludes in not going out with her husband. She demonstrates how she continues to interfere with the analytic process, so that the parental couple, of which she is herself one of the parties, 'do not go out', that is, do not do anything useful and productive. If she did anything productive with the analyst, it would disturb the child in herself, seen as her daughter in the dream. Rather than benefit in the analysis she would do nothing, that is 'stay home' so as not to upset herself.

Klein dates the Oedipal phase earlier than does Freud, according to whom genital desires emerge during the phallic phase, that is from about three to five years of age. Klein considers that sexual and emotional development from early infancy includes genital sensations, and that these constitute the first stages of the Oedipal complex. The genital sensations are experienced alongside desires and phantasies related to oral, urethral and anal urges and needs, and are permeated by anxiety derived from aggressiveness roused by envy and jealousy. 'Anxiety, guilt and depressive feelings at times drive the libido forward to new sources of gratification, at times they check the development of the libido by reinforcing the fixation to an earlier object and aim.'[9]

This is not the place to trace the effects of anxiety on the emotional and libidinal development; those interested are referred to Klein[9, 10] or to Segal.[6] It is important to know that Klein associates the infant's Oedipal relationship with the depressive position, at which time, in normal development (that is at about six months) the infant becomes aware of his parents as people separate from himself, who have a relationship with each other from which he is excluded. The adult, genital meaning of the relationship is of course absolutely beyond his comprehension, but he endows it with phantasies derived from oral, anal, and urethal impulses, as well as from genital ones.

External environmental influences and internal phantasy life

Kleinian analysts are sometimes accused of not taking sufficient account of the effect on the personality of external environmental influences. From the foregoing it would be apparent that since impulses and emotions shape the individual's relationship to others, major emphasis is not placed on external events. However, those who use a Kleinian framework consider that external events can exacerbate or alleviate certain characteristics. If the environment is warm and loving, phantasies related to internal needs are invested with warmth and love. If the environment is cold and destructive, envious and destructive phantasies receive confirmation. If an infant has phantasies of destroying his object in hate and anger, and a parent is ill or dies, then the illness or death serves to confirm his omnipotent destructive phantasy and he has an added task of distinguishing his impulses from the external reality. On the other hand, if the object of his attacks not only remains alive and well, but also can tolerate his projections of hate and hostility without negating them, he is helped to accept his destructiveness as his own.

On the other hand, since unconscious phantasy permeates all levels of functioning, Kleinian analysts consider that it is an extremely important influence on the ways that people deal with themselves and with others. If one observes newborn babies in nurseries, as Middlemore[11] did, one can see that some babies take their feed quietly and contentedly, while others fuss and turn away from breast or bottle. These reactions are not necessarily related to what the infant has experienced; some who have had severe birth difficulties tolerate frustration in waiting more patiently than do others who have had no apparent external trouble. The latter may react to the least frustration as if it were of catastrophic proportions; the frustration leads to such angry phantasies that these infants feel overwhelmed by their need. They require considerable help and patience to establish a rhythm. No environment, no matter how benign, can avoid subjecting infants to frustration, nor would it be advisable to do so. It is only by being helped to tolerate moderate amounts of frustration over a period of time that the infant develops a sense of reality, as opposed to living in his phantasies.

Example of the effect of external environmental influences and internal phantasy life

I should like to give some details from the analysis of a woman patient that may help to illustrate some of the points I have made, particularly with reference to the effect of detrimental environmental factors. At a point early in her analysis, this patient gave evidence that she thought that she had driven her mother insane. Although she was not conscious of this idea, she knew that her mother's behaviour was strange and bordered at times on the bizarre.

Once incident that indicated that she had this unconscious thought was a dream in which a woman she knew, the wife of a psychoanalyst, had a hole in her head. The image in the dream of the hole in the side of woman's head filled the patient with horror of nightmare proportions.

The hole was interpreted to her as representing the result of attacks she made on her analyst's mind and thinking. The attacks had been going on for some time and were many and varied. They took the form of her deliberately withholding information that she knew would be helpful in the analysis, of her taking the meaning out of interpretations, or of shifting the bases of discussions, or of evading the implications of what was being said, and other such manoeuvres. It was not surprising that the idea of a hole in the head, standing for a hole in the analyst's mind, should arouse such intense anxiety since she was dependent on the analyst having an intact mind and ability to think clearly, if she were to benefit from the analytic work. In the dream the hole was in the head of the wife of an analyst, rather than in her analyst's head, to disguise the significance of the dream and to indicate, too, that the attacks were being made on the maternal aspects of the transference. In infantile terms the attacks were comparable to those made on the feeding function of the mother, on her breasts; in analytic terms, the attacks were on the head, the part of the analyst that 'feeds' mental well-being and sanity.

Since the mother evidently showed psychotic features in her personality, although she was never hospitalized, it is understandable that the patient felt alarm when she had the unconscious thought, expressed in her dream, that she made someone, representing the analyst, have a 'hole in her head'. At a conscious level the patient did not think that her destructive behaviour could drive anyone insane. She was aware that aspects of her personality could have a detrimental effect on others; her coldness and lack of involvement with her family, children and friends had brought her for help in the first place. In her unconscious she showed repeatedly that she considered that as she took the life out of the analytic situation, so she attacked life in all her objects. That included life in her husband's work, in his creativity, and potency, in her children's development, and even in her own occupational endeavours, as she saw them fostered by others, and so belonging to those others, be they parents, teachers, or the analyst. By paying strict attention over a long period to all her reactions in the analysis, it was possible to show her how destructive her manoeuvres were to the whole analytic process, and to the work of the analyst, and that this destructiveness permeated all areas of her life.

The patient's behaviour in the analysis suggested that at the unconscious level she thought that she had made her mother and her breasts as lifeless and impotent when she was a baby, as she tried, at times, to make the analyst. Her mother's severe emotional disturbance reinforced the phantasy that her methods of mental functioning had a pernicious effect on others. The logic behind this phantasy lies in the idea that if her beliefs and behaviour affect others, then she can stop them, if she desires, and thus can restore the mental equilibrium of others. Inappropriate behaviour in the mother obviated the need to tolerate painful feelings of envy of, and dependence on, a mother who is sane, as well as obviating the need to deal with psychotic features in her own behaviour. She could continue in the delusion that she managed disturbing aspects of her own personality by projecting them into others, but then she suffered by living in a world in which she was deeply immersed in the disturbances and distress of others. Her mother's inappropriate behaviour strengthened the patient's impression that projection of unwanted emotions is a successful process and hampered the differentiation of phantasy from reality. She thus avoided admiring and fostering positive, appropriate attributes in herself and her family, since according to 'talion' punishment, described by Freud, if the sanity of others is to suffer because of her, then her own sanity must suffer in retaliation. This process robbed her of her productivity and creativity. As a consequence her work suffered as did her life in general, socially and sexually, so that her methods of avoiding psychic pain (including the pain of having a severely disturbed mother) had to be understood in many contexts, and her analysis took a long time.

Summary of the chapter
In summary, Kleinian psychoanalytic technique involves a process whereby the individual is helped not only to remember his past, in order not to repeat it, but it involves helping him to know his impulses, so as not to be at their mercy. It attempts to make explicit the ways impulses distort relationships with others. To accomplish this, the patient goes through what Meltzer[12] has called the 'natural history' of the psychoanalytic process. He experiences and observes with the psychoanalyst ways in which he splits off and disowns his feelings and suffers as a consequence. As he acknowledges over a period of time his own destructiveness, feelings of persecution and of being attacked lessen. As he can acknowledge too his envy of the attributes of others, his relationship to them and to himself becomes more benign. He is then able to experience more fully and consistently feelings of depression and of guilt over what he has lost or spoilt. He learns to deal with feelings of dependency on objects even

in their absence, and to accept the loneliness implied in his separateness from them at the same time that he accepts the possibilites of loving someone essentially different from himself.

Behavioural therapy

William Yule

Behavioural approaches to the treatment of psychiatric disorders differ fundamentally in a number of respects from other psychotherapeutic approaches discussed in this book. It is the aim of this chapter to make these differences explicit. Both the rationale on which behaviour therapy is based and some of the techniques employed in behaviour therapy will be described. The behavioural approach will be illustrated with applications to disorders of adulthood and childhood. Finally, some common criticisms of the behavioural approach to therapy will be discussed.

Introduction

Most of the forms of psychotherapy discussed elsewhere in this volume derive ultimately from the psychoanalytical writings of Freud and his followers. The view of man, his functioning and mal-functioning, put forward by Freud owed much to his own clinical experience, and to his medical training. In particular, Freud adopted an *illness model* of psychiatric disorder. By this, he viewed the phenomena of psychiatric disorder (the behaviour shown by the patient) as being merely symptomatic of some deep, underlying illness. This is analogous, in medical terms, to regarding the surface spots of chickenpox as merely symptomatic of the real illness. Whilst it is undeniably true that symptomatic treatment of the skin-deep manifestation of chickenpox by rubbing on some soothing lotion will do nothing to cure the basic illness, it is not necessarily true that this model holds for all disorders.

The psycho-dynamic psychotherapist largely views the phenomenological aspects of the disorder as symptoms of an underlying illness. Removing the symptoms does nothing to cure the illness. The patient is only cured when the illness is successfully treated. By contrast, the behaviour therapist concentrates on the observable behaviour and directs treatment at the symptoms. When the symptoms are removed, the patient is 'cured' because there is no *illness* there to explain. In other words, behaviour therapists believe that concepts and methods which have been valuable in the field of physical illness do not necessarily have any place in the field of mental disorder.[1, 2, 3] This, then, is one of the major differences between a psycho-dynamic view of psychiatric disorder and a behavioural view.

If psychiatric disorder is not an 'illness', how is it to be regarded? To answer this, behavioural therapists turn to the large literature of psychological studies of learning. Since experimental psychology was founded in the late nineteenth century, psychologists have been studying how men and animals learn. Many major laws of learning are now clearly established. Behavioural therapists point out that it is not only adaptive forms of behaviour which are learned. Maladaptive behaviour can also be acquired through learning. If one concedes that some maladaptive behaviours can be learned, why, then, can they not also become unlearned? Much of the behavioural approach to treating maladaptive behaviour is concerned with the quest for discovering ways of replacing existing maladaptive behaviour with new adaptive behaviour.

Thus, the second major difference in approach to treatment rests on the different theories forming the rationale of treatment. Behaviour therapy is strongly allied to the applications of the findings of modern experimental psychology, particularly those findings related to learning. As Meyer and Chesser[4] point out, 'Learning theories . . . accept that both genetic and environmental factors are important in determining abnormal behaviour, and that mental disorder is the result of the interaction between a more or less predisposed individual and his changing environment. It is, therefore, appropriate to consider the extent to which psychiatric symptoms are a form of learned behaviour' (p. 18).

Behavioural therapists do not claim that *all* maladaptive behaviour is learned. Clearly, in the case of organic psychoses such a view is untenable. However, they ask of all maladaptive behaviour, 'to what extent is it learned and to what extent is it modifiable?' Learning theory approaches to psychiatric disorder are, therefore, basically optimistic.

So far, the rather clumsy terms 'behavioural approaches to therapy . . .', 'learning theory approaches . . .', and 'behavioural therapy' have been used. This has been to emphasize, as will shortly be seen, that a related group of therapeutic techniques is under discussion. It has been shown that these techniques differ from more traditional psycho-dynamically oriented psychotherapy in two major respects: 1) their concern with the actual behaviour, rather than supposed underlying causes, and 2) their alliance to modern learning theory. It has become customary to group all these techniques under the simpler heading of 'Behaviour Therapy'.[5, 4, 2] (In the United States, the term 'Behaviour Modification' is sometimes preferred.[6])

As Eysenck[7] points out, the term 'Behaviour Therapy' is of fairly recent origin, but the techniques of behaviour therapy have a long and respected history. There have been sporadic attempts to apply learning principles to the treatment of maladaptive behaviour since the early 1920s. In the decade following J. B. Watson's famous demonstration that some fears commonly found in children were learned by a conditioning process, there were many isolated instances of therapists using conditioning techniques to eradicate such fears.[2] However, it was not until the late 1950s and early 1960s that a growing dissatisfaction with the results of traditional psychotherapy[8, 9, 10, 11, 12] caused psychologists to look again more closely at this early work.

In summary, most critical reviews of the effects of psychotherapy with adults are agreed that approximately two-thirds of patients show some level of improvement. This holds for adults[8, 6] and for children.[12] However, it must not be assumed that the changes have been caused by the psychotherapeutic treatment. In fact, on average, untreated groups do just as well.[6] In other words, what these writers have argued is that there is little concrete evidence to suggest that psychotherapy is an effective form of treatment.

Even if such evidence is forthcoming from future studies, there are two further objections to psychotherapy as a preferred mode of treatment. Firstly, it is expensive in terms of skilled manpower. It would be economically impossible to provide the number of therapists needed to deal with the community's problems. Secondly, psychotherapy is rarely offered to people presenting antisocial disorders, such as delinquency, bullying or destructive behaviour. Yet many of the problems causing most unhappiness in the community as a whole are centred on antisocial problems. Dissatisfaction of this sort with traditional psychotherapy acted as a major stimulant to the search for new methods of treatment.

What is behaviour therapy?

Behaviour therapy has been defined as '. . . the attempt to alter human behaviour and emotion in a beneficial manner according to the laws of modern learning theory'.[7] Meyer and Chesser[4] state that: 'Behaviour therapy aims to modify current symptoms and focuses attention on their behavioural manifestations in terms of observable responses. The techniques used are based on a variety of learning approaches. Although behaviour therapists adopt a developmental approach to the genesis of symptoms, they do not think it is always necessary to unravel their origin and subsequent development.'

Meyer and Chesser's definition is explicitly somewhat broader than Eysenck's earlier formulation. They agree that the techniques of behaviour therapy are derived from the experimental literature on the phenomena of learning. Yates[2] would widen the definition further to include techniques derived from any branch of experimental psychology. He holds that the distinguishing features of behaviour therapy is the overriding concern with the experimental investigation of each individual case. No matter how 'standard' a technique might be, its application to an individual requires unique modifications. These modifications are made in accordance with the experimental findings, and the effects of the 'treatment' on the patient are likewise experimentally validated.

Behaviour therapists are agreed that the focus of their attention is on the actual behaviour of the patient. They require detailed *behavioural* descriptions of what the patient (or society) is complaining of. For example, a mother may complain that her four-year-old is 'jealous' of his younger sister. The behaviour therapist will immediately ask, 'How does he show his "jealousy"?' 'How often does he show this behaviour?' 'What do you do when he shows this behaviour?' and so on. Vague, every-day descriptions of behaviour such as 'jealous', 'scared', 'destructive' are translated in this way into precise behavioural descriptions.

Having obtained a description of the presenting complaint (and a history of its development as far as can be re-constructed), the behaviour therapist will then try to pinpoint events in the patient's immediate environment which are either maintaining the undesirable behaviour or are preventing the patient from learning a new mode of adjustment. In doing so, the therapist is guided by his knowledge of the literature on the ways in which behaviour is learned and maintained.

Perhaps the one single feature which most clearly differentiates behaviour therapy from traditional forms of psychotherapy can now be described. Having obtained a precise behavioural description of the presenting complaint, and having begun a treatment intervention based on a learning theory model, the behaviour therapist is then concerned with the problem of evaluating the efficacy of the treatment. As has been seen already, it is not just enough to show that the patient gets better following treatment. It is necessary to demonstrate that the improvement was caused by the treatment. Few other methods of treatment have been so concerned with evaluating outcome.

Applications of behaviour therapy to adults

The actual techniques of behaviour therapy can be grouped together in a variety of ways. Some authors have followed traditional medical models and discussed techniques brought to bear on separate illnesses.[2] Others have grouped the techniques according to the theoretical models of learning from which they were derived.[6, 13, 4] Most authors have discussed applications to children separately from applications with adults.[14] Below, applications to children and adults will be separated. Whilst specific techniques are frequently used with both age groups, desensitization and aversion therapy will be discussed only as applied to adults, and operant conditioning and modelling will be discussed mainly with reference to children.

There are three major techniques of behaviour therapy used with adults. They are:

1) Desensitization
2) Aversion therapy
3) Operant conditioning

In addition, there are a number of miscellaneous techniques such as the bell-and-pad treatment for enuresis and the 'negative practice' treatment for tics which do not fit in adequately to the major theoretical models.

Desensitization

Systematic desensitization is perhaps the most commonly used method of behaviour therapy with adults. It is regarded as the most effective way of treating phobic disorders (i.e. severe fears of particular objects, people, places or events).

The technique of systematic densensitization was largely developed by Wolpe.[15] He was influenced by the earlier work of Pavlov, and of Watson and Jones. Not only had these latter two investigators demonstrated in the 1920s that phobias could be learned, they had also experimented with means of unlearning the fears. Wolpe replicated their early work, first with cats and then with humans.

He showed that cats which had been given electric shocks in the presence of a particular object soon learned to fear that object (a simple application of Pavlov's classical conditioning model of learning). The cats refused even to eat in the presence of the object. They would eat in the absence of the feared object. Wolpe gradually introduced the object to the cats while eating.

As soon as they showed any sign of fear, the object was withdrawn, and then re-presented when the animals were again eating.

By controlling the gradual presentation of the feared object whilst the animals were eating, Wolpe found that the cats were no longer afraid of that object. Put simply, Wolpe argued that the animal cannot be both relaxed and afraid at the same time. The state of relaxation induced by eating is incompatible with the state of fear. Wolpe said that the relaxation *reciprocally inhibited* the fear. Put more formally:

> If a response antagonistic to anxiety can be made to occur in the presence of anxiety-evoking stimuli, so that it is accompanied by a complete or partial suppression of the anxiety responses, the bond between those stimuli and the anxiety responses will be weakened.[15]

Clearly, inducing an anti-anxiety response in adults by asking them to eat is impractical, not to say messy.

Patients can be taught to relax their muscles, and once they are completely relaxed, they can be gradually reintroduced to the anxiety-provoking stimuli.

It is important to note that patients are re-exposed to the feared objects only very gradually. If they show signs of anxiety, the objects are removed. Wolpe originally worked with the objects being physically present. However, this poses problems when the patient is phobic of situations other than single specific objects. Good, if not better, results were obtained by getting the patients to imagine the feared situations whilst remaining relaxed.

In presenting the situation gradually, the therapist again focuses on exact behavioural descriptions. Before desensitization training commences, the therapist builds up a *hierarchy* of feared objects. The patient describes each phobic stimulus and states whether it is more or less feared than every other one. Therapy commences with the least feared object and systematically other items from the hierarchy are presented.

Rachman[14] divides systematic desensitization into four stages:

1. Preliminaries (history taking, etc.).
2. The patient is trained in progressive relaxation.
3. Hierarchies of phobic stimuli and/or anxiety-provoking situations are constructed and ranked in ascending order of intensity.
4. The patient is required to imagine the phobic stimuli in gradually ascending order while in a state of deep relaxation.[14]

Initially, systematic desensitization was used mainly with monosymptomatic phobias. Recently[4] it has been recognized that the technique can be generalized to deal with more complex phobic disorders. Multiple hierarchies can be desensitized simultaneously, or in sequence. Difficult, more generalized anxiety of social situations such as is involved in *agoraphobia* (an intense fear of being out alone in public places) also responds to this form of treatment, although recent studies indicate that 'flooding' (see later) is an even more successful technique.

Reviewing the literature on the efficacy of systematic desensitization, Meyer and Chesser[4] report success rates ranging from 62 per cent to 100 per cent. The better figures tended to come from studies of monosymptomatic phobias. Agoraphobia was found to respond better to desensitization than to individual or group psychotherapy. One of the obvious advantages of behaviour therapy is that it takes a much shorter time than traditional psychotherapy. Many studies report treatment being successful in as few as ten sessions. Follow-up studies show that gains are maintained and that the removal of the unwanted fear has not resulted in the appearance of new 'symptoms'.

Aversion therapy

A phobia is one type of distressing behaviour that the patient wants to be freed from. There are other types of behaviour which the patient finds pleasurable but are regarded by other people as socially unacceptable. Thus, various addictions such as alcoholism, smoking, and the drug addictions, gambling and sexual perversions, may bring pleasure to the individual in the immediate short-term, but he and society disapprove of the long-term consequences. The aim of behaviour therapy in treating disorders of this sort is for the patient to learn that indulging in the behaviour leads to unpleasant consequences.

Originally, aversion techniques were most widely used in the treatment of alcoholism. Patients were administered a nausea-inducing drug. Then, just before they started retching and vomiting, they were allowed to pour themselves a glass of their favourite drink. The aim was to build up an association between the sight and taste of the alcohol and the overpowering feelings of nausea.

The treatment procedure was cumbersome. Patients had to be in-patients in hospital. It was difficult to time the interval between the injection and vomiting so as to present the alcohol at the crucial stage. Instead, electric shock has been substituted as the aversive element.

Progress in treating sexual deviations by aversion methods has been monitored in a number of ways. One of the most precise measures of change of sexual orientation involves measuring the strength of penile erection when fetishistic objects are shown. Marks and Gelder[16] paired each of a number of sexually exciting objects in turn with the shock. Among other things, they demonstrated the high specificity of this form of treatment. Only the particular object which had been paired with the shock became no longer attractive to the patient. However, since this was so, there was no doubt that it was the particular form of treatment which was having this dramatic effect.

A wide variety of other adult sexual disorders have been treated both by aversion therapy and other techniques. Interested readers are referred to standard sources for more details.[17, 4, 18, 19] It should be noted, however, that on its own, aversion therapy does nothing to make the socially desirable alternative behaviours more attractive for the patient. For this reason, most therapists nowadays attempt to modify the patient's social environment so that newly acquired alternative responses have an opportunity of appearing and being reinforced.

Aversion therapy is one of the most widely publicized forms of behaviour therapy. It is also one of the most controversial. Ethical issues which are implicit in all forms of treatment are somehow highlighted. The value judgements of society are clearly seen to operate. The question is often posed, 'What right does the therapist have to stop a patient from his homosexual practices?' The answer is that the therapist has no more right than he has to try to teach a new skill to any other patient. In both cases, the patient has asked for the therapist's help to encourage behaviour which is more socially acceptable. Where there is no alternative form of treatment that has been shown to work as well, there can surely be no objection to aversion therapy, provided the patient understands what is going to happen to him.

There is no doubt that aversion therapy is unpleasant. No therapist likes to use it, and as soon as equally effective, more pleasant forms of treatment can be devised, these techniques will be used less frequently. Already, in a search for a less unpleasant form of treatment, a technique called 'covert sensitization' is being experimented with.[2] In this, the patient is asked to imagine some unpleasant scene immediately after imagining the behaviour which he wants to decrease. The unwanted behaviour becomes associated with the unpleasantness, and decreases in frequency. Thus, aversion therapy is practised totally in imagination.

One point needs to be emphasized. Aversion techniques are very rarely used with children. Unlike adult patients, children are not voluntary patients. Moreover, it is doubtful if they would understand how unpleasant the techniques might be. Without the informed agreement of a voluntary patient, aversion therapy would only be employed as a last resort. For example, there are a number of cases reported where subnormal children have engaged in self-injurious behaviour to the extent that they have been in danger of permanently damaging themselves. Normal restraints had proved of no value, so aversion therapy was considered justifiable.

Operant conditioning

In dealing with phobias and with sexual disorders, the therapist is
helping the patient to get rid of an already existing maladaptive
response, and to replace it with a more acceptable and better
adapted behaviour. A further problem is how to build up a new
response or how to strengthen an existing, but weak, behaviour.
For this, the principles of operant conditioning are mainly
employed. These will be discussed in greater detail below with
reference to the literature on children's disorders.

Operant procedures have been successfully applied not only to
individual patients, but also to groups of patients. Ayllon and
Azrin[20] describe the setting up of 'token economies' within institutions whereby chronic, previously passive patients can be
motivated to participate in group activities by rewarding them
with tokens which are later exchanged for privileges, sweets or
cigarettes. These techniques are powerful means of changing
behaviour in a wide variety of patients in a wide variety of
settings.

Other techniques

It is only possible within the confines of this chapter to give a
brief introduction to behaviour therapy techniques. Two other
techniques must be mentioned.

Firstly, 'flooding' or 'implosion' therapy. One of the characteristics of phobic patients is that they never allow themselves to
come into contact with the object that they fear. Thus, they never
have the opportunity to learn that there is little basis in reality
for their fear – that nothing catastrophic is going to happen to
them. The techniques of desensitization take the phobic patient
gradually towards the feared object. The technique of 'flooding'
presents the most feared object immediately and forcibly keeps
the patient in contact with it for long enough for the induced
anxiety to begin to diminish. This form of treatment is still in
the experimental stage, but there is evidence that it is very successful with some phobias.[2] Clearly, it can be more economic in
terms of therapist's time.

The second technique which deserves brief description is that of 'Response prevention'. It is mentioned here because one recent case study[21] has explored its use with obsessional-compulsive patients (patients who act as if compelled to repeat various ritualist acts such as hand-washing, over and over again). This group has proved notoriously difficult to treat by any traditional method and it is not infrequent to find such patients being given brain surgery in a desperate attempt to relieve their misery. Rachman, Hodgson and Marzillier[21] show that a patient with a washing compulsion following exposure to dirt was successfully treated by making him watch a therapist handle dirty, 'contaminated' objects. The patient was able to copy the therapist more easily than to handle the objects on his own. He was then prevented from washing for increasing periods of time following his modelled contamination. The time spent by the patient in toiletry and washing dropped from four hours twenty-one minutes per day during the first week of treatment to one hour twenty minutes a day during the last week of treatment, some seventeen weeks later. The improvement was maintained at six months following discharge.

This latter approach to treatment is mentioned here because it illustrates an application of behaviour modification principles to a most difficult form of psychiatric disorder. By describing in detail exactly what the patient's disorder was, the therapists were able to manipulate the environment and effect a change in the behaviour. By monitoring the patients' behaviour during treatment, they were able to demonstrate which of a number of strategies was most beneficial. This continuous monitoring feeds back directly to the treatment process, and speeds up the whole process. Immediate knowledge of results guides the therapeutic tactics, and again illustrates one of the distinctive features of behaviour therapy.

Application of behaviour therapy to children – There is a very large literature on the application of behaviour therapy to children.[2, 22] The problems presented by children are usually qualitatively different to those presented by adults. As Eysenck and Rachman[3] put it, 'Most often the aim in therapy with adults is to break down a behaviour pattern, whereas in treating children the therapist usually has to build up an adequate behaviour pattern.' Thus, whilst desensitization of phobias has a place in treating children, most interest centres around the application of operant conditioning.[23] In addition, the work of social learning theorists such as Bandura[6] on 'modelling' is playing an increasingly important role in child therapy. Finally, we must not forget the continuing use of the 'bell and pad' technique with enuresis.

Operant conditioning

This form of treatment owes much to the experimental laboratory work of Skinner. He showed that certain types of behaviour could be modified by their consequences. What happens immediately after the appearance of a particular behaviour will affect the likelihood of that behaviour occurring again. If behaviour is followed by pleasant circumstances, it is likely to occur again and be strengthened (positive reinforcement). Behaviour which is not positively reinforced is likely to drop out of the child's repertoire. Technically, this is the process of extinction.

[The effects of punishment following the appearance of a particular piece of behaviour are not always predictable, but there is no space to discuss the problem here. Suffice it to say that in our present state of knowledge, punishment is not recommended as a technique for modifying behaviour.]

Positive reinforcement can be either material (sweets, food, toys, money) or it can be social (attention from adults, praise). Only a close study of the child's reaction to different reinforcers will tell whether they are appropriate. Reinforcements must be given *contingently* on the appearance of the desired behaviour if it is to be at all effective. This means that the sweet or the praise is given *immediately* following the appearance of the behaviour, but at no other time.

This very simple principle of positive reinforcement is surprisingly potent in altering children's behaviour. Profoundly disturbed autistic children can be taught some social skills, and in some cases can be taught useful language.[22] Parents have been

trained in operant procedures, and have modified such trouble-
some behaviours as temper tantrums and unco-operative behaviour, at home.[24, 25, 26] In the school, teachers have been
trained in the systematic use of positive reinforcement in the
classroom to control disruptive children, and to socialize withdrawn children.[27, 28, 29]

It is clear from recent surveys of the prevalence of psychiatric
disorder in children[30] that the special psychiatric services cannot
cope with all the problems. Therefore, any techniques which can
be taught to teachers or parents which will help them to deal
with the problem behaviour in its natural setting are to be
welcomed.

A typical programme of behavioural modifications involves
four main stages.[22] Let us here consider an application to classroom practice.

1) *Identification of target behaviours* – The teacher (or parent)
specifies the behaviour which she finds unacceptable, and outlines
the desired behaviour. The psychologist then translates these
complaints and goals into observable, behavioural terms.

2) *Baseline period* – The 'target' behaviours are counted to obtain
estimates of their naturally occurring, pre-treatment level.

3) *'Therapy'* – In the case of classroom behaviour, teachers are
instructed to ignore completely the child's bad behaviour, but to
praise him immediately for any acceptable behaviour. Teachers
often find it difficult to 'catch the child being good'. Initially,
they reward the child for any behaviour which approximates to
the desired goal. Gradually, more is demanded of the child before
the reinforcement is given.

4) *Evaluation* – The child's behaviour is monitored periodically
throughout treatment. Those unacceptable behaviours one wishes
to eliminate should decrease, whilst the desired behaviours should
increase. To demonstrate to the teachers that it is the change in
her behaviour which produced the change in the child's be-

haviour, it is sometimes necessary to revert to the pre-treatment conditions when once again the undesirable behaviours will reappear. Finally, the treatment conditions are reinstated. These techniques of classroom modification using the principle of operant conditioning are widely used in the United States, and have been shown to be equally applicable in the very different English school system.

Perhaps the widest application of operant techniques has been in the field of mental subnormality. Programmes have been worked out to teach subnormal children basic self-help skills such as feeding, toiletting and washing. Nurses are taught to administer these, and to train the children's language.[31] Parents, too, can be taught the techniques.

Only a few examples of the application of reinforcement principles have been given. Even from these, it is clear that operant conditioning is a flexible method of treatment applicable to establishing many desirable new behaviours.

Modelling

One of the difficulties of operant conditioning can be the time involved. If the therapist has to teach a child a particular gesture, it will take a great many trials if the child is only reinforced for successive approximations to the desired action. However, if the child is first shown the desired behaviour and is rewarded for a reasonable attempt at copying that behaviour, the process will be speeded up.

Bandura is the name most closely associated with work on the phenomena of copying, imitation, or modelling. Social learning theorists were interested in the process of 'identification'. Bandura and his colleagues concentrated in their early work on how children learn aggressive behaviour by watching others. They showed that under certain circumstances, children will imitate the aggressive actions of their peers, particularly if they see the models being rewarded for their aggression. Through observation, children may *learn* new behaviours, but they may not *perform* this until later. Bandura argues that modelling procedures are most useful in instituting novel responses. Once established through modelling procedures, they can be strengthened by positive reinforcement.

One recent study by O'Connor[32] will serve to illustrate a behaviour treatment based on modelling. Thirteen socially withdrawn, isolated nursery school children were the subject of this experiment. Six children were in the modelling group which was shown a twenty-three-minute film of children joining in social activities with obvious rewarding consequences. The seven children in the control group saw a film about dolphins. All children were observed before and after the films. Whereas initially they had shown very few social interactions with their peers, after this one exposure to the film, the modelling group showed a five-fold increase in social interactions, making them indistinguishable from their well-socialized peers. The control children did not alter in any way.

Modelling procedures have also been used in desensitization therapy, in which the child watches non-phobic children playing happily with, say, dogs.[4] Training in imitation has a valuable place in all sorts of behavioural treatments.[6]

Treatment of enuresis

Bed-wetting is a common, and particularly uncomfortable behavioural disorder. There are many theories about the causes of enuresis, some more plausible than others, but none entirely convincing.[2] Beyond the age of five, many more boys than girls are persistent bet-wetters, and this is often taken as an indication that enuresis is a developmental disorder, i.e. an abnormality of development which is related to biological maturation.

Whatever the causes, the treatment most successful with enuresis is the bell-and-pad. The child sleeps on a special pad placed in his own bed. When he wets himself, the urine completes an electric circuit on the pad, and an alarm bell or buzzer is set off. This immediately wakes the child.

Success rates with this form of treatment are usually around 80 per cent, varying in different studies from 50 to 100 per cent, after about eight weeks of treatment. The relapse rate can be as high as 40 per cent, but the majority of them usually respond to a booster course of treatment. Good accounts of this work appear in Yates,[3] Lovibond[33] or Turner and Young.[34]

Concluding remarks

Through long discussions following introductory lectures on behaviour therapy, it is clear that there are many criticisms of this approach. Some of the commonest can be dealt with here.

Firstly, the charge is often levelled, 'You are only treating the symptoms, not the cause'. As was briefly argued at the beginning of the chapter, the question begs a more fundamental question. It assumes that behavioural disorders stem from an illness on the traditional medical model. By now, it is obvious that this assumption is not borne out by the evidence.

If the medical model were correct, one would predict that removal of one symptom leaving the illness untreated would result in 'symptom subsitution'. Despite thorough searches for such phenomena, none have been documented so far.[2]

Secondly, some critics claim that it is the patient–doctor relationship, and other non-specific factors in treatment that are the effective agents of change. If this were so, why then is it only with behaviour therapy that 'cures' are not only more common, but also quicker? Of course, behaviour therapists make use of the reinforcing aspects of the relationship, but this is not a sufficient condition for the treatment.

The third most common criticism is that the whole approach is over simplistic. The answer of Eysenck to this sort of criticism would be to ask what does one expect at this stage of our knowledge. All science starts in this way. By simplifying, certain issues can be seen more clearly. This is not to deny that human beings are complex creatures. However, at this stage in trying to help those with problems, their needs are best met by ignoring the complexities and concentrating on those aspects of human behaviour which can be understood. No one is saying that all human behaviour can be understood in learning theory terms, but let us at least push this sort of explanation to the limit as long as patients benefit from it.

However, the overriding answer to all these criticisms is really quite simple. None of the alternative forms of treatment have been shown to work as well. Belief in drug therapy or belief in psychotherapy can be no substitute for evidence on efficacy of treatment.

In the space of this chapter, it has been possible to provide only the most cursory introduction to a rapidly expanding area of treatment. It has not been the purpose of the chapter to prove that behavioural approaches to psychiatric disorders 'work'. For that, the reader will have to consult the psychological and psychiatric journals. If the chapter has resulted in anyone wanting to study the subject in more detail, then it will have succeeded in its major aims.

Acknowledgements
I would like to record my sincere thanks to my colleagues, Mr M. Berger and Dr H. C. Philips for their helpful and critical comments on an earlier draft of this chapter. I am grateful to Mrs B. Hunt for typing the manuscript.

Jungian psychotherapy

Irene Champernowne

Introduction

Jungian psychotherapy is a way of healing for the neuroses or psychoses, but also for the so-called 'normal' person who finds life empty and meaningless, or who is so overwhelmed by the social sickness of our time that he feels unable to develop life to the full. Dr Jung paid great attention to the work with so-called 'normal' people.

The psychology of C. G. Jung is called analytical psychology, in contradistinction to psychoanalysis, which is the term now reserved for the treatment offered by followers of Freud. Analysis by a Jungian method is a process of readjustment and development included under the heading of psychotherapy. It is a psychological happening in depth in a recognizable form, including both analysis and synthesis. Professor Jung, who had for some years worked as an assistant to Freud at the beginning of his professional career, gave full credit to the great psychologist but developed his own psychological method away from a psychology based purely on cause and effect and on a sexual theory of repression. Jung's psychology did not only try to answer the question 'where from', 'how', but was also interested in the question 'whither' and 'to what end'. For Jung a neurosis or psychoneurosis had an aim as well as a cause. It is itself an attempt at healing which needs to be understood.

Individuation

The development of a conscious 'ego' as the centre of consciousness is a process commencing in childhood. It is the building up of the 'I' of the conscious personality. The original identification with the surroundings and the state of undifferentiation slowly disappears and an individual identity develops. The individuation process, though initiated by the ego, continues more strongly in the second half of life, where the preoccupation with the inner world of the psyche becomes more pronounced. Young people, however, can sometimes be precipitated into the later stage too early because of excessive pressures and difficulties. The individuation process is a process of healing, or making whole, taking place within the psyche itself. As Jung says, 'It is a vital happening which brings about a fundamental transformation of personality'.[1] Jung did not believe in the conditioning of a man to external circumstances, that is, a forcing of social adaptation by external methods: He says:

> Inasmuch as a man is merely collective he can be changed by suggestion to the point of becoming or seeming to become different from what he was before. But inasmuch as he is an individual he can only become what he is and always was. To the extent that cure means turning a sick man into a healthy one, cure is change.[2]

Jung then points out that many people just do not want or require this sort of change.

> The Doctor must leave the *individual* way to healing open, and then the cure will bring about no alteration of personality but will be a process we call 'individuation' in which the patient becomes what he really is.[3]

The psychotherapeutic process

This process includes a great deal of work on unconscious material, dreams and other art forms, which communicate from the depths of the personality both to the patient himself as well as the doctor. This work is carried out *between* doctor and patient. They meet and spend some fifty minutes to an hour at a time talking together. The number of times a week varies with individuals; at the beginning perhaps two or three times a week, later about once a week or possibly less. The whole work may last some years. But Jung was always ready to adapt to the need of an individual's life. He did not want, if he could prevent it, the psychotherapeutic work or analysis to become the life of the patient. He said that the psychological work or treatment should feed into the existing life of an individual and he encouraged everyone to continue living and working normally if he could. The world of the conscious ego and its values had to be maintained as far as possible *vis-à-vis* the new discoveries in the psyche.

Jung made it quite clear to all his students that the psychotherapeutic work was the mutual responsibility of both doctor and patient. He sat face to face with his patients or students, setting no barrier of a desk between them. Each brought to the matter in hand, that is, the patient's life and problems, his own share in the search for understanding of this individual's life within the context of life as a whole. I remember how impressed I was in the summer of 1936, when I first talked to Professor Jung, by his attitude. He made one feel at once a fellow worker. Sitting face to face beside the windows of his study, which looked out on Lake Zurich, I was struck by the way he made himself absolutely available and totally present in the situation of the moment. The matter in hand for both doctor and patient was all important and constituted the immediate material, i.e., the patient's life itself, for research into the mystery of life itself. Individual life problems became possible, enriched by their position within the collective problems of human life and by the fact that Jung himself gave them the honour and attention they needed. One felt at once a fellow-worker, albeit a humble one (not a guinea-pig under observation or an object to be experimented upon). Jung himself says:

When I set myself up as a medical authority over my patient and on that account claim to know something about his individuality, or to be able to make valid statements about it, I am only demonstrating my lack of criticism, for I am in no position to judge the whole of the personality before me. I cannot say anything valid about him except in so far as he approximates to the 'universal man'. But since all life is to be found only in individual form, and I myself can assert of another individuality only what I find in my own, I am in constant danger either of doing violence to the other person or of succumbing to his influence. If I wish to treat another individual psychologically at all, I must for better or worse give up all pretensions to superior knowledge, all authority and desire to influence. I must perforce adopt a dialectical procedure consisting in a comparison of our mutual findings.[4]

and he continues:

[psychotherapy is] a kind of dialectical process, a dialogue or discussion between two persons. Dialectic was originally the art of conversation among the ancient philosophers, but very early became the term for the process of creating new syntheses.[5]

Psychotherapy is not a technique to be applied in a stereotyped fashion in order to reach a set goal. It includes discussion of the individual's life and conscious personal standpoint, an analysis of the family life and recapitulation of early experiences, related to the present position, that is to the immediate problem brought by the patient. Jungians are often accused of neglecting the early personal life of the individual, of becoming so fascinated by the unconscious and its contents as to be drawn too deeply into that material to the detriment of the whole person. I think this criticism is sometimes justified, but individual needs differ. Jung himself says:

Modern psychotherapy is built up of many layers, corresponding to the diversities of the patients requiring treatment. The simplest cases are those who just want sound common sense and good advice. With luck they can be disposed of in a single consultation. This is certainly not to say that cases which look simple are always as simple as they look; one is apt to make disagreeable discoveries. Then there are patients for whom a thorough confession or 'abreaction' is enough. The severer neuroses usually require a reductive* analysis of their symptoms and states.[6]

The treatment of children in relation to the family unit

Although there are a number of Jungian psychotherapists who work predominantly with children, especially through play and creative activities and are very successful in this work, Jung felt that a child's problem was nearly always rooted in that of the parents and family. The unrecognized and unconscious complexes in the family can manifest themselves through the most vulnerable member, who most often is the child. The child can dream the dream, or manifest the symptom, for the father, mother or the family as a whole. It is important in psychotherapy to discover which member of the family is more likely to be open to treatment; a child's symptoms can disappear through the treatment and growth in consciousness of a parent or even a more available sibling. It is often seen that a sickness in a family seems to travel from one member to another. If one manages to isolate a child psychologically and protect it from the sickness in its family another child, or one of the parents, may then start to show the same or equivalent symptoms of the psychological ill health.

In one family the youngest boy had terrible nightmares. He was treated at a Child Guidance Clinic by a Jungian analyst and was relieved. But at once the eldest sister fell psychologically ill. After some long time she was helped to readjust to life. At that point the mother began to steal, falling into a state of confusion and having hysterical faints. She was given treatment. It was not until the father began to see that in some way he, too, was psychologically responsible for his sick family and went for treatment, that the sickness began to abate. One child alone, for some strange reason, seemed to escape the psychic infection.

From Jung's point of view the psychic environment and the unconscious psychic participation in problems of others lies

*The 'reductive' method treats the unconscious product in the sense of a leading back to the elements and basic processes.

behind a child's sickness as a rule. So for Jung, child treatment is very closely bound up with adult treatment, and can often be met by changing the child's psychic environment within and through the adults' life.

Psychotherapeutic material: life-history, dreams and art forms

The analytic or psychotherapeutic process usually consists in the patient telling his life story and 'confessing' his part in it. A great deal of emotion is discharged in doing this and the individual is often much relieved in the early stages. The 'confession' is followed by 'elucidation' or explanation and a mutual discussion of the problems that have arisen. The present situation is reviewed in the light of the early years. Dreams or other art forms are studied and used to expose the conscious situation to the modification and compensatory influence of the unconscious. As Jung says:

> The doctor can only look on and try to understand the attempts at restitution and cure which nature herself is making. Experience has long shown that between conscious and unconscious there exists a compensatory relationship, and that the unconscious always tries to make whole the conscious part of the psyche by adding to it the parts that are missing, and so prevent a dangerous loss of balance.[7]

Jung says that 'a dream that is not understood remains a mere occurrence; understood it becomes a living experience'.[7] Nevertheless, just having a dream is therapeutic in some more limited sense, and this applies to all creative expression in whatever art form which springs from the depth of the psyche, from the hidden and unconscious levels of experience. So much more, however, can be derived from the 'occurrence' if attention is given to it afterwards and some understanding of it achieved.

Professor Jung was one of the pioneers of so-called art therapy as a handmaiden of psychotherapy. For well over half a century he used the creative expression of his students and patients –

painting, writing, sculpture, etc., in the same way as he used dreams. The ego became involved and related to that which was previously unconscious. By receiving the mysterious messages within the dream, painting, sculpture, poetry, dance, mime, music and drama, created by the patients or students, modification, re-education and development takes place. Thus the life of the individual can be adjusted, balanced or radically changed from within the psyche itself.

The figures in the personal and collective unconscious

Deeper than the personal historic layer of memories and experience there is a level of the universal experience of man within the psyche, that Jung calls 'the collective unconscious'. There we encounter the ancient types, patterns of experience called the archetypes in dreams and art forms of all kinds. In speaking of the collective unconscious Jung says:

> The psychologist of the unconscious proceeds no differently in regard to the psychic figures which appear in dreams, phantasies, visions and manic ideas, as in legends, fairy tales, myth and religion. Over the whole of this psychic realm there reign certain motifs, certain typical figures which we can follow far back into history, and even into pre-history, and which may, therefore, legitimately be described as 'archetypes'.

Jung continues:

> The archetypes* seem to me to be built into the very structure of man's unconscious, for in no other way can I explain why it is that they occur universally and in identical form.[8]

At this point we could do well to look at the way in which psychotherapeutic practice in general and Jungian psychotherapy in particular leads an individual to meet the figures in the un-

---

*The concept of the archetype is a specifically psychological instance of the 'pattern of behaviour'. Hence it has nothing whatever to do with inherited ideas, but with modes of behaviour.

conscious. This must not be taken as a stereotyped or set path of progress. There is, however, a general picture of the way the aspects of the psyche appear to the dreamer or artist. We are so much more than our conscious ego, the 'I' we call ourselves. Until we begin to understand more, we simply say, 'I was not myself' when we act out an unconscious aspect of our personality, taking no responsibility for it. A great deal of the psyche which really belongs to the personal aspect of our life has been discarded, repressed and rejected in the course of our training and under social pressure. Thus a great deal of vitality and capacity has for various reasons not been lived. This psychic energy is constellated into a figure Jung calls 'the shadow'. In psychotherapy and analysis this appears in the dream as a being, the same sex as the dreamer's ego. The appearance of this figure is the psyche's attempt to bring an unknown aspect into consciousness and to the notice of the ego, and thus to enlarge the field of the ego by much that is complementary and compensatory to the individual's existing narrower field of consciousness. Behind this lies the contrasexual opposite, the 'Eve' in man, the 'Adam' in woman, which Jung calls the 'anima' and the 'animus' respectively. These contrasexual images have been formed partly by the historic experience in the individual, of woman or man respectively in early years, generally of the parents or other prominent parental substitutes. Secondly, by the masculine and feminine qualities inherent in the individual himself and lastly, by the archetypal nature of man and woman respectively, that is, man as hunter, judge, king, etc., etc., woman as virgin, prostitute, queen, etc., etc. The possibilities of an inner psychic marriage of these sexual opposites is brought closer to inner reality through the growing consciousness and experience of the inner images. The actual outer relationship between a man and woman is much affected by this inner situation, as indeed the inner psychic life situation is by the outer reality of relationship. The inner drama can be externalized in dream, picture, drama or other art form, as well as in a phantasy relationship of flesh and blood. Much work on this is the business of psychotherapy.

The temperamental types

The question of the opposites brings before us the fact of differing individual temperaments and their methods of functioning within the healing process. In Jung's theory of psychological types there is a division into introverts and extroverts, the former, an introverted individual who lives mostly within himself via the images of actual objects and events, and the latter, an extroverted individual, who lives in an outgoing way in continuous external relation with the objects or situation.

These two temperamental types Jung divides into four functional types. Although we all function via thinking, feeling, intuition and sensation we are inclined to develop in consciousness one or two functions to a greater extent. The most undifferentiated function lies practically unused within the psyche and is related to the unconscious shadow figure. The accompanying diagrams give some guidance. If the individual is a philosopher the craftsman in him on the opposite side will lie in the unconscious as an undifferentiated shadow figure. If the individual is a technical scientist in consciousness he has left the intuitive artist undeveloped in the shadow of the unconscious and so on. The inferior or undeveloped side is best reached in psychotherapy via an auxiliary function which is one of the other two more closely related to consciousness not entirely in the unconscious. For instance, the technician will get nearer to his intuition via his thinking or nearer to his feeling via his sensation.

The self

Behind these personal shadow figures and contrasexual figures lie the archetypal images of the collective unconscious deep in the psyche and deeper still, where conscious and unconscious meet is a central point Jung calls 'the Self'. This begins to show itself in dreams and art forms, especially later in life as the individual person develops. The 'Self' is a container of all opposites, the ego and the non-ego.

Jung says:

A heathlful compensatory operation comes into play which

DIAGRAM I

(Shading indicates unconscious part of psyche in a thinking type)

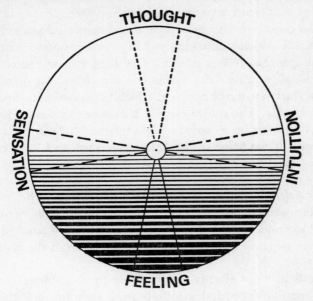

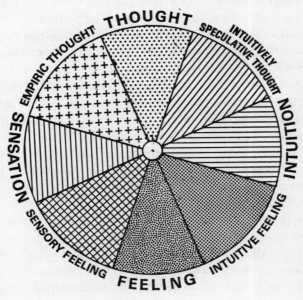

DIAGRAM 2

each time seems to me a miracle. Struggling against that dangerous trend towards disintegration there arises out of this same collective unconscious a counteraction characterized by symbols which point unmistakably to a process of centring. This process creates nothing less than a new centre of the personality which the symbols show from the first to be superordinate to the ego, and which later proves its superiority empirically. The centre cannot, therefore, be classed with the ego but must be recorded a higher value. Nor can we continue to give it the name of 'ego', for which reason I have called it 'the Self'.[9]

The *Self* is a concept or experience which cannot be described and disposed of in a few words. In the *Grail Legend*, written by Mrs Jung and Marie-Louise Von Franz there is a passage which helps us to grasp something of the importance of the symbol:

The Self is not already present from the beginning in a comprehensible form, but manifests itself only through the outer and inner realizations of a life lived to its end. For this reason Jung has likened it to the crystal lattice present as a potential form in a solution but which first becomes visible in the process of crystallization, although crystallization does not necessarily take place. The Self is, therefore, not complete but is present in us as a potentiality which can become manifest only in the course of a specific process. Certainly the Self is not invariably realized through the unfolding of the natural biological life processes . . . As the threads of fabric are woven into a pattern so the Self as the living garment of divinity is woven out of the many decisions and crises, in themselves possibly insignificant, by which we are affected in the course of our lives.[10] . . .

Psychologically the term 'Self' denotes the psychic totality of the human being which transcends consciousness and underlies the process of individuation and which gradually becomes conscious in the course of this process. The psychic totality which comprises the conscious and unconscious parts of the personality is naturally present as an *entelechy* of the individual from the very beginning. In the course of the process of maturation, however, the various aspects of totality enter the field of consciousness thus leading to a widening of the continually changing horizon of awareness. Beyond this there is often a numinous experience of this inner psychic wholeness. This experience is usually accompanied by a profound emotion which the ego senses as an epiphany of the divine. For this reason it is practically impossible to differentiate between an experience of God and an experience of the Self.[11]

The individual's meeting with the figures foreshadowing the experience of the Self, is a later happening in the psychotherapeutic process and usually in older people. Youth is the time chiefly for ego-building and assimilation of the shadow and the meeting of the contrasexual images as has already been explained, though in reality the process of individuation begins at birth with the physical separation from the mother and continues as the development of consciousness progresses and with increasing experience of life.

Relation of doctor and patient

Here I should like to return to the relationship of doctor and patient and the question of the transference which is given such a prominent place in Freudian psychoanalysis. Here it is suitable that Jung speaks for himself and makes clear his position *vis-à-vis* the patient. He has said that the transference phenomena is only very acute when the relationship between doctor and patient is difficult to maintain. Nevertheless, he treats this part of the analytic and psychotherapeutic process as of vital importance. He says:

As a result of reductive analysis the patient is deprived of his faulty adaptation and led back to his beginnings. The psyche naturally seeks to make good this loss by intensifying its hold upon some human object, generally the doctor. . . .[12]

This can cause confusion and tension, the patient seeing in the doctor what he found in his parent or what he hoped to find in a parent, whether it is really in the doctor or not. This uncomfortable situation is like a concrete dream drama being worked out by two people who understand, or come to understand, what is happening, and this is truly a psychotherapeutic and healing opportunity.

Jung continues:

> Even if these projections are analysed back to their origins . . . the patient's claim to human relationship still remains and should be conceded, for without a relationship of some kind he falls into a void.[13]

The doctor or analyst must be the more conscious member of this 'freely negotiated bond or contract', for this person to person relationship is essential for the success of psychotherapeutic work and at the very least the doctor must understand as fully as possible its meaning. The personalities of doctor and patient probably decide ultimately the success or failure of the work more than what is actually said. Quoting again from Jung:

> For two personalities to meet is like mixing two different chemical substances: if there is any combination at all both are transformed.[14]

Professor Jung is ruthless and humble in the way he puts responsibility upon the doctor or psychotherapist, and in his book on psychotherapy he volunteers a great deal of information about the weakness of the doctor's position because of the latter's human frailty. He says:

> It is futile for the doctor to shield himself from the influence of the patient and to surround himself with a smokescreen of fatherly and professional authority. By so doing he only denies himself the use of a highly important organ of information. . . . The doctor is as much in the analysis as his patient.[15]

This seems to me a very profound, courageous and illuminating statement, exacting, humbling, but with the most creative possibilities for all concerned. Jung continues:

What is now demanded [is the doctor's] own transformation, the self-education of the educator . . . The doctor can no longer evade his own difficulties by treating the difficulties of others.[16]

This mutual way of working lies at the heart of our work as Jungian psychotherapists. The transference and counter-transference are far-reaching opportunities of growth and development, if brought into consciousness for both doctor and patient.

What was formerly a method of medical treatment now becomes a method of self-education, and with this the horizon of our psychology is immeasurably widened. The crucial thing is no longer a medical diploma but the human quality.

For as soon as psychotherapy takes the doctor himself for its subject it transcends its medical origin and ceases to be merely a method for treating the sick. It now treats the healthy, or such as have a moral right to psychic health, whose sickness is at most the suffering that torments us all.[17]

Individual and society

Although Jungian psychotherapy concentrates so pronouncedly upon the individual and his fulfilment, Jung points out that the microcosm and the macrocosm are really one. The health of the individual affects the health of society and vice versa. But we have to start in each individual human psyche; only there can we really effect change. We must begin with ourselves for we cannot 'take anyone further than we have gone ourselves'. At the end of Volume 16 of the *Collected Works* Jung makes the following statement:

We live in a time of confusion and disintegration, everything is in the melting pot. As is usual in such circumstances unconscious contents thrust forward to the very borders of consciousness for the purpose of compensating the crises in which 'the psyche' finds itself, . . . what our world lacks is the *psychic connection*; and no clique, no community of interests, no political party and no state will ever be able to replace this. It is, therefore, small wonder that it was the doctors and not the sociologists who were the first to feel more clearly than anybody else the true needs of man, for as psychotherapists they have the most direct dealing with the suffering of the soul.[18]

Jungian psychology in its exploration of the personal and collective unconscious has given us so much greater knowledge of the creative process through images and symbols. This has developed widely into the field of art therapy in painting, sculpture, drama, movement, music and poetry writing, and art therapy is used much more extensively in hospitals and clinics. Jungian psychotherapy has also explored group methods in therapeutic communities and in hospital wards, as well as family therapy, including marriage guidance with both husband and wife, but through all these methods Jung made central the psychotherapeutic work with the individual in a *tête à tête* situation. Most Jungian psychotherapists stand firmly by this, whatever other methods are explored through art therapy as a handmaid of psychotherapy or group therapy, not as an alternative method but as an addition. However, as I have just quoted, 'No clique, no community of interests, no political party and no state will ever be able to replace . . . the direct dealings with the suffering of the soul.'

Adlerian psychotherapy

*Hertha Orgler**

Alfred Adler, the founder of Individual Psychology (for meaning see p. 158), was born in Vienna on 7 February 1870, the second of six children. His health was delicate during childhood. Having been near to death himself and having also experienced the death of his younger brother in the bed next to him, he decided from an early age to overcome death and with this goal in mind to become a doctor. He studied medicine at the University of Vienna and also Psychology and Philosophy. He obtained his medical degree in 1895. Working first as eye specialist then as general practitioner he became a neurologist and psychiatrist. At the turn of the century he married Raissa Epstein. Two of his four children carry on his work. His daughter Alexandra, his second child, is Clinical Professor of Psychiatry at New York University and Medical Director of the Alfred Adler Mental Hygiene Clinic, New York. His son Kurt, MD, PhD, is Medical Director of the Alfred Adler Institute of New York and Medical Director of the Jamaica Center of Psychotherapy, New York.

In 1902 Adler accepted Freud's invitation to join his discussion group. From the beginning Adler made it clear that he disagreed with some of Freud's ideas, and when his divergent views became stronger he left Freud's circle in 1911 and founded another society, subsequently called in 1912 the Society for Individual Psychology. Adler was never a Freudian analyst. He had not followed his classes, nor been psychoanalysed himself. I think that Adler's different views have their origin in their fundamentally different attitudes towards life. Adler had the

*Also author of *Alfred Adler: The man and his work triumph over the inferiority complex,* London, New York, Paris, Rome, Utrecht, Vienna, Munich.

opportunity of applying his new theories in the war hospital work he was doing during the 1914–18 war. After the war he practised in Vienna but frequently accepted invitations to lecture abroad. He continued his pioneer work in Child Guidance Sessions in front of doctors, teachers, social workers and others. In 1926 he was appointed Visiting Professor at Columbia University, New York, where he lectured until he was called to take up the lectureship of Medical Psychology at Long Island Medical College, New York in 1932, which he kept up to his death. He died from heart failure on 28 May 1937, in a street of Aberdeen, Scotland, while giving a course of lectures at Aberdeen University.

Alfred Adler called his psychology 'Individual Psychology', because he saw in a human being not a bundle of drives and instincts, but an indivisible unity, as the meaning of the Latin word *individuum*, not to be broken into parts, from which our word 'individual' is derived, clearly shows. As the term Individual psychology has often been misinterpreted, his psychology is now internationally known as *Adlerian psychology*. Adler emphasized the unity of body and mind. He did not think that heredity and environment determine the development of a human being, but that heredity gives certain potentialities and environment gives certain impressions. These potentialities and impressions are the bricks an individual uses in his own creative way to build up his *life-style*.

It should be stressed that the term life-style, which is used now almost everywhere, was coined by Adler. This life-style is unique and distinguishes one single individual from all others. To understand the life-style one has to discover the goal towards which an individual is striving. Adler saw a human being always in movement towards his life-goal; this movement is from below upwards, from a minus position to a plus position. This striving is not so much influenced by the facts as by the opinion the person has of the facts. The individual does not relate himself to the world in a predetermined manner. He relates himself according to his own interpretation of himself and of his problems. He sees everything from his own self-created perspective. To help patients who have an erroneous opinion to get insight and thus to change their life-style is one of the most important tasks of Adlerian psychotherapy. To reveal the life-style and the secret goal Adlerians use the interpretation of the position among brothers and sisters, of dreams and of first memories.

Family constellation, another term Adler coined is now discussed everywhere. It matters whether somebody grows up as an only, first, second or youngest child, as an only boy among sisters or an only girl among brothers, for the development of the life-style varies according to the child's position in the family. The eldest child is for a while an only child and is the centre of interest. When a second child arrives, he often feels 'dethroned', which he bitterly resents. So, through looking back to his lost Paradise, the eldest mostly has a tendency to be interested in the past. The second born has a pacemaker in front of him whom he tries to outdistance. The youngest born often has several pacemakers and no one coming after him as a challenge. So he has never to look back and can concentrate on running forward with the aim of catching up or overtaking his older brothers and sisters.

A detailed description of this theme can be found in a publication entitled *The position of the child in the family and its significance* by Neil R. Beattie, formerly Dean of the Royal Institute of Public Health and Hygiene, and Principal Medical Officer, Ministry of Health, London.[1] When writing about the first, second, youngest, middle, only child, the only boy among girls and the only girl among boys, he says: 'While these characteristics have always been obvious, for they could not have been missed, they were accepted as inevitable and unavoidable, for which nothing could be done. It was, however, due to the penetrating genius of Alfred Adler that the causes of and the reasons for the development of these particular types of children were made clear; it was because of him that we are enabled to become aware of the fact that these human characteristics were not purely accidental, but that, on the contrary, they were chosen and deliberate . . . The Family Constellation, therefore, is one of the basic principles of Adlerian or Individual Psychology, and . . . it is true, it is real, it exists; . . .'

Adlerian *dream* interpretation is different from that used in Freudian psychoanalysis. According to Adler the purpose of the dream is *not* that it shall be understood, but that it shall arouse feelings and emotions that cannot be aroused by logic or common sense, in order to give us more impetus to solve immediate problems. Adler's use of dream interpretation is shown in his own account of a young offender:

N. was a particularly handsome youth who had been released from prison after six months for good behaviour. He had stolen a large sum of money from his employer's till. In spite of the great danger of having to complete his three years' sentence if he committed another crime, he again stole a small sum. However, before the police got wind of the affair, his people sent him to me. He was the eldest son of an extremely respectable family, and his mother's spoilt darling. It turned out that he was very ambitious and wanted to be the leader in everything. He chose as friends only those individuals who were inferior to him, and thus betrayed his inferiority feeling. His earliest childhood memories always pictured him as the getting type. In the post he had when he stole the money from the till, he always saw very rich people around him and, at the same time his father lost his own position and could not support his family. Flying dreams and dreams of situations in which he was the hero characterized his ambitious striving and, at the same time, his feeling that he was predestined to be certain of success. A tempting opportunity led him to the theft as he thought that he could thereafter be superior to his father. The second little theft was carried out as a protest against his being released on parole and against the subordinate position in which he found himself. While in prison he had once dreamt that his favourite dish had been served, but remembered during the dream that this was not possible in prison. His greediness is evident in this dream as well as his protest against his conviction.[2]

First memories allow a deep insight into the human mind. What a person selects out of the multitude of memories indicates on what his interest is still focused. What can be found by interpreting first recollections is stated by Adler: 'Proceeding with great caution and equipped with long experience, we are now able to discover by means of early recollections, any erroneous direction of the life-style, lack of social interest or the contrary. Much light can be thrown on the individual by his selection of a "we" or "I" situation, by mention of his mother. Recalling a danger or an accident, or a punishment, shows great inclination to look at the hostile side of life. His recollection of the birth of a brother or sister shows his retained sense of having been dethroned. The rememberance of the first day in kindergarten or school shows the great impression made by a new experience. The recollection of illness or death is often connected with fear, but more often with the desire to face these dangers better equipped as a doctor or nurse. The recollection of a country holiday with the mother, or the mention of certain persons as mother, father, grand-parents in a friendly atmosphere shows preference for these people and the exclusion of others. Recollections of one's own misdeeds, such as theft or lies or sexual vagaries, shows the endeavour to avoid such misdemeanors in the future. First memories reveal distinctly different trends, visual, auditory, or motor; these can help us to discover the cause of failures in certain subjects at school, or of a mistaken choice of occupation. They aid us in helping the individual to select a profession which better suits his preparation for life.'[2]

Sometimes a first memory reveals an Inferiority Complex. *Inferiority Complex* is for ever linked with the name of Alfred Adler. He distinguished between the normal inferiority feeling and the Inferiority Complex. 'To be a human being means to feel oneself inferior,' wrote Adler. He believed that every human being required security and that the small child with his intelligence far surpassing his physical power has a keen appreciation of his own inadequacy. Thus a feeling of inferiority is created. This inferiority feeling spurs him to activity and is a stimulus to every upward striving. In contrast, the Inferiority Complex acts as a restraint.

There are three sources of the Inferiority Complex: First, 'organ inferiority'; second, neglect; third, spoiling. *Organ inferiority*: Already in 1907 in his *Studie über die Minderwertigkeit von Organen und ihre seelische Kompensation*[3] (*Study of Organ Inferiority and its Psychical Compensation*[4]) Adler pointed out that an organ inferiority may have an effect on the mind. An inferior organ may lead to an Inferiority Complex, but on the other hand may be compensated and lead to a striving for the highest achievements; Demosthenes, a stutterer, said to be incurable, trained himself to speak and became the greatest orator of Greece. Beethoven and some other famous composers became deaf. Many famous painters have suffered from eye defects. Adler stressed that investigations in art schools have shown that up to seventy per cent of art students had anomalies of the eyes, specially colour-blindness. See also today's findings by Professor R. W. Pickford on *Colour vision defective art students*.[5] That is not to say that these famous people became great because of their organ inferiority, but by courageously compensating for it. Some organic inferiority only comes to light under the stress of mental tension. *Neglect*. Whether somebody actually was neglected in early childhood or only thinks he was neglected, hated, unwanted or too ugly to be loved, all have the same harmful effect. The opinion one has of the facts, rather than the facts themselves, matters most. *Spoiling*. Adler considered spoiling means pampering a child so as to produce dependency. Many spoilt people get on very well in life as long as their path is smooth. As soon as there is an obstacle they fail, because they have never learned to use their own abilities. They do not know that life involves *the overcoming of difficulties*. As they are not aware that they suffer only from a lack of training, they understandably believe in a lack of ability and dare not solve problems by themselves. (See also the chapter on 'Environmental handicap and the teacher' by Stephen Wiseman, late Director, National Foundation for Educational Research in England and Wales.[6])

Adler defined the Inferiority Complex as 'inability to solve life's problems'. The three great problems of life are love, occupation, social interest.

Love. Adler's views about love have often been misunderstood. Adler never undervalued the importance of sex. Adler propounded that sex is directed by the life-style and is not an uncontrollable drive. However, he saw in love much more than sex and thought that in the harmony of a couple true happiness can be found. Much disharmony in love and marriage is caused by the wrong view that women are inferior to men. Adler, a champion of woman, emphasized that the 'superstition' of woman's inferiority is harmful to men as well as to women. Many women who wrongly believe that women are inferior reject the woman's role. Those men who wrongly believe that they have always to demonstrate their masculine superiority get into an unnatural mental and physical tension.

Masculine protest was coined by Adler to mean 'being emphatically masculine'.

Social interest is another term of Adler's that is often misinterpreted. In the original German Adler called it *Gemeinschaftsgefühl* and later *Mitmenschlichkeit*. It is more than just interest in others, it involves actively helping others. Children lacking social interest are open to various dangers. Passive children are potential neurotics and active children lacking social interest are potential delinquents. To prevent neurosis and crime all educators should do all they can to develop social interest in the young.

There are three possibilities with an Inferiority Complex:

1) One may overcome it by one's own efforts or by psychotherapy.
2) One may not overcome it, but suffer from it throughout life and limit oneself.
3) One may not overcome it but hide it under a Superiority Complex.

A *Superiority Complex* can be manifested in the exaggerated demands an individual makes on himself and on others. For the most part people with an Inferiority Complex only harm themselves, but most of those with a Superiority Complex are potentially harmful to others. Those who depreciate others to savour their own superiority can even undermine the physical health of those they denigrate. The strongest expression of a Superiority Complex is *power striving*. It is essential to see through power striving, as it is harmful to the mental health of the power strivers and of the people affected by them. The deeply hidden doubts in their abilities drives the power strivers on to prove always to themselves and others that they are superior and never allows them any rest. It is futile, therefore, to give them all they want in the hope that they will stop their demands. As they strive towards the goal of personal power and superiority over others, they can never be satisfied. This is demonstrated in everyday life in all human relationships.

Modern educational research brings out the correctness of Adler's views that man is not a bundle of drives and instincts, not a mere product of heredity and environment, but builds up his unique personality with his own creative power. See the findings of Professor P. E. Vernon, formerly London University, Institute of Education[7, 8] and of Dr W. D. Wall, Dean, Institute of Education, University of London, formerly Director, National Foundation for Educational Research in England and Wales. Many other thoughts of Professor Wall are in accordance with Adler's ideas, for instance in his Convocation Lecture at the National Children's Home, he said: '. . . They should come to accept that difference is neither necessarily a threat nor a sign of inferiority – and indeed that difference of view and of culture is enriching and stimulating. . . .'[9]

This point that difference is not an indication of inferiority, is important in psychotherapy, as many people who are gifted above the average feel wrongly inferior because they are 'different'.

Many ideas of Adler are acknowledged as the basis of many new schools of thought, especially in medicine. I myself heard Sir Walter Langdon-Brown, Emeritus Regius Professor of Cambridge University, speaking at a symposium on Adler, at which he stated: 'There is hardly an aspect in medicine which has not undergone some change as the result of Adler's teaching. It has even had effect upon the views of many who have never read him, but who are conscious of a change in the medical atmosphere that surrounds them.' In the field of psychosomatic medicine in particular Adler's ideas are acknowledged to be the basis of psychosomatics.

Psychosomatics. After testing Adler's theories on organ inferiority in the psychosomatic wards of Vienna neurological university clinic, the heads of this clinic Professors, Dr H. Hoff and Dr E. Ringel, both of Vienna University, concluded that Adler's views were fully confirmed. They call him 'one of the fathers of modern psychosomatic medicine'[10] and acknowledge that 'The theory of organ inferiority by Alfred Adler represents not alone a useful contribution but can be considered an indispensable adjunct in the management of psychosomatic disease'.[10]

Professor O. Spiel, Vice-President of the Austrian Society for Mental Hygiene, called Adler's *Study on Organ Inferiority, Grundstein der heute als stolzes Gebäude sich erhebenden 'Psychosomatik'.*[11] '. . . the foundation stone of today's proud edifice "psychosomatics".'[11]

Social psychiatry which today is a world-wide movement, is also based on Adler. Dr J. Bierer, Professor of Social and Community Health, Southern University Florida, USA, a founder of 'Social Psychiatry', calls Adler 'the grandfather of Social Psychiatry', as Adler was the first to emphasize the importance of social factors in psychopathology. Dr Bierer, who now lives in London, is a former pupil of Adler. Today he is President of the 'International Association of Social Psychiatry'.

The founder of Logotherapy, Professor Dr Viktor Frankl of Vienna University comes from Adler's circle and his work is based on Adler's Psychology. Adler's view that life has value and meaning and that an individual has the freedom of decision can be found in Frankl's teaching. Professor Frankl, President of the 'Austrian Medical Society of Psychotherapy', is now Professor for Logotherapy at US International University, San Diego, California. He calls his teaching 'Existential Analysis' as well as 'Logotherapy'. He wrote: 'Existential Analysis (*Existenzanalyse*) and logotherapy . . . represent a certain aspect of one and the same theory . . .' *Logos* signifies first of all 'meaning'. Thus logotherapy is a psychotherapy that is orientated towards meaning . . . Logos now means not only *meaning* but also the *spiritual*. . . .[12] In his book, *Theorie und Therapie der Neurosen,*

Professor Frankl states: 'Logotherapy does not intend to replace psychotherapy in the narrower and previous sense of the word, but only wants to supplement it.'[13]

Adlerian psychotherapy has four main aspects: 1) establishing contact with the patient; 2) elucidating his life-style; 3) encouraging; 4) developing his social interest.

The psychotherapist lets the patient choose a seat. The psychotherapist best establishes *contact* by maintaining an unchanging friendly attitude. He has to be a reliable fellow human being. It is best to approach the patient on a non-authoritarian basis and never force him. In order to *elucidate the life-style* the patient is allowed to speak freely. Usually he starts by talking about his present problems. Many find it difficult to talk at all. And this is where from the very beginning of the treatment, *encouragement* plays an important role. Although the therapist might recognize the life-style early on in the treatment, he should postpone giving his opinion until the patient feels able to interpret with him. Gradually his dreams, first memories and his family constellation are interpreted. The unity of his personality is revealed in his thinking and feeling in his movements and actions. He is encouraged to find his secret goal. (Adler's concept of 'goal-directedness' is of great help in psychotherapy.) His answer to the question, what he would do when cured often reveals the meaning of his illness.

The current general tendency is to blame parents for the children's difficulties. In contrast, Adlerian psychotherapy helps the patient to overcome his bitterness about this. After all as nobody knows the future, one is bound to make mistakes, and as parents are only human it is futile to expect their behaviour to be perfect. The attitude towards the parents is linked with difficulties that have arisen through the position in the birth order. How often intelligent patients of any age think they are stupid, because they have grown up in the shade of a very intelligent brother or sister. How much jealousy in later life can be traced back to an often wrong assumption that a sibling is or was preferred. Far from provoking or enlarging feelings of guilt, which lower the self-valuation, we stress that one can only go from a greater error to a smaller error and thus raise the patient's self-esteem. He gets insight into the discrepancy between the facts and his erroneous self-valuation by the therapist's stressing of his former or present achievements, which show he has abilities. How much more could he achieve, if he gave up his self-limitation. Dr E. Weissmann, the present Chairman of the Alfred Adler Society of Great Britain, finds that every patient had a wrong training and is therefore not sufficiently equipped for some aspects of life. He should gain new encouraging experience in a process of careful and continuous step-by-step retraining to develop some of his untapped abilities.

After the patient has discovered in co-operation with the therapist where his main interest lies, he trains in this field. When the therapist realistically praises his successes, the patient acquires the joy of achievement and his self-confidence is increased.

With growing self-esteem of the patient, the therapist will find it easier to enlarge his *social interest*. It is not enough to bring him into the company of others, the therapist has first to help him to realize his links with other human beings and rouse his wish to make contact with others. The Adlerian therapists do not regard the symptoms in isolation but as part of the whole life-style. The patient gets insight into the meaning of his symptoms and towards what goal they are directed. Adlerian therapists are not content with the mere disappearance of the symptoms but only consider the patient cured when besides losing these symptoms he strives towards a constructive goal, takes responsibility, courageously solves his problems and acts as a *Mitmensch*, fellow human being.

Duration and frequency. It is most helpful to the patient to get some points clear at the beginning of the psychotherapy. His justified question of duration is difficult to answer precisely. We Adlerians point out that it is advisable to have some weeks' treatment before deciding definitely how long the whole therapy may be. Adlerian methods, although very thorough, involve on the whole a short period of time. The question of frequency is also handled on the same lines as Adler advised. Dr Herbert Schaffer, present Chairman of the Société Française de Psychologie Adlérienne, Paris, like Adlerians in other countries, writes that three sessions a week is the most to begin with, soon after reducing to two weekly. Duration and frequency depend on the co-operation of the patient.

What can be done with Adlerian psychotherapy of schizophrenic patients is best described by Dr Alexandra Adler, Alfred Adler's daughter:

Schizophrenia

Adlerian psychiatrists have always accepted schizophrenic patients and have devised various methods for keeping them out of hospitals and on an ambulatory basis. In order to help the schizophrenic patient cope with his environment, which he usually looks upon as hostile, his whole life situation must be taken into consideration. An effort must be made to prevent him from withdrawing from society and its demands on him; he must be taught to deal with his fears. To achieve this objective, constant attention is given to the patient's current activities, rather than to attempt to explain to him the possible causes of his illness on a symbolic level, which in our experience, is likely to increase his tendency toward mystic thinking . . .*[14]

A good example of what is being done today in USA with applied Adlerian Psychology is the following report on the work done by Professor M. Sonstegard of West Virginia University, a well-known Adlerian:[15]

The Mid-East (USA) Society of Individual Psychology has been slow in developing; however, Parent Study Groups were recently organized in the Morgantown area. The Morgantown Family Education Centre, where parents and children are counselled with the techniques Alfred Adler used in his

*Based on a paper read at the session, 'Alfred Adler – a hundred years later', at the 123rd Annual Meeting of the American Psychiatric Association, San Francisco, 1- 15 May 1970.

Centres in Vienna, was founded by Dr Manford Sonstegard four years ago. From this beginning developed the television programme 'Growing Him Up'. The one hour weekly programme is a live telecast of the Family Education Centre. Parents and children are counselled with an added feature, TV viewers call in questions which are discussed and answered by the parents and counsellors attending the Centre. Dr Sonstegard is the counsellor for the programme which is produced and televised by West Virginia University educational television station WVU TV. Dave Wilson is the producer and director of the programme.

The Family Education Centre in Willington, Delaware, is sponsored by the Association for Study and Action and has an extensive programme which not only includes the Centre where parents and children are counselled each week, but also Parent Study Groups and a programme for training para-professionals. On an average a hundred and ten parents attend the weekly counselling session at the Centre. More than fourteen Parent Study Groups meet each week. It is estimated that between nine thousand and ten thousand parents in the Wilmington area have studied or have some contact with Adlerian Psychology.

The para-professionals who have been trained in Adlerian Psychology by Dr Sonstegard are now being invited to work in the schools counselling children individually and in groups as voluntary workers.

The Individual Psychology Association of Great Washington, D.C., instituted a programme of the same type as Wilmington's. It is not as extensive because it lacks the trained personnel to provide leadership in forming Parent Study Groups and volunteer workers in the schools. The Family Education Centre is attended by parents of the area to learn better methods of raising children in a democratic society.

The Albert Gallatin Area School District serves a practicum facility for West Virginia University to train counsellors by using Adlerian methods. The University students not only counsel children in groups and individually in the elementary and secondary school, but also parents two days per week under supervision of a Professor of the Counselling and Guidance Department of the University. The practicum students are helping the teachers initiate parent study groups for parents of the children enrolled in their classroom. Mrs Carrie Sonstegard is serving as consultant for the teachers in the implementation of the programme. The parents who attend the Study Groups are being trained to lead the study groups, thus freeing the teachers for other professional work and insuring more involvement by parents of the community.

A two-way involvement of students learning to become counsellors, and the parents of the community learning techniques of child rearing is the establishment of a Family Education Centre based on the Adlerian model. Leaders for the implementation of this Centre are Ron DeGusepie, a counsellor in the Albert Gallatin School District, and Dr Sonstegard.[15]

Adlerian psychotherapists today follow on the lines of Adler. There is Adlerian treatment for individuals or groups. In many countries more emphasis is now laid on the latter. Dr R. Dreikurs, University Professor in Chicago, USA, specially advocated Adlerian Group Therapy. Adler's Child Guidance technique which he himself demonstrated in front of doctors, teachers, social workers, etc., is now successfully used in many parts of the world.

There is an International Association of Individual Psychology to which Adler Societies in many countries are affiliated. A directory of members of this Association is edited by Nahum E. Shoobs, New York.[16] The largest of these Societies is the American Society of Adlerian Psychology (ASAP) of which Joseph Meiers, MD, New York, is the historian.[17]

Prevention. Adlerian Psychotherapists are profoundly concerned that much more should be done with the young to prevent mental disorders. Educators can play an important role by applying Adler's new method of education. Should there, however, already be an indication, among other traits, of an anti-social attitude, this can be more easily corrected in the formative years of the life-style by Adlerian psychotherapy.

Today the problems of aggressiveness, vandalism and delinquency concern every human being. The practical positive results of Adlerian Psychotherapy are widely acknowledged. As former co-worker of Alfred Adler I know that Adler himself and Adlerians in many countries have succeeded in helping even hostile anti-social individuals, specially teenagers, to turn into beings with social interest. This is best shown in the 'Autobiography of an "Incurable" Burglar' cured by Alfred Adler, published in my book *Alfred Adler: The man and his work triumph over the Inferiority Complex*.[18] Adler introduced this man to me and I know that he has gone straight ever since and has been very helpful to others.

This cured 'incurable' burglar is another proof for Adler's statement: 'For difficult times like ours, the inherited potentiality for human cooperation does not suffice. It must be further developed. The necessity and importance of this development are inherent in the discoveries of Individual Psychology – and the scientific method by which it may be accomplished is its contribution to the advancement of mankind.'

To all those who doubt in themselves and feel they cannot cope with life's problems – and the most valuable people are among them – Adlerian Psychotherapy shows that their worry is based on an error, which they can overcome. They are only lacking the right preparation to cope with life's problems. This preparation they can acquire at any age.

Drug therapy

S. D. McGrath, J. McKenna, J. J. Stack

Summary

Current usage of drugs in psychiatric practice is considered in the context of developments in the recent past. A classification of drugs is proposed and detailed consideration is given to the effects of specific drugs on both children and adults suffering from different types of emotional disorders. Advances in drug therapy are discussed, *lacunae* are highlighted and predictions are made about probable advances in the near future.

Introduction

One of the most important aspects of the developing use of psychotropic drugs in practice is the fact that, within the past two decades, practically every physician in general practice has become a drug therapist. This is borne out by statistics which indicate that a large proportion of the funds set aside for health programmes in these islands has been spent on drugs which influence human behaviour. Twenty years ago the psychiatrist was the specialist who took decisions about the kind and the amount of drugs to be administered for specific mental disorders. Today the family doctor, the nurse, and in some cases the patient himself may decide the nature and amount of drugs to be taken.

Many factors are responsible for this dramatic change; for example, the modern trend towards community care in the treatment of psychiatric disorders has removed the emphasis from psychiatric hospitals and psychiatrists and has involved the family doctor much more in the treatment of these disorders. This is but right – however, it raises questions about the teaching of mental health in medical schools, both at undergraduate and post-graduate levels. Again, the dramatic increase in our basic knowledge of the biochemical effects of neurophysiological functioning has brought about an increased optimism about the favourable results of pharmacological intervention.

Along with this growth of basic scientific knowledge, there has been a concomitant growth in the collection, analysis and dissemination of this knowledge. Sophisticated retrieval, dissemination and advertising systems have been developed so that each new discovery is on the desk of every physician, advertised in every professional journal and, in some cases, discussed in the newspapers, radio and on television very soon after the completion of research. This knowledge appears to have created a chain of dependencies. The organically oriented physician, with little or no training in the complexities of interpersonal difficulties and their effects on behaviour, is only too ready to fall back on the easily available psychotropic drugs with their promise of quick results. In many cases the drugs do bring about favourable changes but it is doubtful whether such results are attributable solely to the drugs. Placebo experiments suggest that there are complex interactions between the physician and patient in the treatment situation and in the illness itself, which may also contribute to the patient's improvement.

Despite the frequently voiced fears over the consequences of the abuse of drugs, practitioners with experience are more aware of the beneficial effects of new discoveries in psychopharmacology. On the positive side there have been dramatic changes. Today most psychiatric hospitals have a rapid turnover of short-stay patients, and long-term patients are diminishing in number. While community care programmes may claim a share in this advance, many attribute it in great part to more effective psychopharmacological agents. There has been a marked decrease in those admitted to hospitals with depressive illnesses. Violence in association with psychotic episodes is now almost a memory of the past. The increased acceptance of psychiatric patients in general hospitals, while betokening a more realistic concept of illness on the part of the medical and nursing professions, is made possible because of the more widespread and refined knowledge of suitable drugs for regulating behaviour. The rapid response of some schizophrenic patients to the antipsychotic group of drugs is in dramatic contrast to the long-term hospitalization which was looked upon as the inevitable lot of most of this severely disturbed group in the past. In child psychiatric practice, patients who were once regarded as intractable are now responding positively to drug therapy and to concomitant psychotherapy. These include children with the hyperkinetic syndrome, brain damage syndromes, and depression. Because of the lack of appropriate stimulation at optimal learning periods the outcome for many of these patients once was secondary mental deficiency. Tranquillizers, stimulants and antidepressants have changed the picture considerably and now many patients respond to milieu therapy.

Practitioners in psychiatric hospitals, general hospitals and in child psychiatric clinics are well aware of the great benefits bestowed on individual patients over the past two decades by new drugs for a wider range of emotional disorders. Psycho-active drugs are probably the main factor in making the most severely disturbed patients more amenable for other concomitant therapies, and pharmacologically assisted psychotherapy is probably one of the most characteristic features of child and adult psychiatry of the past two decades.

Classification

Various classifications of drugs with a tranquillizing effect have been used. We incline to accept the logic of the division into 'antipsychotic' drugs and 'anti-anxiety' drugs. This is in keeping with other terms such as 'antihistamine', 'antibiotic', which are in common use and does not necessarily imply that they are curative. As Pfeiffer and Murphre[1] point out, it is purely academic as to whether their antipsychotic action occurs through killing the roots (biochemical action) or pruning the foliage (symptomatic effect).

The terms 'major tranquillizer' and 'minor tranquillizer' are the common alternative to those which we use.

There are two main groups of antidepressant drugs: the tricyclic derivatives and the monoamine oxidase inhibitors.

Antipsychotic drugs

Until the introduction in 1952 of Rauwolfia and shortly afterwards Chlorpromazine, drugs used for the control of disturbed behaviour produced a predominantly somnolent effect. The characteristic feature of the new drugs is their ability to modify behaviour while leaving the patient accessible to other forms of therapy.

Physiologically this is related to the fact that they act on subcortical structures such as a) the hypothalamus, which influences the functions of the automatic nervous system, b) the limbic system which is concerned with emotional reactions and the integration of emotions with general behaviour and c) the reticular system which is intimately concerned with maintenance of the state of alertness.

This was a marked advance on the older sedatives such as barbiturates which acted predominantly on the cerebral cortex and so disturbed consciousness and accessibility.

These initial drugs have proved to be of greatest value in the treatment of seriously disturbed patients, particularly those suffering from schizophrenia or mania. It has been said that their effect on psychiatric hospitals has been revolutionary but it is probably more accurate to say that they greatly facilitated the transformation of mental hospitals which had been initiated by the introduction of physical methods of treatment such as electro-convulsive therapy and insulin coma therapy ten years before.

These treatments had removed the emphasis from custodial care to active treatment and in a small number of hospitals experiments with reduction of restraints and the opening of locked doors had begun. The new drugs hastened these developments and made possible further changes in attitudes, leading to the present emphasis on community psychiatry with the accent on out-patient treatment, day-centres, hostels and a shorter period of in-patient treatment.

The remarkable feature of the action of these drugs is that they have far more than a tranquillizing or sedative action. They appear to act on the 'core' symptoms of schizophrenia, such as emotional withdrawal, hallucinations, delusions, thought disorder, paranoid projection, belligerence, hostility and blunted effect.[2]

As with all powerful therapeutic agents, skill in administration is necessary for most effective use. In the acute stages of illness failure to give an adequate dose is a frequent cause of poor response, e.g., although the usual recommended dose of Chlorpromazine is 150–300 mgs. daily, some therapists use up to 1600 mgs. daily. In the later stages, when the control of symptoms has been achieved, it is important to reduce medication to the minimal dose which consistently and effectively alleviates symptoms. Toxic effects such as pigmentary deposits in the eye are related directly to high dosage prolonged over many years.

Maintenance treatment in correct dosage is, however, vitally important and may have to be carried on for a very prolonged period. It has been clearly shown that it reduces the incidence of relapse. Fortunately, addiction to these drugs is virtually unknown and does not create a problem in prolonged administration.

As they have varied pharmacological effects, it is not surprising that they have numerous side effects most of which have not been found to be dangerous and are readily reversible on reducing or stopping medication.

In a brief review of drug therapy, such as this, an exhaustive list of drugs and their pharmacological effects would not be appropriate. Readers interested in a more detailed exposition are referred to one of the many textbooks dealing with the subject.[3, 4]

A short account of those drugs or groups of drugs in common use may, however, be helpful.

Rauwolfia, although an effective tranquillizer,[5] was dropped from use as it was found to precipitate severe and suicidal depression in a proportion of cases. This fact proved to be of considerable importance in elucidating the biochemistry of depression and the action of the Monoamine Oxidase Inhibitor (MAOI) group of drugs. In the major psychoses the phenothiazine group of drugs rapidly established a predominant role.

Four main groups of drugs have become established in this field:

a) Phenothiazine derivatives
b) Thioxanthines
c) Butyrophenones
d) Diphenylbutylpiperidines

(a) *Phenothiazine derivatives:* chlorpromazine (Largactil, Thorazine) the first to be introduced is still the most widely used and the one by which others are measured. Changes in the side chains of the Phenothiazine Nucleus result in compounds with varying degrees of potency. Many such drugs were introduced into clinical practice following the success of Chlorpromazine but few have stood the test of time. Some such as the Piperazine group, e.g., Perphenazine (Fentazin, Trilafon), Trifluorperazine (Stelazine) and Fluphenazine (Moditen, Anatensol, Prolixin) have established a place in therapy. They are effective in much smaller doses and also have a more marked tendency to produce extrapyramidal side effects, e.g. Parkinsonian rigidity and tremor.

An extensive multi-hospital study by National Institute for Mental Health[6] failed to show any particular advantage as a therapeutic agent for any one of these drugs over others of the group, nor did it show that any particular drug was more specific than another in the control of particular symptoms. In such a study it is possible that the large numbers may have affected the more subtle variations in response of individual patients and may have obliterated minor differences in reaction. Most clinicians tend to believe that one drug will help a particular case more than another and fall back on their experience to match the drug with the individual. Certainly cases which have proved impervious to one drug have responded positively to other drugs from related sub-groups.

(b) *The Thioxanthines* are closely related chemically to the Phenothiazines and not surprisingly have rather similar properties. They are more widely used in North America than in Britain, examples are Chlorprothixine (Taractan) and Thiothixine (Navane).

(c) *The Butyrophenones* are chemically quite different from the Phenothiazines, although they have rather similar pharmacological properties. They are effective in low dosage, have marked extrapyramidal side effects and have been found to be particularly useful in the control of mania. Haloperidol (Serenace, Haldol) is the most commonly used member of this group.

(d) *The Diphenylbutylpiperdines* are a very interesting recently introduced group which seem to have some unique properties. They are longer acting and so can be given in more convenient dosage. This is useful with many patients, such as schizophrenics who are notoriously unreliable in taking medication.

Pimozide (Orap) is usually given as a single dose in the morning time. It is particularly effective in the treatment of inactive and withdrawn schizophrenics and has less tendency to produce extrapyramidal and autonomic side effects.[7] The fact that it has such a powerful action in schizophrenia with less effect on the extrapyramidal system may prove to be of considerable importance in the study of the pathophysiology of this disorder.

Fluspiriline has similar properties to Pimozide but when given by intramuscular injection has a duration of action of five to fifteen days. Even more remarkable, Penfluridol given by mouth need only be administered once weekly and is effective in the maintenance treatment of chronic schizophrenics.[8]

Long-acting preparations – The development of these drugs with inherently long-acting properties and of long-acting preparations of Phenothiazine derivatives, e.g. Fluphenazine (Anatensol, Moditen, Prolixin), Decanoate in Sesame oil, provides a very useful weapon in the control of symptoms of chronic schizophrenics treated on an outpatient basis.[9] Relapse in these cases has often been related to inconsistency or to actual failure to take drugs by mouth. It has been shown that over fifty per cent of chronic schizophrenic patients neglect maintenance medication.[10]

Anti-anxiety drugs

Shortly after the introduction of the phenothiazines, Meprobamate was made available and, thanks to widespread advertising and to the increasing interest in drug therapy, was widely acclaimed as a very effective treatment for anxiety. It was alleged that it produced this effect with little or no sedation.

The acceptance of Meprobamate in a non-critical and almost

hysterical manner by the profession and general public has been well described by Greenblatt and Shader.[11] It was an object lesson in the power of suggestion and the necessity for careful scrutiny and scientific investigation of the effects of drugs in the treatment of psychological disorders.

Following the initial remarkable claims about its effectiveness and safety, controlled clinical trials tended to show that, although better than placebo in relieving anxiety, it showed little or no advantage over Sodium Amytal, a barbiturate. It is now considered to have little place in therapy.

In the late 1950s, a new group of substances, the Benzodiazepines, of which the leading examples are Chlordiazepoxide (Librium) and Diazepam (Valium) were developed and have proved to be effective in the alleviation of anxiety. They have been almost too successful in that they are now prescribed virtually indiscriminately for the relief of minor stresses of life and are one of the most frequently prescribed of all drugs. More than twelve and a half million prescriptions were dispensed in the United Kingdom in 1968.[12] They tend to have a mildly euphoriant effect and so there is a considerable risk of habituation. The over-prescription of these compounds may lead to the suppression of symptoms in many patients with neglect of their underlying problems. It may, too, prevent young persons from developing more appropriate and natural means of dealing with stress. Despite this, they have a very useful role as an adjunct to supportive psychotherapy and may be invaluable in treating acute stress reactions or in relieving the crippling anxiety of phobic states. Frequently, in the latter cases, there is a depressive element and it is necessary to use an MAOI drug in combination with a benzodiazepine.

Further drugs of this group, such as Medazepam (Nobrium), have been introduced but despite vigorous promotion have not so far established a specific role in therapy, although they may be a useful alternative.

On the other hand, Nitrazepam (Mogadon) which has a more marked hypnotic effect has proved to be a safe and effective 'sleeping tablet' and is very extensively used.

With the vast market for minor tranquillizers, it is not surprising that a wide variety of compounds have been made commercially available but none have shown themselves to be of great value.

Antidepressant drugs

Depression, to a greater or lesser extent, is an unavoidable experience of the human condition. Some individuals disintegrate as a reaction to environmental setback to the extent that they could be described as suffering from neurosis. A neurosis is an affective crisis personally structured, determined by objective events and subjectively experienced, so that what would appear objectively to be similar precipitating causes may have significantly different consequences in different individuals. In both mild and severe depressive reactions drug therapy has made a significant contribution in reducing both the intensity of the depressive feelings and the time span of the illness itself. Again, it should not be forgotten that anxiety states, obsessive-compulsive illnesses, phobias and other recognized neurotic entities can themselves be associated with depression.

On the other hand, the severe, depressive illnesses which manifest themselves in patients with little or no external precipitating factors appear to be of a different order. Psychologically they may be accompanied by delusional thinking, agitation and feelings of worthlessness and guilt. Such depressions are assumed to have a genetic or biochemical basis[13] and traditionally are called the endogenous or psychotic depressions. The distinction between the so-called reactive and endogenous depressions is not, however, universally accepted and the ongoing Maudsley/ Newcastle controversy well illustrates some of the issues involved.[14]

Drugs have been in wide use in the treatment of depression since the turn of the century. Such hypnosedatives as barbiturates were the drugs of choice for depression in the early decades of this century, but while they helped the patient to cope with the distressing problems of agitation and insomnia, they had little effect on the basic mood disorder. The psychomotor stimulants, particularly the Amphetamines, were favoured in the 1930–40s but their antidepressant action was too short-lived and their sympathomimetic action often increased the patient's anxiety and nervousness. Furthermore, some patients became addicted to them and their overuse sometimes caused a schizophreniform psychosis.[15, 16] The non-Amphetamine psychomotor stimulant, Methylphenidate (Ritalin) was not a success as an antidepressant, but it is enjoying a return to favour in the treatment of the hyperkinetic syndrome in childhood,[17] an illness that sometimes has a depressive basis.

Convulsive therapy – Many of these drugs might have continued in use in the treatment of depression for a longer period of time, but for the discovery and general acceptance of electro-convulsive therapy (ECT) as the treatment of choice for patients with endogenous depression. Convulsive therapy was introduced in 1935 and since 1940 it has been widely used in psychiatric practice, particularly if the depressed patient has suicidal tendencies. However, since this procedure proved anxiety-provoking for certain patients, doctors were relieved when presented with alternative approaches.

Modern antidepressants – Fifteen years ago two new classes of antidepressants were discovered which replaced electro-convulsive therapy in the successful treatment of some depressive states, or when used in combination with ECT, cut down the number of applications required. Current discussion of anti-depressant drug therapy is mainly concerned with the use of the iminodibenzyl compounds popularly known as the tricyclic drugs or of the monoamine oxidase inhibitor group (MAOI).

Research into the aetiology of endogenous depressions indicates that most of these disorders are related to abnormalities of the neurochemistry of the brain and that antidepressant drugs tend to correct these abnormalities.[18] Gibbons,[13] in his review of the biochemistry of depressive illness, indicates that depression and its relief by antidepressant drugs may be due to changes in the monoamine concentration in the brain. The tricyclic and the

MAOI drugs alter the monoamine concentration and they probably owe their difference in clinical action to the particular ways in which they bring about this change.

Tricyclic antidepressants – These drugs are so named because of the three contiguous benzene rings in their chemical make-up. Imipramine (Tofranil) the first tricyclic in clinical use was introduced by Kuhn[19] who noted that it had no beneficial effects in chronic schizophrenia but that it had sustained mood-elevating properties. Controlled trials[20, 21] on Imipramine and related tricyclics indicate that they are superior to MAOI antidepressants and to placebos in the treatment of depressed hospitalized in-patients. The large study reported by Bennett[22] confirmed this superiority and further showed that ECT is more effective than tricyclics in the treatment of the severely depressed patient. It is now clear that the tricyclic group of drugs are not effective in neurotic depression.

Clinicians may choose from a large number of tricyclic compounds all of which have antidepressant properties but some have more anxiety-relieving or sedating qualities than others and, depending on the clinical picture, the doctor can choose the appropriate drug for his patient. Some drugs such as Trimipramine (Surmontil), Amitriptyline (Tryptizol, Laroxyl, Elavil) and Nortriptyline (Aventyl, Allegron) have sedating effects while Protriptyline (Concordin, Vivactil) is more stimulating in its action. Recently a slow release preparation of Amitriptyline has become available (Lentizol). It is given as a single dose at night which is more convenient for many depressed patients. Doxepam (Sinequan) and Opipramol (Insidon) are interesting new drugs which relieve anxiety and are also antidepressants.

Monoamine oxidase inhibitor drugs (MAOI)

It is fairly generally accepted that MAOI drugs are less effective than tricyclic antidepressants in the treatment of patients with typical endogenous depression and they are more effective with patients suffering from reactive or neurotic depressions. It is our experience too that they are of especial value in the treatment of the group of acutely phobic anxious and depressed patients so well described by West and Dally[23] and we find that many of these patients, particularly children and adolescents, are available for psychotherapeutic approaches only when their acute distress is lessened by medication. Phenelzine (Nardil) is a potent MAOI and causes few side effects but Tranylcypramine (Parnate) and Isocarboxazid (Marplan) are also widely used.

Combination of tricyclic and MAOIs drugs – Physicians are often reluctant to use tricyclic and MAOIs in combination because of the increased danger of serious side effects. However many experienced clinicians[24, 25, 26] have in recent years reported favourably on the combined use of these groups of drugs and they note that few side effects occur. Pare[18] rightly points out that depression can be a serious incapacitating illness and in discussing the British Medical Research Council[20] trial refers to the fact that one-sixth of these hospitalized depressed patients showed little improvement after six months of active treatment with antidepressants used alone or in combination with ECT. We agree that in such intractable and distressing illnesses, in spite of some risk, a combination of antidepressant drugs is often justified. While this may strike one as a purely empirical approach based on a trial and error procedure with little regard to the patient's needs or to the possible unfavourable consequences, practice has shown that the probable gains outweigh any possible deleterious side effects. It should be recalled that the serious step of psycho-surgery (leucotomy) was frequently used twenty to thirty years ago (and apparently still is on occasions) for these patients.

It is, of course, important to give detailed and accurate instructions to patients and their relatives concerning the dietary and other precautions that they must take as long as they are on MAOI medication. Some pharmaceutical firms issue cards with printed instructions for patients on these drugs and all doctors who prescribe them should have these cards available for each patient.

Initiation of drug treatment – Most clinicians commence the treatment of endogenous depression with a tricyclic preparation gradually increasing the dose over the first two weeks and if there is no response after four weeks of treatment a change to an MAOI compound should be considered. Both groups of drugs have a latent period of about seven to fourteen days before they become really effective but in general the MAOI group tend to act more quickly than tricyclics.

The findings of Angst,[27] Pare *et al*[28] indicate that the response of a patient to a particular group of antidepressants can at times be predicted. They found that if there is a history of a successful response in a close relative of a depressed patient to one group of antidepressants then the probability is that he will respond to a drug from this same group. These findings tend to support the theory that there may be genetically specific types of depression.

Lithium therapy

Lithium was first discovered to be effective in the treatment of mania by John Cade in 1949. Although most psychiatrists would agree that it is not an antidepressant, we are including it with the antidepressants because of the evidence from recent articles by Shou[29] and Coppen,[30] that it can be used successfully in the prophylaxis of recurrent affective disorders. They indicate, and it is our experience too, that it may be as effective in cases with recurrent endogenous depression as in those with cyclical mania and depression. Lithium therapy is an exciting new advance in psychiatry as, for the first time, a chemical substance has been developed that not only effectively controls a psychotic illness but its continued administration prevents further episodes of the illness. It is also important in that its mode of action is different from the other psycho-active drugs, particularly interesting being its effect in decreasing intracellular sodium levels which are known to be differentially increased in mania and depression.[13]

Drugs in childhood and adolescence

Child psychiatry is of relatively recent origin in the history of medicine. This is principally because emotional disorders of childhood were totally neglected at the beginning of this century and if emotional disturbances in children were of a sufficiently severe nature the consequences inevitably were that such children developed secondary mental handicap and were treated as mentally deficient. This was one of the few mental disorders of childhood which was recognized in the past. As medicine has become less adult-centred with the growth of specialties such as paediatrics and child psychiatry, it is becoming increasingly evident that nearly all adult mental illnesses have their childhood models. The main difference is the fact that symptomatology in childhood is fluid and changing, and adaptive resources and flexibility greater in children than in adults. As a consequence the focus of care and prevention programmes has been directed more to children and the possibilities of child-directed therapeutic approaches have increased markedly. Drugs which have proved successful with adults are now used with children and adolescents[25] and in fact it is commonly felt that drugs are equally important in the treatment of childhood disorders as in that of adult disorders.[31]

However, since children and adolescents have relatively little control over their environment, and since they are rarely self-referred for treatment, it is of paramount importance to treat their problems in the context of the total family situation and of the social institutions which form a background to their development. Our clinical experience is that many children can benefit from the use of drugs, just as adults do, but drug treatment requires back-up services with family and community oriented approaches.[32]

An interesting development in child psychiatry has been the use of Haloperidol (Serenace, Haldol) in children with psychogenic tics and in those with stammers. It is our experience that patients with Gilles de la Tourette Syndrome respond remarkably to treatment with Haloperidol when resistant to all other forms of treatment. We sometimes use Haloperidol in psychotic states where children have self-destructive tendencies and we find that it decreases these tendencies and they participate better in milieu therapy programmes.

We have already referred to the use of Methylphenidate (Ritalin) in the hyperkinetic syndrome. It is also useful as part of the drug programme with children with other organic brain syndromes, where it appears to facilitate the learning process.

Anti-anxiety drugs, particularly Chlordiazepoxide (Librium) and Diazepam (Valium) can be of value in dealing with crisis situations, particularly where other measures have failed, for example, in initiating a return to school in children with school phobia. This condition may also, like anxiety phobic states in adults, respond dramatically to treatment with one of the MAOI drugs as do some of the other acute phobic disorders of childhood and adolescence. However, we tend to use psychoactive drugs only in these conditions and with those patients who have failed to respond to other therapeutic approaches.

The future

A recent editorial in the *British Medical Journal*[33] poses the question of why research into the nature, pathogenesis and treatment of functional mental disorders has made such little progress during the past half century. Two of the possible culprits mentioned in this connection have been the stress on sociocultural factors as determinants of psychiatric illness and the predominance of psychoanalytic practice unsupported by experimental evidence of its efficacy. While epidemiological studies and psychopharmacological research hold out hopes for improvement in the current position, the article sees most hope in a coordinated multi-disciplinary approach directed towards early ascertainment of vulnerability and the devising of prophylactic regimens. It rightly indicates that while the paucity of available funds is often blamed there is in fact little evidence of lack of financial support for promising developments.

The relationship between research and the economics of its subvention is generally a much more complex one than scarcity of money. Selective influences generally play a significant part in the deployment of resources. These influences stem from the attitudes, values and needs of those who control the allotment of resources or of those in institutions in a position to determine the direction of research projects.

It is to be hoped that in the next decade a more rational approach towards the funding of research will emerge. Research resources are generally divided between categorical and generic approaches and at present more financial resources seem to be available for the former type of research. The categorical approach is based on attempts to combat specific mental illnesses and in contrast to this the generic approach hopes for advances in basic knowledge by giving priority to research on say, brain functioning, the biochemical effects of neurophysiological function, the chemistry of learning, and other such fundamental problems. If there is no interest in specific projects to combat discrete illnesses then the problems of patients are apt to be neglected. This is basically the approach of the sickness-oriented physician and it is probable that financial support for this type of research will continue to be made available especially by drug firms.

In contrast to this, however, the generic approach holds out more hope of extending our knowledge of basic principles of mental health and of making advances on a broad front. In the absence of basic research psychiatric intervention is likely to remain a series of patchwork jobs with the psychiatrist waiting until imminent breakdown or frank decompensation has indicated the need for his attentions. For balanced progress both the generic and categorical approaches are essential if knowledge and its applications are to be utilized and advanced.

There is no doubt that progress in the development of specific drugs for mental illnesses has created a climate of optimism in which further advances are confidently expected in the near future. It is almost certain that by the end of the next decade a wider range of more effective psychoactive drugs will be available for the treatment of the neuroses and psychoses.

While it is literally a fact of life that those who live long enough will personally experience decrements in intellectual functioning and eventual deterioration, it is probable that an increased understanding of premature dementing processes and their treatment by drugs will forestall these processes in many cases and reduce the incidence of organic psychosis. Again the control of psychosis with a genetic and biochemical basis is likely to improve considerably judging from recent advances in behavioural genetics, in neurobiochemistry and psychopharmacology.

However, the hopeful light cast by advances in research on brain disorders and on the neuroses and psychoses does not appear to shed its rays on our efforts to combat personality disorders. Our knowledge of the complexities of the interactions between innate factors, physical experiences and the social environment at present is so crude that much more fundamental research with a wide multidisciplinary approach is envisaged before light will be thrown on disorders which are experienced currently by psychiatrists as almost totally refractory to either psychotherapeutic or psychopharmacological intervention.

Nevertheless, some light is being thrown upon the essential reciprocity between organisms, their experiences and environment by work reported by Krech.[34] This study indicated that an enriched environment in terms of educational stimulation changed the status of brain chemistry in the rat. As compared with a control group reared in a stringently improverished environment, a stimulated group of rats had significantly higher acetylcholinesterase levels, heavier cerebral cortices and the data were consistent with the notion that they also had more glial cells per neuron. It is probable that similar findings about human brain chemistry will emerge in the near future and it is not unreasonable to assume this as an analogue of what happens fortuitously in unfavourable circumstances with humans. In fact deprivation studies with children where early basic physical and psychological needs have not been adequately met indicate that the personalities tend to be permanently distorted or marred in some way.

A review of research in the chemistry of learning in the 1960s[34] indicates that there was then available a fairly extensive range of drugs which could facilitate learning and memory in animals. In the not too distant future it predicts that educators may be helped in their interaction with pupils by means of 'enzyme assisted instruction, protein memory consolidators and antibiotic memory repellers'.

Genetic research along such lines will probably be the greater source of information about the part to be played by psycho-pharmacology in the devising of prophylactic milieus for the rearing and education of children.

While early ascertainment and treatment of mental disorders will remain an important concern of psychiatric practice, such activities are likely to be speeded up and made more accurate by computer-assisted diagnosis and formulation of treatment schedules for individual patients. This will give the worker in the field of mental health, hitherto mainly sickness-oriented, an opportunity to devote more time to the formulation of more positive health-promoting programmes. The psychiatrist of the future will then become more a social scientist with a heightened awareness of the kinds of milieu which will afford humans not only enhanced opportunities for personal and social interaction but also for more favourable chemical and morphological development.

Social therapy

George Mountney

Introduction

As with many other therapeutic measures, the term social therapy does not lend itself to precision of definition. The expression has been used by many writers from different disciplines to describe both their aims and methods.

Lucille Austin[1] writing about social work suggested that social therapy refers to the attainment of treatment goals by 'the use of techniques designed to influence positively various factors in the environment, and the effective use of social resources'. Such an approach did not ignore the need to provide psychological support or to help the client in dealing with his reality problems.

The term social therapy has also been used in a pejorative sense to refer to all activities that used to take place in mental hospitals before the advent of modern physical treatments. It is suggested that 'reliance on psychotherapy and social therapy was largely responsible for the many seriously suicidal patients who remained ill for years on end'.[2] A more balanced view was offered by Bennett[3] who reviewed the research literature on social therapy and drug treatment, his conclusion was that the evidence suggests, 'that the combined use of both social measures and drugs was necessary to produce optimal results'.

Another way the expression social therapy might be used is to describe the quite radical changes that have been made in the social structure of many hospitals in recent years. It was during the period to which Sargent refers that there was a public rejection of mental institutions, and the leading psychiatrists came to the conclusion that the hospital itself was a sick organization, with a sick social structure that could not make a positive contribution to help its sick patients.[4] It became increasingly apparent that only by transforming the organization and by exploiting its total therapeutic potential could it make a distinctive contribution to helping the whole person. Such a view required exchanging the concept of cure and emphasizing the need for re-socialization and encouraging social competence, in order that the patient may take his place in the community to which he belongs.

One of the leading writers and exponents of this particular approach is Maxwell Jones[5] who has made a significant contribution to theory and practice on both sides of the Atlantic. Through his initiative a traditional psychiatric hospital with a preponderance of long stay and elderly patients has been established as a therapeutic community. The customary clinical hierachy has been exchanged for patient participation, and executive control is in the hands of a multi-disciplinary team, answerable to the community as a whole – patients and staff.

Having markedly changed the social organization of the hospital in order to try and reverse the effects of institutionalization, they are now seriously questioning the merits of admitting patients to hospital, without compelling reasons for so doing. It is recognized that affording hospital patient status to an individual who has been selected for this role by others, i.e. members of his family, general practitioner, or other medical and social agencies, should be preceded by an intensive social and psychiatric investigation.* What happens in practice is that the patient and the referers are usually interviewed by a hospital team, this includes a psychiatrist, nurse and social worker. Some important issues that are often overlooked are raised, i.e. what can be achieved by hospitalization that could not be obtained by the patient remaining at home? Are there any disadvantages to admission – in a particular case – that might outweigh the benefits? Will re-enforcement of the sick role by admission to hospital adversely affect the patient's eventual re-establishment in the community? These and other topics are raised by the team

---

*A more usual approach is for a thorough psychosocial investigation to post-date the admission to hospital.

with the patient, his family and usually the general practitioner. From the discussion a plan is evolved, and if hospitalization is not indicated, other therapeutic strategies are introduced with one member of the team accepting primary responsibility for their implementation. The success of this particular approach is clearly dependent on the community being prepared to accept an increased responsibility for its deviant members. Local authority financed facilities are vital but this cannot be the limit of the community's involvement and concern. Increasingly it will have to contain behaviour that previously was thought to be the responsibility of the authorities.

It is too soon to evaluate the effectiveness of these methods, and even if it was possible to show a measure of success, it would be unrealistic to assume that such procedures could easily be transferred to the larger urban areas, with their formidable and complex social and community problems.

Jurgen Ruesh, describing the development of social psychiatry in the USA, says of social therapies, 'They are designed to alter existing conditions and they approach this by influencing both the social system and the individual.'[6] To ensure that we are left in no doubt as to the breadth of the goals of social therapy, he explains that community psychiatry, group therapy, family therapy, and a therapeutic community are different names for social therapy. He contrasts the clinical approach with its aim at improving individual functioning, with social therapy which attempts to better the group as a whole. Social therapy is seen as being particularly useful for helping the seriously ill patient who does not function socially, and perhaps never did, whose condition may require long-term care, and where short-term somatic or psychological therapy either has been exhausted, or is inapplicable. In short, the focus is on the social functioning of people, rather than their psychopathology, so that the therapist will be concerned with influencing groups, social organizations, community networks rather than persons seen in isolation one from another.

As we have seen then, social therapy like social psychiatry is used to describe a wide range of not very specific procedures, in fact it would be fair to say that both terms often refer more to a policy, than to a particular method of helping a patient.

Perhaps it would be appropriate at this stage to clarify how the term social therapy will be used in the remainder of this chapter. Social therapy, community psychiatry and social psychiatry will be used interchangeably and will refer to a system of supplying treatment and care based on the following principles.

1. A recognition that the environment including the family and the sub-culture are important determinants of how deviant behaviour is expressed: how it is formally and informally handled, and these factors must be taken into account, and used in any therapeutic intervention.

2. It is accepted that there is no clear line of demarcation that separates individual or family malfunctioning in a way that would define it unambiguously as a medical or a social problem. This being so, adequate help efficiently delivered to where it is needed will often require the assistance of an inter-disciplinary team, after a multiple assessment of the nature of the problem.

3. A properly conceived mental health service will be based on the recognition that both the hospital and a comprehensive range of local authority facilities are inter-dependent parts of a total service serving the same population.

4. Because both medical and social services are administered by different bodies, formal and informal methods of ensuring coordination at all levels of work must be introduced.

5. Hospital patient status in a psychiatric establishment has dangers as well as being a necessity for some grossly disturbed patients. The social system of the hospital will influence the norms of the patient groups. These norms must be consistent with progress towards self-realization and independence.

Discussion

Social psychiatry in its oldest form has found few protagonists in this country. There are many reasons for this, not least in importance is that the role expectation of the consultant psychiatrist is seen as being analogous to that of specialists in other branches of medicine. They are expected to 'treat' patients referred by G.P.s and other medical colleagues. Both the agency that employs the psychiatrist and those that refer patients, not to mention the patient and his family, all impose certain constraints on how the psychiatrist will act. He is expected to admit into hospital patients who are a problem to others, i.e. members of his family, doctors, police, other social and medical agencies. The general practitioner will expect to receive information from the consultant that is comprehensible in terms of his own medical training, so that if necessary he can use his own skills to help the patient. The consultant is likely to have beds in hospital and it is in this setting that his image as a medical specialist will best be exemplified. Additionally there will be pressures on him from outside and inside the hospital to ensure that beds are fully used. These factors, coupled with the absence of training opportunities in this country for doctors to specialize in community psychiatry, are sufficient explanation why there is relatively little interest by psychiatrists in the community from where their patients are recruited.

In looking at the development of hospital psychiatry since 1959 we see much to praise and criticize. Some hospitals have responded as if psychiatric disorders were really analogous to physical illness and have organized the regime of the hospital accordingly. Fortunately the considerable literature on milieu and administrative therapy and on the therapeutic community has encouraged an increasing number of hospitals to experiment in re-shaping the pattern of daily life of middle and long stay patients so as to minimize the secondary effects that we have come to expect from long-term exposure to institutional life.

Perhaps the most far-reaching failure of the hospitals is – with one or two exceptions – their inability to collaborate and coordinate their work with the expanding local authority psychiatric services.

Turning to the developments in the local authority services we see that the 1959 Mental Health Act gave expression to the need for developing an adequate psychiatric community service. However, while the concept of community care has received much publicity and vocal support, the fact remains that community care has yet to be tackled in a systematic and comprehensive way. The reasons for this are manifold, but one fundamental obstacle was recognized at the outset by Titmus,[7] 'Many people believe that, without a revolution in local government and its financial resources, the new mental health provision for community care will remain virtually a dead letter.' To understand some of the other major difficulties obstructing progress it is necessary to look briefly at the events following the introduction of the 1946 National Health Service Act.

This Act required local health authorities to develop a range of personal health services, including mental health, and the Medical Officer of Health was made responsible for their overall administration. The staff of the local mental health service was largely untrained and the opportunities to establish a professional style of service were few and largely discouraged. This is not surprising, the medical training of the chief officer perhaps tended to encourage an authoritarian approach which was strongly reinforced by the local authority hierarchical method of administration. As Etzioni[8] suggests the use of knowledge and professional authority places a strain on the organization, for the application of knowledge is an individual process for which the professional has the responsibility, and the ultimate justification for his professional act is that it is to the best of his professional knowledge the right act. This individualized principle is in conflict with the administrative procedures that place emphasis on rules and regulations and acts that have been approved by a senior officer.

This style of administration and the lack of career prospects ensured that the mental health services were generally ill prepared to respond efficiently to the expectations embodied in the Mental Health Act. This Act clarified the permissive clauses in the National Health Service Act, and required local authorities to initiate prevention and aftercare services, although special funds to finance them were not made available.

During the 1960s many local authorities took seriously their responsibilities to develop a mental health service. The majority found it easier to build, or adapt premises for training centres, day centres and hostels, than to recruit professional staff to service and manage them.

This often resulted in a serious displacement of aims, the alleged primary purpose of a hostel or day centre might be to establish social competence and encourage independence of those using the facility. However, because of inadequate managerial and professional competence those two units, instead of offering a complementary service, may well be working in opposition to each other. Furthermore it often served the interest of those in charge of hostels or training centres to retain their best workers rather than to persistently pursue the goal of rehabilitation.

If local authority mental health services had problems in coordinating the facilities under their own administrative control, it is not then surprising that it was rather rare indeed to find any significant degree of coordination between local authorities and hospital services. Clearly it required a quite fortuitous set of circumstances for this to happen, some of the more important are as follows.

1. That the catchment area of both the hospital and the administrative area of the local authority are broadly the same.
2. The key members of the hospital staff and the local authority service recognize that their work is complementary and are highly motivated to tackle the formidable problem of joint planning.
3. The mental health service is given sufficient priority to ensure that adequate resources are allocated for its development.
4. Delegation of responsibility by the Medical Officer of Health to an appropriately experienced and qualified worker, capable of developing a psychiatric social service.
5. A recognition that there are inherent complications in two differently administered organizations working together – especially when this requires the co-operation of a number of professions – and to evolve formal and informal methods of meeting and resolving these difficulties.

Bearing in mind the multiple obstacles in developing a coordinated service it is perhaps surprising that a measure of success has been achieved in a number of areas. This has usually been accomplished by mental health social workers and sometimes psychiatrists having joint responsibilities to both hospitals and local authority services, which have enabled multi-disciplinary teams to concern themselves with both treatment and a wide range of supportive services.

Future developments
Even in those relatively rare cases where collaboration has flourished it has usually been restricted to the staff of the hospital and the mental health service, whereas if the maximum influence was to be brought to bear on helping families under stress, general practitioners and other social and community agencies will need to be brought into the picture.

There are grounds for slight optimism in that the restructuring of the local authority social services into a unified department, the re-drawing of local government boundaries, and the expected major modifications in the health service may contribute to a more rational way of supplying health and social services to those in need. It is, however, impossible to forecast the final pattern of such complex and manifold changes. The only thing that we can be fairly certain of, is that the personal social services will be administered and financed by local government and the medical services will be nationally financed and administered independently of local government. We may also expect that the family doctors or at least their representatives will fight hard to retain their almost unique position of being private contractors within a national and publicly financed service.

Let us now examine how the re-organization of the local authority social services into one department might affect the development of community psychiatry. Here are some of the possible advantages:

1. The whole range of facilities administered by the new department could be made available for use by the mentally disordered, whereas previously both the children's and welfare

departments were often resistant to offering a service to clients whom they considered to be the responsibility of another agency. An example of this might be an adolescent girl who committed a self-poisoning act and is ready for discharge from the casualty department, and who would be better dealt with by using one or more of the range of facilities open to a child care officer rather than establishing the young person in the role of a psychiatric patient. Likewise the mentally sub-normal child who needs substitute family care, and who previously was likely to be admitted to a hospital for the mentally sub-normal, could profit from having access to the child care services. One would hope that the reverse equally applies, i.e. that psychiatric help would be as readily available – where appropriate – to the whole range of users of the social service department, as it usually is to the clients of a well developed mental health department.

2. Mental health services and psychiatric hospitals have been denied a fair supply of senior qualified social workers, largely arising from the restricted promotion opportunities compared with some other agencies. The re-organization of the departments should facilitate a more equitable distribution of professional and management personnel. Perhaps some of the more ambitious workers who left the psychiatric services may resume an active interest in their original specialty.

3. Now that there is one department concerned with providing a comprehensive family service, it should be possible for greater emphasis to be placed on preventive psychiatry. This could provide a common theme for team work with psychiatrists, family doctors, and social workers. Furthermore social workers are becoming increasingly interested and active in working with groups and communities where an exclusive individual approach is inappropriate. This interest in the community may be brought into sharper focus as departments of social service systematically collect and analyse important social data pertaining to areas with special problems. Perhaps what might be seen in the future is social workers exerting pressure in the direction of those with political power, having recognized that the model of individual inadequacy is sometimes inappropriate for certain groups of

clients and patients. Just as in the nineteenth century improving the environment was more efficacious than clinical medicine in dealing with the scourge of infectious deseases, so similar attention on the quality of life in certain communities may also be shown to be more effective than an exclusive concern with individual psychopathology. As the departments re-organize and experiment with the concept of generic social work there are likely to be many problems as workers have to learn new skills and practices. Provided there is appropriate leadership these difficulties should be transient and in the not too distant future the benefits of amalgamation should emerge.

If we now turn to some of the possible disadvantages that might arise from the change we should first of all record that few other countries have attempted to offer such a range of treatment in supportive services to all its citizens in need. A possible danger is that the Department of Social Services, in its eagerness to meet the new demands made upon it, may give inadequate priority to those whose essential requirements include both medical and social intervention. Furthermore, senior professional staff of the department may be suspicious and reluctant to develop too close an association with doctors because of their traditional assumption that medical training automatically equips the individual to undertake the leadership role.

Perhaps the biggest challenge that has to be faced by both the social services departments and the hospital service is to find a way of reconciling the need to support and encourage an individualized professional service within an organizational structure that possesses a reasonable degree of public accountability. There are obvious extremes to be avoided; both complete professional autonomy and a highly structured vertical chain of command can result in a waste of resources and an inability to respond to new requirements in a swiftly changing society.

The contents of the first annual report of the Hospital Advisory Service[9] suggests that this is one useful method of focusing attention on issues that are of public and professional concern. Clearly the personal social services under the administration of the local authorities need equal attention. One interesting development that might help to keep both professionals and administators alert is the introduction of volunteers into hospitals and local social service departments; not only does this add a new dimension to the customary use of the term community care, but it enables responsible people unencumbered by the usual constraints on career staff to know something of what goes on in organizations, and as a last resort to make this information public.

In conclusion, no apology is made for treating the topic of social therapy largely in terms of a need for broad organizational changes. It must be apparent to even the most dedicated practitioner offering individual therapy that his effectiveness is increasingly dependent on the system and quality of management of the service that employs him.* We have now become increasingly aware that only an administratively healthy organization can adapt to the changing needs of patients, the staff employed to help them, and the community generally.

---

*And other community supportive services.

Religious therapy

Eamonn O'Doherty

Introduction
The psychologist, the psychiatrist, the pastor and minister of religion, find themselves confronted from time to time with problems on the frontier between psychology and religion. The psychiatrist finds himself face to face with the religious convictions and moral principles of his patient, while the priest and minister of religion find the sub-rational and irrational life of their flocks intruding, sometimes in obvious ways, sometimes in subtle and insidious ways, into the spiritual life and practice of religion.

Religion and psychotherapy
The history of the relationship between religion and psychotherapy can be summarized in a few sentences. Up to the early nineteenth century, before any real understanding of psychopathology had emerged, it is probably true to say that all forms of psychopathology were widely regarded either as punishment from on high or as some form of demonic possession. The concept of mental illness as punishment from on high is seen perhaps at its clearest in the story of Nebuchadnezzar. The judgement of God against Nebuchadnezzar for his pride resulted in a picture closely resembling a serious psychosis:

> He was driven from among men, and ate grass like an ox, and his body was wet with the dew of heaven till his hair grew as long as eagles' feathers, and his nails were like birds' claws (Daniel, 4: 30).

But on his repentance later he says:

> My reason returned to me . . . my majesty and splendour
> returned to me . . . and I was established in my kingdom.

The concept of mental illness as punishment

The concept of mental illness as punishment for sin has in its
explicit form disappeared from our culture, but survives in
disguised ways. Patients can still be heard repeating such phrases
as

> I know it is all my own fault;
> If only I had said my prayers . . . , behaved better . . . ,
> been better brought up . . . , been a better child . . . ,
> been a better adolescent . . .

The second and more important way in which this concept
survives is in the confusion between the functions of religion and
psychotherapy, or more accurately between the roles of minister
of religion and psychotherapist. The problem that has to be
faced here is that of the relation of mind and soul, or psyche and
soul. This is a very important problem, not only for the theore-
tician, but also for the practitioner, especially in the light of the
enormous influence of Jungian thinking on some theologians and
psychologists. The Jungian idea appears to be that there is in fact
no real distinction but only a logical one, between soul and psyche.
But 'soul' in the language of religion, refers to man's spiritual
principle, capable of the life of grace and of survival after death,
whereas 'psyche' is the psychologist's term to indicate, not a
spiritual principle, but a set of functions.

There is a third way in which the concept of a link between
mental illness and punishment for sin survives. It lies in the confusion between religion and psychotherapy, as though spiritual
well-being and mental health were one and the same. This
confusion is best illustrated by reference to Jung:

'Not only Christianity with its symbols of salvation', he said in a lecture in 1935, 'but all religions, including the primitive with their magical rituals, are forms of psychotherapy which treat and heal the suffering of the soul, and the suffering of the body caused by the soul' (*Practice*, 20); 'since the only salutary powers visible in the world today', he writes in a work published in 1946, 'are the great "psychotherapeutic" systems which we call the religions . . .' (*ibid.*, 390); and in an article published in 1951, 'for not only is religion not the enemy of the sick, it is actually a system of psychic healing, as the use of the Christian term "cure of souls" makes clear (*sic*), and as is also evident from the *Old Testament*' (*ibid.*, 249; he cites Psalm 147:3 and Job 5:18, but the opinion expressed is more important than the reasons he gives for holding it). Since Jung holds this opinion, it should cause no surprise that he also believes that 'religious statements are psychic confessions which in the last resort are based on unconscious, i.e. on transcendental, processes', which 'demonstrate their existence through the confessions of the psyche'.[1] In other words, Jung thinks that religious statements, when properly understood, are statements which reveal the nature of the human psyche, and he applies this theory particularly to statements about God: but it must be added that he regards the 'psyche' as quite as numinous and incomprehensible as religious people regard God.[1]

With Freud's *Future of an Illusion*,[2] the issues are most clearly stated. Religion itself is a neurosis – the universal obsessional neurosis of mankind. Freud's case was threefold: 1) he thought that religion was generated as a defence against unconscious fears, by infantilism, regression, introjection, repression, projection and rationalization. These are among the better known defence mechanisms, and refer to the processes whereby the individual under stress reproduces behaviour patterns appropriate to earlier phases of development. Thus, infantilism refers to the condition of behaving in ways appropriate to the infant, usually with reference to emotional dependence and the enacting of repetitive, non-productive modes of stereotyped behaviour. Repression is the unconscious process whereby emotionally loaded thoughts experienced as threatening are prevented from entering consciousness. Projection is the process whereby one's own inadequacies or undesirable impulses are seen as belonging to or emanating from others, and rationalization is the process whereby reasons acceptable to consciousness are provided to account for behaviour the true or real reasons for which are unacceptable to consciousness; 2) he thought religion was a refusal to cope rationally with reality; and 3) he noticed certain similarities between religious practices and the behaviour and thought-contents of psychoneurotic and psychotic patients. Jung's *Modern Man in Search of a Soul*,[3] by contrast, appeared to be on the side of the angels, especially his claim that he had never had a patient whose illness was not due to his lack of religion, nor had he ever cured a patient whose cure was not due to his return to religion.

The confusion of 'psyche' and 'soul'

Jung, who claimed in his Introduction to Victor White's *God and the Unconscious*[4] that he was an empiricist and an agnostic, identified the religious usage of the term 'soul' with the psychologist's meaning of the term 'psyche'. Whatever was true of 'psyche' must therefore be true of soul, whatever is good or bad for the one must therefore be good or bad for the other. In this way, 'sin' and psychopathology, 'grace' and mental health respectively are only different names for the same realities.

Some of Jung's followers (e.g. Father Victor White) rightly understanding the religious usage of the term soul, appear to have reversed the logic of Jung's thinking, but with essentially the same result: where Jung identified the 'soul' of religion with the 'psyche' of psychology, White conversely identifies the 'psyche' of psychology with the soul. In this way a series of identifications became possible which have caused great confusion. Thus, whatever is good for the soul is good for the psyche, and vice versa, since they are one and the same. *Holiness* is *wholeness*. Whatever is bad for the one is bad for the other. Mental illness and sin are indistinguishable. Religion is a form of psychotherapy, an instrumental value in making man healthy, integrated, happy. Cure of soul is cure of mind.* Conversely, psychotherapy or *cure of the sick mind* becomes an alternative to religion. The end result is the Huxley point of view, which has climaxed in the 'religion' of drug-taking, in the concept that lysergic acid is a short cut to mystical experience. It has been pointed out (by Fromm, Zilboorg and others) that Jung's notion of religion and its relation to mental health is even more bizarre than Freud's. It therefore becomes necessary to say a word about religion and psychotherapy. Religion is a public set of beliefs, associated with a set of public behaviour patterns, whose function is to express a transcendental relationship, man's dependent relation on his Creator. The use of the term religion in such phrases as 'religion of man', 'religion of nature', would seem to deprive the word of any *specific* meaning. It becomes identical with the term 'value system of any kind'. It has taken many forms historically, but its many forms are not our concern here. But ever since William James's *The Varieties of Religious Experience*[5] it has been widely accepted that religion is a set of experienced states of the psyche. Religion, he thought, was the 'feelings, acts, and experiences of individual men, so far as they apprehend themselves to stand in relation to whatever they may consider the divine'. The assumption that religion is a set of feelings, acts and experiences is the crucial problem, for this brings religion into the domain of the empirical, the observable, and ultimately the measurable. It brings God within the finite universe. It was perhaps awareness of this that led the Bishop of Woolwich[6] to repudiate the use of mythology in our thinking about God and at the same time to accept this logic and to think of God as somehow the ultimate reality experienced by man. This line of thought would seem to be the most important of the confusions indicated above. These confusions are the more confounded by an extension of the range of application of the term psychotherapy to cover almost any and every form of interpersonal relationship capable of effecting a change in either party or both.

*This is an interesting linguistic confusion. *Cura* in Latin meant 'care', not 'cure' in a therapeutic sense.

Broad concepts like this are important, but not very helpful for a serious discussion. When we use the term 'psychotherapy' we are not concerned with the unstructured, informal set of relationships, which are nevertheless the influence of one mind on another, and may even be 'therapeutic'. Psychotherapy is a definable process, limited in scope, related to a definable set of phenomena, and using certain specifiable means to achieve predetermined goals. The scope of psychotherapy is defined in relation to mental illness. But not all forms of illness are amenable to psychotherapy. Almost from the very first, the special form of psychotherapy called psychoanalysis, was constrained to limit itself to the psychoneuroses (called by Freud himself 'the mental expression' of the *actual neuroses*, which were the 'direct expression' of disturbance of the sexual function). True, later innovators, great and distinguished in their own right, applied psychotherapy to the psychoses as well, notably Sullivan, with apparent success. But on the whole, I think we can agree that the psychoses are discontinuous with the neuroses, and represent a different form of illness. Freud himself has said that 'it would seem that the analytic study of the psychoses is impracticable owing to its lack of therapeutic results'.[7] The psychiatrist in dealing with a patient is not dealing with a section or a part of man, as for instance a surgeon might be considered to deal, but with the total man, body and soul, mind and history, beliefs and convictions. An understanding of such a complex phenomenon cannot be achieved merely by a knowledge of medicine and psychology, but by adding to these a thorough knowledge of philosophy, of ethics, above all of religion. But religion as such is not a form of psychotherapy, and can only be called 'psychotherapeutic' in the same sense in which one can speak of a psychotherapeutic environment.

Psychiatry, of which psychology is a part, is a branch of medicine, using natural means to cure natural illnesses. As will be clear from all the foregoing, this is neither the nature nor the function of religion. However, the initial confusion between mental health and spiritual well-being on the one hand, and their opposites – mental illness and sinfulness on the other – has led to the still prevalent concept that religion is itself a form of

psychotherapy. Here one must tread warily. A religious environment, a religious community, a community of warm affection
and supernatural love ('see these Christians how they love one
another'), is undoubtedly more conducive to the recovery of
mental health than an environment of conflict, turmoil and
insecurity. Nevertheless, this does not turn a well-intentioned
Christian community into a formally psychotherapeutic agency.
Psychotherapy involves the use of certain specifiable means
which are intended to heal pathological conditions of the psyche,
but the term has become ambiguous in much the same way as
the term psychoanalysis itself has become ambiguous. Freud
with his customary curious intuition or foresight in reference to
these things has a very pregnant phrase in the penultimate para-
graph of his autobiography:

By a process of development against which it would have been
useless to struggle, the word 'psychoanalysis' has itself become
ambiguous. While it was originally the name of a particular
therapeutic method, it has now also become the name of a
science – the science of unconscious mental processes. By
itself this science is seldom able to deal with a problem
completely . . .

In much the same way *psychotherapy* has become ambiguous.
The term is now sometimes used to include institutions grounded
in Christian love, which undoubtedly have great value, but which
can only be considered therapeutic by analogy of attribution: the
literary convention whereby, for example, one can predicate
'healthy' of a place, a climate, or a food.

It is not the function of religion as such to cure psychiatric
illnesses any more than it is the function of religion as such to
cure organic illnesses.*

*A psychotherapeutic efficacy in regard to the neuroses has sometimes been
attributed to the sacramental system as such, but this is a mistake. The
sacraments of the Christian church *as such* have only a supernatural efficacy
in the order of grace. But since they are also human experiences (e.g. being
absolved from sin) they can have also a temporal psychological effect – not
formally as sacraments but incidentally as human experiences.

The confusions in this area are due in part at least to a confusion between the concept of mental illness on the one hand and that of immaturity on the other. Undoubtedly, religion, through its beliefs, values and practices, ought to be one of the great maturing influences in human life. The idea of mental health means a great deal more than mere absence of mental illness. It connotes a degree of maturity of mind and emotional development commensurate with an individual's chronological age. It demands a high level of integration of the personality; it means judgement freed from the distortions of emotional pressure, and consciousness freed from an obsession with self. It demands a degree of extroversion which yet leaves sufficient room for introversion in the form of insight leading to self-knowledge. And it demands good interpersonal relations: with oneself, with others and with God. It is greatly to the credit of such authors as Victor Frankl, O. Hobart Mowrer,[8] Rollo May and others, that they have seen clearly that man, in order to reach his full stature as man, needs these three dimensions of mental health. Hence the development of such concepts as egotherapy, logotherapy, religious therapy, etc. These processes consist essentially in a conscious mind to conscious mind relationship in which values, life-choices, self-initiated activity and self-realization prevail over the analysis of the deep unconscious. Thus the individual is regarded as a self-actualizing being, whose growth to maturity or to full mental health depends more on his mobilizing his own resources than on extraneous help from without on the part of the therapist.

It is difficult to see that any one of these is a specific mode of therapy, least of all so-called 'religious' therapy.

Egotherapy, logotherapy and religious therapy
It would seem, however, that the concepts of egotherapy, logotherapy and religious therapy as such are not so much *psychotherapeutic* processes as processes geared to the further moral and characterological formation of otherwise healthy personalities.

On the assumption (made by Freud, and not necessarily

accepted by anyone named in this article) that all guilt is neurotic, religion 'becomes a means of getting rid of neurotic guilt'. Religion, however, properly conceived, has as one of its functions the seeking of absolution from the 'real' guilt of genuine wrong-doing, and reconciliation with God. Relief from 'neurotic' guilt is a matter for the psychiatrist. Two problems arise at once: one centres around the distinction between the morally good and the mentally healthy person, the other centres around the incidental or epiphenomenological therapeutic consequences of some of the practices of religion. The first problem can be stated as follows: is every criminal to be considered mentally ill. For instance were the custodians of Belsen mentally healthy and responsible, or mentally ill and, therefore, not responsible agents, because they had chosen evil? In the case of the 'Moors murders' no evidence of psychopathology was adduced in court either by prosecution or defence lawyers. Were they, therefore, mentally healthy persons but responsible for moral evil? Or because of the nature of the acts done, are these alone sufficient evidence to conclude the presence of psychopathology? In the literature on forensic psychiatry it would appear to be assumed that the more reprehensible the crime the more psychopathological its perpe-trators. But this is in effect to ignore or deny the possibility of man's choosing evil or even the possibility of his being a respon-sible agent in any sense. Undoubtedly, in many instances the agent is clearly psychopathological or psychopathic. But there is always the possibility, however unpalatable, that a healthy man may choose evil. Otherwise one would have to exonerate all the great criminals of history.

Religion a therapy or neurosis?

It is not the formal function of religion as such to relieve us of our anxieties, but rather to glorify God, to enable us to express our finiteness and dependence, to return thanks for the gift of existence. But if we need some means to relieve ourselves of our primitive infantile pre-rational anxieties, and if we should have had recourse in any case to some ritualistic performances in order to do so, if moreover we must needs confess our conscious rational guilt as well, and make atonement for it, as well as protesting (symbolically in sacrifice) our finiteness, is it surprising that in one and the same act we should achieve all these purposes simultaneously? This is really divine economy. This point has been made in many different ways, perhaps in one of its clearest forms in Mowrer's[8] note on 'confession as sacrament or therapy', where referring to Wilson's *Pardon and Peace* he subscribes to the idea that 'confession is unmistakably and powerfully therapeutic'. Here again, however, the word 'therapeutic' has been extended far beyond any psychopathological reference to embrace the much more generalized concept of *anything conducive to man's felt states of well-being*, e.g., in the relief from anxiety or self-reproach. Once again one may be forgiven for repeating that the extension of the word 'therapeutic' in this manner makes possible the concept of religion as therapy, but at the same time substitutes a metaphorical meaning for a literal one. The practices of religion, being the acts of human beings, may and do have many consequences for the human person as distinct from or incidental to their function as acts of divine worship. In this way, acts of religion will sometimes be found to serve as incidental means of allaying anxiety, guilt feelings, depression, relieving conflict, insecurity, etc. It is also possible, and indeed quite common, to find individuals subordinating these incidental consequences of religious acts to their primary purpose. This may be done consciously or unconsciously. When this is done, however, we are concerned with a dimension of human behaviour, rather than with an aspect of religion as such.

It was Freud's great genius to discern how this mechanism (whereby religious acts can be carried out as means whereby states of well-being can be achieved) can be used unconsciously and therefore be used to illumine the nature of neurotic behaviour patterns. Freud thought, however, that by doing this he had shown the neurotic character of religion as such. This on Freud's part was the same error in reverse that one perceives in the behaviour of those who in fact use religion in an exclusively instrumental way to achieve their own well-being. But while claiming that religion was in itself psychopathological, *viz*. a neurosis, Freud[9] also conceded the right of the believer to go on believing. He said:

> I still maintain that what I have written is quite harmless in one respect. No believer would let himself be led astray from his faith by these or any similar arguments.

Earlier he had said:[10]

> Nothing that I have said here against the true value of religion needed the support of psychoanalysis; it had been said by others long before analysis came into existence. If the application of the psychoanalytic method makes it possible to find a new argument against the truths of religion, *tant pis* for religion.

He went on:[11]

> But defenders of religion will by the same right make use of psychoanalysis in order to give full value to the affective significance of religious doctrines.

There is considerable evidence that religious people with psychiatric interpersonal or intrapersonal problems, tend to seek help in the first instance from the minister of religion rather than from the family doctor or specialist:

> Where did they go for help? Forty-two per cent consulted clergymen, twenty-nine per cent physicians in general, eighteen per cent psychiatrists or psychologists, and ten per cent social agencies or marriage clinics.[12]

Evidence of this kind has tended to reinforce the concept of religion as therapy, while at the same time it has obscured the nature of therapy itself, since many of the people in such surveys were not in fact psychopathological or in need of psychiatric help but were suffering from the normal hazards of human living.

As Rümke[13] has pointed out, human life free from all unhappiness and suffering would not be human life as we know it. It is true that mental illness causes great unhappiness and suffering, but this proposition has often been confused with its converse, *viz.* that all forms of unhappiness and suffering are forms of mental illness and need psychotherapeutic help.

It has been contended above that one may be mentally healthy while guilty of moral wrongdoing. In the same way, one may be mentally ill while well advanced in sanctity. There is no reason to suppose that all the saints were a hundred per cent free of all psychopathological symptoms, in fact, quite the converse could be shown to be the case. All the phenomena of the 'mystical states' can be duplicated in psychopathology. If we recognize, as we do, that mental illness in its many forms is a perfectly normal, natural illness, and is not linked with concepts of sin and demonic possession as stated above, there is no reason to suppose that God could not, if He so wished, lead a neurotic person to the heights of sanctity. This has been controverted, particularly by followers of Jung, and by some theologians arguing on *a priori* grounds. Thus Father Victor White says:

> Psychological disorder, in the broadest sense, is thus 'normal', and indeed universal, for fallen man, that is to say for empirical man as we know him.[14]

Not all the consequences of man's disorder are pathological by psychiatric standards, but Father White thinks 'some may very well be so'. Many, like Father White, who adopt this position, are loath to draw the full consequences of their teaching, which would involve the following propositions: sin is a disorder of the soul, and, therefore, of the psyche. Psychotherapy and religion have the same purpose, the rehabilition of a disordered psyche. One result of this line of thought is the formal training of ministers in some of the Christian churches, in techniques of psychotherapy; another is the suggestion that sacramental participation *as such* has a psychotherapeutic function. A third consequence is the doctrine that sanctity and mental illness, however mild, are

incompatible. The objection is perhaps stated in its clearest form
by Aumann as follows:

> . . . therefore sanctity requires a certain integrity in the psychic
> order. This does not mean that neurotics cannot have utmost
> confidence in God and an intense love for God, but they
> still lack that integrity which is required for sanctity (pp.
> 290–1).[15]

And again:

> If we ask whether truly pathological states may have preceded
> the mystical state or sanctity of an individual, the answer is
> 'YES'. But we hasten to add that the cure of the pathological
> condition is a necessary prerequisite to true sanctity and the
> mystical state. If we further ask whether truly pathological
> phenomena may be concomitant with the mystical state and
> sanctity the answer is 'NO' (pp. 291–2).[15]

These presumptions yield to fact. There is considerable evidence
to show that many incontrovertibly sanctified persons and mystics
did not achieve total freedom from psychopathology, the integrity, the perfection of mental health, required by such a theory.

The roles of the minister and psychotherapist

The formal roles of psychotherapist and minister of religion
are radically distinct, precisely because the formal roles of
psychiatry and religion are distinct. The one aims at the healthy
functioning of the psyche, the other at the spiritual well-being of
the soul. The two roles of minister and psychiatrist are related,
they are complementary, but they remain distinct. The psychotherapist's role is the healing of the sick mind, the helping of an
individual through forces within himself to overcome or remove
pathological processes, and thus to free his personality from
distortions of an emotional or instinctive character. The role of
the minister of religion on the other hand is to be a minister of
grace, to help a person to make right choices, to enable him to

solve his conscious moral or spiritual problems, and to choose right means for the attaining of spiritual and supernatural goals. This does not mean that he neglects, depreciates or decries true human and temporal values. It only means that he must integrate these with his formal concern, which is the transcendent.

Educational therapy

Irene Caspari

General remarks

Educational therapy is a method of therapeutic intervention for children with severe learning disability. It has been developed over the last fifteen years in the Department for Children and Parents of the Tavistock Clinic, and it is used by a number of psychologists and teachers who have received some training in this method.

These children have no detectable physical or neurological handicap. They are of average or above average intelligence, but suffer from an inability to progress in one of the basic subjects, *viz*. reading, spelling or arithmetic. However, the majority of the children treated in the department suffer from reading disability and thus the description of the treatment will be limited to cases who had difficulty in learning to read.

Educational therapy is based on empirical evidence suggesting that some emotional disturbance is present in most cases. The problem of treatment is, therefore, approached with particular regard to the child's emotional needs and great importance is attached to the understanding of the child's feelings, and of his emotional reaction.

This kind of approach does not, of course, exclude other aetiological factors, such as inadequate teaching as suggested by Morris[1, 2] or some kind of neurological dysfunctioning put forward by supporters of the hypothesis of specific developmental dyslexia, such as Newton, Critchley and Vernon.[3] Other workers in this field look specifically for perceptual difficulties, such as Frostig,[4, 5] Tansley,[6] Franklin and Naidoo[7] and Naidoo.[8] It merely assumes that amongst the variety of possible factors, some degree of emotional instability will be present as well.

Our method of treatment rests on the Freudian hypothesis that unconscious mechanisms are very important determinants of human behaviour. To this extent, educational therapy can be described as a psychoanalytically orientated type of treatment. In as far as the therapeutic intervention focuses on a particular aspect of dysfunctions, *viz*. inability to read, spell or to do arithmetic, it can be seen as focal therapy. In addition, it shares with most kinds of 'remedial teaching' the special emphasis on carefully planned and programmed instruction. As a psychotherapeutic type of intervention educational therapy is based on the understanding of the child's behaviour in the relationship with the therapist and this understanding can, of course, be used in many different ways. This makes a theoretical discussion of the technique difficult and liable to be fraught with misunderstandings. For this reason we shall restrict this presentation to a description of some of the techniques we commonly use and leave the reader to make his own comparison between educational therapy and other therapeutic interventions.

Some of the children treated in this way have been studied in greater detail. A more detailed account of the findings is to appear in 1975. However, it seems important that the reader should have some information about these children so that the description of the treatment can be put into perspective.

They were children aged eight to fourteen at referral. Only twelve per cent were girls. Seventy-one per cent of them had a reading age of less than five years eleven months on Schonell's Graded Vocabulary Scale and only ten per cent had a reading age of seven or above. The highest reading age was seven years ten months. Sixty-eight per cent of these children were of low average or average intelligence, sixteen per cent were above this level and sixteen per cent were of limited intelligence. These children were only accepted if there were indications that the test result was an underestimate of their intellectual capacity. No correlation between the intellectual level and the reading ability could be found, i.e. children with the lowest reading ages could be found on all levels of intelligence, and some of those with reading ages of seven years or above were amongst the children of low average intelligence.

The children showed many of the usual manifestations of reading disability. Most of them were inclined to reverse letters and words; ability to memorize and powers of concentration were poor. Seventy-eight per cent were unable to synthesize words, i.e. to blend ke-a-te to make 'cat', and fifty-three per cent showed great resistance towards learning this simple skill which is usually acquired by infant school children without great difficulty.

In addition to the reading difficulty, about half of the children had one or more recognizable symptoms of maladjustment, such as delinquency or severe behaviour problems, another thirty-three per cent were over-docile or withdrawn. Almost half of these showed overt behaviour problems when they began to learn. Only fourteen per cent had no obvious emotional difficulties; but underlying their overtly well-adjusted behaviour severe emotional problems were found in the course of their treatment. Information gathered about their home conditions suggested possible emotional instability in at least sixty-one per cent of the families. These figures must be regarded with caution, for the sample comprised only fifty-one children.

The children were seen individually for an hour twice a week, most of them over two to three years. At the end of the treatment half of the children had a reading age of eight years or above, but only six per cent could read with ease and enjoyment. Almost all the children learned to blend words with simple sounds. Those that did not, broke off treatment prematurely.

This is, of course, a very modest result, but a large number of these children had previously not shown any improvement in spite of being given a considerable amount of extra help with reading in their schools. We would be inclined to see the modest results as an indication of the severity of the disability.

The description and generalizations of the technique that follows are derived from detailed reports of observed behaviour of each child in each session, and of his interaction with the educational therapist, as recorded by the latter. There is unavoidably a subjective element in these reports. Nevertheless, as most of the educational therapists were trainees, their reports were studied by an independent observer, the tutor, who also queried and discussed inconsistencies in the material. In addition, there were almost as many educational therapists as there were patients.

Interpretation of observed behaviour can, of course, be biased. In this study this applies to the extent that the understanding of the patient's behaviour depends on the interpretation of this behaviour by the educational therapist and his tutor. However, this bias was substantially reduced by an insistence of reporting the sessions in terms of observed behaviour rather than in terms of inferences. For example, the success in reading would be stated in terms of number of pages read, number and type of mistakes made rather than 'he read fairly well'. Discussions with parents and teachers provided a further source of information and constituted an additional check to the possible bias of the educational therapist. We, therefore, feel fairly justified in regarding the evidence from the reports as sufficiently reliable clinical material to provide the basis for some tentative generalization concerning the treatment technique.

The treatment technique
The teaching element in educational therapy – Throughout treatment conventional teaching methods are seen as tools to be employed according to the needs of each child and the preferences of the teacher. Therefore, the teaching techniques in educational therapy differ from case to case. To explain this more fully I should like to draw attention to those aspects of the interaction between teacher and pupil that appear to have some similarity to the mother–child relationship in the feeding situation.

Perhaps this analogy appears to be strange to some readers, but they may be reminded of the frequent use of terms like 'taking in' and 'digesting' in respect of knowledge, suggesting that a symbolic equation of learning and feeding is built into the imagery of common speech. This equation, of course, does not cover the whole range of interactions between teacher and pupil, but we have found it to be a relevant analogy in discussing how we approach the problem of teaching these children to read.

It is generally accepted that successful feeding of infants depends not only on the interaction between the mother and the child, but also on the appropriateness of the food and the manner in which it is given. These three factors are closely interlinked. If a baby is given whisky instead of milk, or milk in a glass instead of a bottle, he will cry and refuse the food however positive the relationship between him and his mother might be.

Similarly in a learning situation, when the teaching matter is perceived as food, three factors are interdependent: the interaction of the teacher and his pupil, the degree to which the teaching material is gauged to the pupil's appetite and whether or not it is presented so that he can take it in.

Generally, there is a fairly wide range of variation between these three factors without any adverse affects on a baby's feeding. However, if a particular baby develops a feeding difficulty, the mother will take special care to see that the food is appropriate and to present it to the child in the way he can take it and at the right time for him.

Similarly most children will be able to learn even if the task does not particularly appeal to them or if the lesson is slightly above their heads; but the child with a severe learning difficulty will reject the learning at once if it is not given under optimal conditions. Just as there is no general rule that will guarantee successful feeding, there is no one particular teaching method that will ensure successful learning. Just as it is useful for the mother to know the many known ways in which babies with feeding difficulties have been helped, so it is important for the teacher to know the range of teaching methods that have been successfully used with children who have difficulty in learning to read.

These children have some characteristics in common: their progress in reading is generally very slow and is characterized by specific learning blocks, mainly to do with blending and synthesizing sounds into a word or with phrasing. In contrast to ordinary children, they are unable to make use of 'latent learning'. Skills can only be acquired if they are systematically practised. They find it very difficult to transfer their knowledge from one situation to another; for instance, there is often a time-lag of about three months before they show at school any improvement they have made in the educational therapy sessions. They are also extremely sensitive to failure. Any mistake results in an immediate reduction of efficiency in reading. If, for instance, they are unable to read a word in a story, their fluency in reading usually deteriorates for several minutes, even if they have been helped to correct their mistakes themselves. They also have a very unreliable memory. It is quite common for a child to read a particular word correctly several times within, say, ten minutes and to be entirely unable to recognize it a minute later. Lastly, it may be repeated that most of these children are unable to synthesize simple sounds into words.

This leads us to formulate some general teaching principles:

a) Whatever method is used, the teaching has to be carefully programmed. This means that, whatever method is used, the educational therapist needs to work out the various steps by which he intends to teach the skill of reading and he has to devise means by which he can determine whether the child is sure of that part of the skill. For instance, if the phonic method is used, the sounds of letters have to be learned before synthesis of simple words can be attempted and the educational therapist needs to plan how to ensure that the child is familiar with the sounds. For example, if a teacher decides to use the 'touch cards' of Stott's Programmed Kit,[9] for this purpose, he needs to repeat this game every lesson until he has ascertained that the child knows the sounds spontaneously and without help from the teacher every time he is presented with them. This may appear common sense, but if the child's performance varies from day to day, and this happens very frequently, one is tempted to take the child's effectiveness on his 'good days' as a guideline, while it is necessary to continue practising until the child can recall the sounds reliably also on his 'worst days'.

b) We have learned from experience that any change of books or apparatus results in deterioration of performance. Thus, it is more useful to keep to a limited series of books and a very limited amount of apparatus, rather than use a variety of teaching material. I have never found any confirmation of this observation in the literature, but some of the most successful and widely used teaching methods, such as Stott's[9] and Moxon's[10] and i.t.a.[11] do, in fact, follow this rule although it is not explicitly stated.

c) These children are also observed to have a low failure tolerance. The teaching has, therefore, to be introduced in such a way that the child never fails to accomplish the task he is given, and it is necessary for the educational therapist to give him individual attention, whether the child is seen alone or in a group. The larger the group the more difficult this becomes and this might be seen as an argument for the need for individual tuition, or at least for tuition in very small groups for these children.

d) All these children need to acquire phonic skills. To some degree this is true for all children. Even in the controversy between phonic methods and 'Look and Say' methods, the basic difference would not appear to be so much *whether* word-wholes or phonics are learned, but *at what stage* in the child's acquisition of reading skills phonics are taught. Almost all teachers introduce reading by presenting children with meaningful words to demonstrate that the symbol in print represents a meaningful symbol in speech. However, some prefer to introduce the phonic rules early, while others wait until the children have built up a considerable 'sight vocabulary'. For the majority of children the learning of phonic rules is extremely difficult because of their irregularity. Children with severe reading disability very frequently show great resistance towards learning these rules, yet we found that they need to know them as a prop that can help in the recognition of a word when memory fails. Our experience taught us that the aphasic-like incidents mentioned above diminish as the child gains confidence, and so does his anxiety in respect of word recognition, with the consequence that his memory becomes more and more reliable.

Teaching and underlying emotional conflict
Our attempts to remove the specific learning block in synthesis of simple words led to considerable evidence of a link between this

difficulty and underlying emotional problems. In some of our cases, these appeared to be connected with phantasies about the analysis of the word which precedes the synthesis. For example, Jack, aged nine years, with a reading age of five years ten months, on Schonell's Graded Vocabulary Test and of above average ability, showed great difficulty about synthesis. He learned the sounds quite easily, but could only synthesize a word after having recognized it as a word-whole. In the first session in which synthesis was systematically introduced, the educational therapist gave him some apparatus consisting of seven postcards each showing a three-letter word, such as 'cat', underneath the appropriate picture. (See example below.) Jack was presented with each card in turn and asked to sound and read the words, without seeing the picture. He had considerable difficulty with this. He was then shown the picture and was asked to cut each card up, separating each letter, and also cutting through the drawing so as to make a jigsaw puzzle. He did this

Illustration of apparatus for cutting-up procedure

enthusiastically, making short, sharp rather jagged cuts in spite of his very efficient motor co-ordination.

This is an extract from the report of the subsequent session:[12]

I then told Jack that we had several cards left to cut up this session, and he said 'Oh, yes, let's do that!' The cards I gave were *dog, hat, red, net*. Both the pictures and the words were uncovered. He correctly and quickly recognized these words as wholes (from the picture clue?). When it came to the cutting up he grasped the first card tightly – *dog* and went 'arrrgh!' and jabbed the point of the scissors towards the picture of the dog, saying 'there's blood, lots of blood', in a very aggressive, tense way. He then grasped the scissors tightly and most aggressively, going 'arrrgh' as he did it, slashed into the card in an attacking way, saying 'I'm killing it'. He repeated this statement. He carried out this violent cutting attack on each of the cards, making aggressive sounds as he did so, at one point saying: 'I'll cut it all to bits'. With the second card, *hat*, he again referred to blood, saying: 'there's no blood here'. When he came to the last card, *red*, in which the picture was a red patch, he said: 'here's the blood' in a blood-curdling way, and if anything he slashed this card even more than the others.

During the next few sessions Jack became less reliable in synthesis than he had been before, until the educational therapist verbalized his fears:

I reminded him how he had cut up the word cards . . . telling him that it didn't matter how much he cut up or slashed the word into bits, it didn't harm or destroy the word—it would still remain a whole word which could be built up again after being cut up.

Following this explanation there was a dramatic reaction. For the first time Jack synthesized with keen interest. For the first time he was able to synthesize a word he had never met before, and laughed with pleasure when he realized that he could read new words by means of synthesis. He finished that part of the session by 'strutting around a little saying "I'm good, I am!" '. Four sessions after this he could synthesize three-letter words reliably. The whole procedure had taken nine sessions.

This is one of the most vivid accounts of the reaction to what we call 'the cutting-up procedure', but not by any means the only one. I would suggest that Jack showed very clearly the extent to which analysis of a word meant 'killing it' to him, and also the extent to which the symbol stood for reality. However, this kind of confusion between reality and symbols, combined with the fear of destroying the word, is not always the basis of difficulty in synthesis.

In another case, a ten-year-old boy informed the educational therapist that the first letter was the father, the last letter was the mother and the middle one was the child. His mother reported that her son insisted on watching television at night from his bed. This was only possible if his bedroom door was left open and the parents put their chairs on either side of the door. In this way, the familiar pattern of the child coming between the parents was repeatedly enacted in the home, and the inability to analyse and synthesize a three-letter word seemed to be directly related to this situation.

Such conflict is, of course, not always attached solely to the process of synthesis and analysis of words. For example, with Leonard, aged twelve, the problem was more generally linked with fears that his destructive feelings were so powerful that the person towards whom he had expressed these feelings would be harmed in reality and permanently damaged. He and his educational therapist had for some time played the drawing game of 'hangman', in order to increase the competitive element during the practice of synthesis. The rule was that Leonard could 'hang' the educational therapist (a woman) if the synthesis was correct and Leonard was 'hanged' if it was not. Leonard developed this game into 'torture chambers' and treated the educational therapist-on-paper with great cruelty. His ability to synthesize, however, remained unreliable until the session in which he drew the educational therapist for the first time as a woman instead of a pin-man, and having synthesized nine out of ten words correctly without help, said 'Now I am cutting you loose', and drew a line through the rope.

Leonard seemed to communicate that his inability to analyse and synthesize a word was connected with his doubts at the possibility of reparation after destructive feelings. It seemed that during the hangman game he could only 'destroy' the educational therapist if the drawing did not really resemble a human being. After experiencing, for a considerable time, that the educational therapist accepted and even enjoyed his destructive feelings, and that she, in turn could destroy him and yet like him as much as ever, he was able to represent her as a real person and restore her to life.

Having experienced this, he was able to apply the same mechanism to words. It is perhaps important to add that, before this incident, Leonard had repeatedly played a game in which Leonard, the villain, had tortured the educational therapist and had subsequently been kicked out of the window by Leonard, the rescuer. He had played this game over and over again in a way that is more characteristic of three-year-olds, who play repeatedly at being killed and being alive again.

In most cases, we found a mixture of these more general conflicts and confusion between reality and phantasy in respect of the letters, with these two elements very much blurred. This led us to employ variations of the 'cutting-up' procedure mentioned above, which is not unlike the most successful ways of teaching phonics currently used: Moxon's,[10] Stott's[9] and Daniels' and Diack's[13] methods all incorporate this principle of destruction and restitution.

Another illustration of the use of teaching techniques in relation to the child's emotional problems is the way in which we usually teach the great variety of sound combinations. This needs a great deal of practice, with constant reinforcement of the correct answer, not only by praise, but by more tangible means, such as points or cards won from the educational psychologist. We often arrange it as a competitive game between the educational therapist and the child, in such a way that the child scores words correctly read, while the educational therapist's score consists of the child's mistakes. This way of teaching is, of course, not new. It is often used to motivate a child to perform an essentially dull task. On a deeper level, however, it seems to enable the child to work through his fears concerning rivalry with the adult. It seems to be particularly important that the competition is with the adult and *not* with another child, because the adult does not mind losing and is, in this case, in fact *glad* to lose, as his low scores are the result of the child's competence in reading. It is often surprising to what extent even older children will enjoy this way of practising, and how little they seem to realize that the outcome of the competition is under their control. Andrew, for instance, at the age of thirteen, kept the score until his success had risen to more than a thousand, while the educational therapist had only scored twenty-odd words.

Synthesis of simple sounds into words, however, does not make a fluent reader, nor does the reading of practice words with various sound combinations. Neither is the acquisition of phonic skills identical with fluent reading. In fact, there appears to be a considerable gap between proficency in using phonics in word exercises and the application of this knowledge in the reading of books.

Learning 'blocks' can occur in many areas, particularly in phrasing and fluency. In some cases, inability to read fluently may be as difficult to overcome as the learning block in respect of synthesis. Peter, aged fourteen, for instance, had learned to synthesize simple sounds quite reliably, but whenever he read a sentence he separated each word from the next. He could easily repeat the same sentence when he did not look at the print, but when he was asked to look at the book again he paused after each word. Peter left us before we could find out the reason for this particular difficulty.

At this point it may be useful to discuss how we understand one of the other main characteristics of non-readers, *viz*. the frequent confusion between letters such as 'b' and 'd' or words such as 'on' and 'no', and to describe the various ways in which we deal with this. We very rarely practise these words or sounds specifically, but find that they disappear of their own accord during treatment. Our study of these children has not suggested any definite hypothesis to account for the frequency of this symptom. In some cases, the reversals occur together with minor misreadings, which are generally corrected spontaneously when the mistake is pointed out. The accuracy often improves when the educational therapist places his finger under the text. This may ameliorate some perceptual confusion, but it also seems to be a way by which the child ensures the educational therapist's involvement in the reading.

In one case there was some evidence that the tendency to reverse was caused by an unconscious wish to read the opposite of what was printed. This was again the case with Andrew, aged thirteen, who at that time was reading quite fluently in a book at the reading age level of eight to nine years. Suddenly he started to reverse the usual words, like 'on' and 'no' and 'was' and 'saw', correcting himself immediately when reminded of his mistake. However, he came to an impasse when he tried to synthesize the word 'empty' from the end. He did not know how to sound the 'y'. He knew the different ways of sounding this letter, and tried to use it as a consonant, as would be appropriate at the beginning of a word. At this, the educational therapist stopped the reading and played a drawing game of opposites, with herself drawing a picture of rain and asking Andrew to draw the opposite; then Andrew drew a picture and the educational therapist drew the opposite. This game went on until the drawings depicted feelings like happiness and sadness, and building up and destruction by fire. In the next session, Andrew's tendency to reverse had disappeared and was never a problem again. The clarity of this boy's material was due to the sudden appearance of the reversals, which then disappeared as quickly as they had come. Generally the aetiology for these reversals is far from clear and is likely to be as varied as that of the reading disability as a whole.

The last example is, I think, a very vivid illustration of the interaction between understanding of the child's feeling and choice of teaching approach. In Andrew's case, the educational therapist's observations led her to the hypothesis that he had a need to express negative feelings. He was expressing them in a way that made his reading inefficient and could, therefore, not be accepted by the educational therapist.

The educational therapist, by initiating the game, demonstrated that she understood Andrew's need to express these feelings, that they were acceptable to her, that she herself had similar feelings and these could be expressed in a way that was acceptable to her and not detrimental to Andrew's efficiency in reading.

The use of games and expression work in educational therapy

Games, therefore, offer an opportunity for the actual experience in feeling as well as a 'training' in how they can be handled. Games are used to provide as much scope as possible for expression of feelings, irrespective of whether or not they are connected with reading. For instance, in order to work through the patient's conflict about rivalry with an adult, the educational therapist might decide to use a competitive drawing game in which the patient and the therapist have an equal chance. The best known of these games is 'Beetle', which was a well-known drawing-room game some years ago and is played with a dice, each number allowing the player to draw a part of a beetle until one of them has completed the whole insect. A similar game can be played with the drawing of faces, and we generally prefer this to 'Beetle' because it is more conducive to emotional expression. In fact, we have invented a new game, where the principle is extended to the whole human figure, as this gives even more scope for expression. Most of the games we use are pencil and paper games or can easily be made in cardboard, and if they are well-known games such as 'Battleships and Cruisers' they generally have to be adapted for use with a particular child.

Games are also invented to give an opportunity for dealing with any conflicts that the patient has brought up in the session. Leonard, aged eleven, for instance, frequently drew car crashes in which the educational therapist was often involved, or he acted these out with model cars. So a car-racing game was invented, in which car crashes played a big part and gave opportunity for discussion as well as an experience of the feelings expressed in the original material, in the greater safety of the more formalized game.

Another medium through which feelings can 'safely' be expressed is what is generally called 'free expression work': drawing, painting, acting, clay modelling, cardboard modelling and, particularly for the older patients, writing stories, poems and plays, usually dictated to the educational therapist. An important factor in this kind of work seems to be that the activity is completed comparatively quickly, maximizing, in this way, the amount of opportunity for expression. Although most of the patients under discussion readily used one of these media, they were inclined to use them in a stereotyped way, at first, drawing houses for instance, or isolated figures not in relationship to anyone. It is, therefore, often necessary for the educational therapist to show feelings first, and games like 'Bedlam', in which the educational therapist can express his feelings in the faces he draws, are frequently used for this purpose.

There are, of course, many other ways in which feelings can be stimulated, e.g. the educational therapist can write a story with the child or can draw a picture with him. Even the telling or reading of a story can serve this purpose, for the child will pick up that the educational therapist approves of the feelings expressed in the story and will, therefore, get the message that he is also permitted to express them.

Often the choice of this active intervention on the part of the educational therapist will be in response to some needs of the child, similar to the invention of the game of opposites in the case of Andrew's reversals. Active intervention, however, might have to be made prior to full understanding of the child's feelings.

The choice of intervention, in turn, depends on the psycho-analytic theories the educational therapist holds and on empirical findings with backward readers. The educational therapist can, for instance, safely assume that the child does not express his feelings of hostility, envy or depression, because the child considers these to be unacceptable. Experience with children who suffer from learning difficulties suggests that the child's aggressive feelings are most frequently the most easily available. The educational therapist, therefore, often chooses to express aggressive feelings in his intervention: he draws a shouting face in 'Bedlam', he introduces fighting into the pictures and stories, he chooses a story with a 'good' aggressor such as Robin Hood or a 'Western'. It seems important that the aggression can be considered 'good', as otherwise the child expects punishment and that is precisely what he is afraid of in respect to his own feelings.

Conceptualization and verbalization of feelings in educational therapy

Games and expression work can, therefore, be regarded as a 'comment-in-action' in respect to the child's feelings as well as a vehicle for the child to express these feelings. In addition, however, the educational therapist also conceptualizes these feelings in words. However, verbal conceptualization is generally related only to the feelings made manifest in the expression work, e.g. in the drawing or the story. Sometimes it is linked to the relationship between the child and the educational therapist, but only very occasionally to the child's feelings towards members of his family.

For instance, thirteen-year-old David drew a picture of the Martian King and the Martian Prince, who killed his father, the King, because they both loved the same princess. A whole session was spent on the implications of this, and various solutions were sought but at no time did the educational therapist refer to David's home situation although she knew from reports that this was very relevant to his drawing. Nor did she refer to the feelings of fourteen-year-old Claude towards her when he dictated a story, based on the Superman comics, of the enchantress who endows the weak, lame powerman with superhuman powers to be used in her service. The conceptualization and verbalization was entirely focused on the relationships and feelings of the characters in the stories.

Confusion between reality and phantasy, which quite frequently occurs in the expression work is also treated in this indirect way. The confusion is usually very slight, and the educational therapist needs to be very observant to pick it up. Leonard, for instance, drew a picture of a prison, showing the policeman on a chair with a table in front of him inside the house, which was also depicted from the outside. This is, of course, not infrequent with young children, but Leonard was thirteen years old at the time and had shown similar confusions in many of his pictures. The educational therapist remarked on the impossibility of seeing the inside and outside of a house at the same time, stressing, however, that drawings need not be identical with reality as long as Leonard was aware of this. At this remark, Leonard added a garden to the front of the house and, in this way, transferred the policeman from the inside to the outside, demonstrating that he could now deal with this problem.

In contrast to the 'indirect' conceptualization of conflicts in the expression work, the patient's feelings about the educational therapist and the treatment situation are frequently verbalized directly, if he indicates through verbal or non-verbal behaviour that he has some awareness of the feelings in question and is able to accept such a remark. Such a decision must be left to the discretion of the educational therapist, and the effectiveness of this intervention will depend on his skills. It is, of course, much easier to make an 'indirect' comment. If the educational therapist misunderstands the child's message in the expression work and makes an inappropriate comment, or if he refers to deeply unconscious feelings, the child's anxieties will not be aroused. If he decides to comment on feelings directly he has to take these factors into account. This becomes even more necessary if conceptualizations and verbalizations of feelings are made in respect of the patient and his family. This is done very rarely in educational therapy mainly because these patients do not talk directly about their feelings towards their parents or siblings. Dennis's family, for instance, was disintegrating. He was eleven years old and illegitimate. His stepfather had frequently walked out and finally did not return. His mother had gone to relatives in Cornwall with the new baby and Dennis was staying with neighbours. The educational therapist knew all the facts, and frequently tried to encourage Dennis to talk about this situation, but the child always replied that everything and everybody was perfectly all right. He did, however, express his problems in the form of a story about a lonely little donkey, who had lost his home, and the therapist could discuss Dennis's problems in discussing the donkey's feelings.

Dennis made it very clear that it was too painful for him to talk directly about the devastating reality situation in his family. This is, I think, very often the case. The controversial issue is really whether or not Dennis was able to deal with his feelings of loneliness and depression more successfully because he could discuss the feelings of the donkey with his educational therapist. In the case of Dennis we have very little evidence for it. Very shortly after this episode he was taken into care and we never heard of him again. Our experience with other children, however, lead us to deduce that permanent modification of behaviour does take place as a result of educational therapy and that the 'indirect' comment plays an important part in this therapeutic endeavour. 'Indirect' verbal comments are in fact very similar to the other therapeutic interventions used in educational therapy. Games like 'Bedlam' or teaching devices like the 'cutting-up-procedure' could also be seen as 'indirect-comments-in-action'.

The description of details in comparative isolation used in this paper, leads unavoidably to a slightly distorted picture of the technique. This is not only true of the verbalization of feelings, it applies to all aspects of the treatment. In each session teaching, games, expression work and verbalization of varying kinds are used in varying degrees and are far more intermingled than is shown.

In spite of this, I hope, that the examples are explicit enough to show the fundamental aspects of educational therapy and to give a representative picture of what happens in this particular kind of therapeutic intervention.

Group therapy

Robin Skynner

The field of group psychotherapy has extended so vastly, since it received its main impetus during the Second World War, that it would require a volume of its own to do it justice. It will be necessary, therefore, to survey the field briefly and to suggest where possible suitable reviews and books summarizing the work done in each area, for those interested in a more detailed account.

The 'small-group' models

While the whole field of group psychotherapy is interrelated, it is helpful to begin by reviewing developments in the use of the 'small analytic group' – that is, artificial groups of about seven or eight strangers meeting together with a therapist under strictly defined conditions – in which group processes are more easily studied and in which, consequently, the theories of group interaction and therapy have been mainly worked out.

In England the development of small-group theory has followed two rather separate courses. Both grew from the so-called 'Northfield Experiment', where a number of psycho-analysts, many already leaders in their field, came together at a military hospital during World War II and engaged in lively and productive experimentation in the therapeutic use of group situations along psychoanalytic lines. One of these, W. Bion, working then in association with his former analyst, J. Rickman, later came to take charge of group psychotherapy at the Tavistock Clinic and developed influential theories based on observations with leaderless groups.[1] Having set the group the task of observing and understanding its own tensions and behaviour, he perceived the 'work group' (the group struggling rationally and purposefully to perform the task he had set), alternating with other phases where indulgence in strong emotionally determined patterns would interfere with it. Three main patterns were noted, one characterized by 'dependency' (an attempt to make the leader behave omnipotently and take all responsibility), a second by 'fight-flight' (attempts to find solutions by escape or conflict), the third by 'pairing' (the establishment of relationships between a pair of group members while the rest of the group hopefully anticipated a solution from the interaction between the pair). Bion also studied group behaviour in terms of the psychoanalytic concepts of Melanie Klein and his most valuable contribution is derived from this extension of our understanding to primitive 'psychotic' levels of group behaviour. However, his emphasis on the performance of intellectual tasks (rational understanding, insight, etc.) rather than on processes of growth and integration makes his technique of limited therapeutic value despite its relevance to the study and facilitation of task-orientated situations in training, factory organization, etc. This was the view of Yalom,[2] an independent American observer who spent a year at the Tavistock studying their methods.

Another 'Tavistock' model, also based partly on Kleinian theory, was developed by H. Ezriel.[3] He views the group in terms of a tripartite psychoanalytic model whereby at any moment the group as a whole is seen as undergoing a conflict between a wish for some form of instinctual satisfaction and a fear of the consequences, the actual group behaviour demonstrating the compromise reached. Special needs of the individual are met more than in Bion's method by interpreting, in addition, each member's way of handling the group conflict.

Both these 'Tavistock' models have been worked out with considerable clarity but tend to reduce the group to a two-person pattern which preserves the strictly hierarchical and non-mutual structure of individual psychoanalysis; all comments tend to be focused around the leader, who maintains an artificial withdrawn position valuable for stimulating projection but capable of a defensive use which excludes the leader from the treatment process and so must prevent the group from growing beyond the limits of his own pathology.

The other main British school derives from S. H. Foulkes[4, 5, 6] who had begun applying psychoanalytic ideas to groups before his participation in the 'Northfield Experiment'. After the war he continued to develop his ideas both as Physician to the Maudsley Hospital, where he influenced a generation of young psychiatrists attending for post-graduate training there from all over the world, and also at the Group-Analytic Society and its later offspring, the Institute of Group Analysis. Foulkes made little use of Kleinian concepts (although his followers have attempted to include these), but attempted to work out psychoanalytic ideas afresh in relation to the complexity and potential of the group situation, rather than by reducing the latter to the Procrustean bed of an essentially dyadic mother/child pattern. His main contribution lies in his recognition of inherent growth-facilitating possibilities in the group itself, and his view that the leader's main task is to facilitate this when necessary and indeed to remain open to correction by it himself. Transference to the leader is interpreted where this is dominant, and a 'here and now' emphasis is maintained, but other types of interaction are recognized as equally relevant and communications are not forced into a theoretical mould. The advantages of such an open and growing system have their cost in that it does not provide, in Yalom's words,[7] the 'all-inclusive system [which] satisfies one's need for closure and provides the group leader with a sense of mastery . . .' which the 'Tavistock' models do. Foulkes' methods are difficult to grasp adequately from his writings alone and require an apprenticeship or at least prolonged observation and contact for satisfactory understanding. This is perhaps also due to the fact that some of the main principles have not been worked out explicitly; my own belief is that this may require more recognition of the natural history of growth and developmental processes in groups, sequences which are clear enough in closed, time-limited groups, but obscured in the 'slow-open' groups with slowly changing membership which Foulkes was usually concerned with.

The United States has until recently lagged behind the British schools in sophistication of group theory, though the catalysing influence of new developments in related fields, to be described later, have now put them in the lead. Moreno,[8] an early pioneer in the therapeutic use of groups, has focused mainly on techniques using action and the possibilities of the theatre – 'psychodrama' in which individuals re-enact scenes from their past experience with fellow-patients role-playing other figures involved; and 'sociodrama', where the whole audience participates through identification. Unfortunately, Moreno's work has had less influence than it deserves, mainly because he isolated himself and his school by developing a private language, rejecting past sources and ignoring other current developments. His dramatic techniques have been used extensively in France, often in modified forms, by such authorities as Lebovici,[9] Schutzemberger[10] and others, but until recently have had almost no response in England where a little more emotion and action, and less talk and intellectualization, might be a welcome change.

S. R. Slavson,[11, 12] another early pioneer, has had a vast influence on the development of group psychotherapy generally in the United States and was instrumental in organizing training programmes and setting up the *International Journal of Group Psychotherapy*. Slavson began his experiments in the field of child psychotherapy and his books on groups of children and adolescents are still essential sources. His theories, however, though simple, clear, and so perhaps ideal for beginners, adhere rigidly to an individual psychoanalytic model and do not take much advantage of the group-specific possibilities clarified by the British schools. On the other hand, he has demonstrated more than any other the therapeutic power of well-selected groups where the therapist's analytic understanding is used but deliberately not made explicit, as in 'activity groups' for children and 'child-centred guidance groups' for parents.[13] These approaches extend group therapy to a vast population unsuited to analytic psychotherapy based on intellectual insight and are probably his greatest achievement.

A third influential school has been that of A. Woolf and his collaborator, E. Schwarz.[14] Their technique of 'psychoanalysis in groups' is, as the name implies, an attempt to use conventional Freudian psychoanalytic technique in a highly structured group situation often in conjunction with, or following on from, individual analysis or psychotherapy. They have shown a strong opposition to all techniques based on group processes but, as with the early resistance to conjoint family, and marital groups, this seems based more on an emotional investment in individual psychoanalysis than on any coherent objection arising from factual information.

As is so often the case, the pupils of the pioneers have been more open to cross-fertilization between the schools and have succeeded in integrating many ideas originally seen as irreconcilable by their teachers. Whitaker and Lieberman[15] have succeeded in developing from simple postulates a theory of group interaction which they have been able to submit to some measure of experimental demonstration. This approach, which has had a wide influence on both sides of the Atlantic (Whitaker is now domiciled in Britain and teaches on the Institute of Group Analysis courses), looks at group interaction rather as Ezriel does, as a compromise between a wish for some satisfaction and a fear of its consequences. They view solutions as being 'restrictive' or 'enabling' in so far as the compromises reached are either totally defensive or permit some adequate measure of satisfaction as well as safety.

H. Durkin has written what is probably the best over-view of the 'small group field'[16] with clear descriptions of the British as well as the American schools together with attempts to reconcile some of their ideas and demonstrate common principles. If I describe it as the ideal text for beginners this is not because it is over-simplified or limited, but rather because profound concepts are expressed with exceptional clarity.

Another therapist who has made important contributions to theory and has sought to integrate understanding of 'small-group processes' with knowledge from other areas, latterly including the 'encounter' group approach, is W. Schutz;[17, 18] he has also sought to reduce this knowledge to a set of basic postulates which would facilitate research and further theory construction.

Yalom,[19] a prominent American figure in the field of research, has reviewed the knowledge of small group processes, with a comprehensive summary of research findings to date, in his recent book.

Dominating figures tend to be followed by disciples who work out details within the framework laid down by the master, rather than questioning it or breaking new ground. This eventuality, so characteristic of the major schools of individual psychoanalysis, especially the Freudian, tends to be the case in the United Kingdom where the pupils of Bion, Foulkes, and others, have largely been content to follow in their footsteps. In the United States, by contrast, original contributions to theory and technique have arisen from such a large number of relatively independent practitioners that it is difficult to single out individuals and give proper credit. The greater proportion of these contributions has appeared in the *International Journal of Group Psychotherapy*, past issues of which well repay study.

Applications of the 'small-group' model

Slavson remains the main contributor in the use of group techniques for children, ranging from those based on activity only, suited particularly for children with behaviour disorders or who have limited tolerance for containing conflict, to situations permitting interpretation of behaviour and phantasies through play, mainly for more 'neurotic' problems. Ginott has written a valuable manual based mainly on Slavson's techniques but acknowledging other influences;[20] it is ideal for beginners because of its detailed advice on practical management, though theoretical issues are neglected. J. Anthony, a colleague of Foulkes who supervised my own early groups with children before he left Britain for the United States, has since described techniques with children based on a group-analytic model.[21] A recent review of child group therapy in the United States[22] notes despondently that 'the method has not kept pace with the rest of the field' and that 'one can count on the fingers of two hands the clinical centres offering the traditional method of activity group therapy as part of the treatment armamentarium', explaining this in terms of lack of sanction and of opportunities for training in the field. Until recently I have not been aware of child guidance clinics in Britain, other than my own, making group methods the main focus but this appears to be changing and since the Institute of Group Analysis began offering courses in this and other fields we hear of increasing use of these methods, one authority having sent all but one of its clinic staff for training. However, there has traditionally been extensive use of activity groups and social clubs by social work agencies, usually by relatively untrained staff, directed mainly to the under-privileged and socially deprived. Family service units have been particularly active in this way, and some of the new social service departments are beginning group work of a similar kind.

Group therapy with adolescents, in my experience the treatment of choice at this age and an immensely rapid and effective technique,[23] has also been relatively neglected. Slavson, again, has produced the most useful writings in the United States, already quoted, and J. Evans[24] has been successful in applying Kleinian concepts to hospitalized neurotic and to institutionalized delinquent groups of adolescents. The latter is particularly interesting in his comments on issues of authority and control. A comprehensive review of the work and literature in adolescent group psychotherapy has recently appeared.[25] Both children and adolescents in groups make considerable demands on the adult's resilience and real human capacities, and this challenge may be another important reason why use of these techniques is limited.

Groups for parents of disturbed children are much more widely employed on both sides of the Atlantic, probably because parents have traditionally been entrusted to social workers who on the whole seem to take more easily to group work both by temperament and by the nature of their training. The approaches range between two ends of a continuum. One end is exemplified by H. Durkin[26] who seeks to make the parents aware of their own problems by treating their initial preoccupation with their children's difficulties as a form of resistance; after this the situation is dealt with through interpretation as in any other small neurotic group. At the other extreme is Slavson's 'child-centred group guidance of parents'[27] where the focus is deliberately kept on the children and discussion of the parents' own neurotic difficulties and sexual or marital problems is not encouraged or interpreted. Both approaches complement each other, the second being more suited both to minor difficulties and also to highly defended and even borderline parents too disturbed to tolerate much insight into themselves. In the United Kingdom Thompson and Kahn[28] have recently provided a clear exposition of this group variable, ranging from group analysis or psychotherapy at one extreme, through group counselling to group discussion or education at the other. Skynner[29] has reviewed the use of group techniques generally in child psychiatry.

The need for the National Health Service in Britain to meet the public demand for psychotherapeutic help, rather than to allow this expensive skill to be restricted to those who can afford it, led to the application of group methods to a wide range of intelligence, social class, and diagnosis. Methods suitable for sophisticated, highly motivated, middle-class patients often proved inappropriate, and fruitful experimentation occurred with variations of technique. Deprived or socially inadequate individuals often responded better to more focused, supportive techniques based on increasing ego strength and coping ability rather than insight. Addicts, alcoholics, and delinquents, often found unsuitable for conventional small-group methods because of their poor impulse control and limited capacity to tolerate discomfort and persist in the face of difficulty, could sometimes respond to group influences while contained within an institution by legal sanctions, or when under pressure from others who had struggled successfully with similar problems. Scheidlinger[30] in a review of the development of group psychotherapy in the United States during the 1960s, has noted similar marked advances in flexibility of technique brought about through governmental interest in community mental health and the consequent setting up of comprehensive centres for this purpose with public funds.

Anthony[31] has also provided a stimulating review of the development of the small-group field over the past twenty-five years, emphasizing the widening range of technique. Given this more versatile and carefully matched provision, Pines[32] estimated that about eighty per cent of cases can be helped adequately as well by group as by individual psychotherapy, a figure similar to my own estimate for suitability for group therapy in children.

Large group situations

The facilitation of constructive total group interaction for therapeutic ends in mental hospitals, day hospitals and neurosis units will be dealt with more fully in other contributions to this volume, but this field – perhaps the one in which group techniques have had their widest and most fruitful application – has such important implications for other types of group work that a few comments are necessary. In Britain, Main,[33] Maxwell Jones,[34, 35] Martin,[36] Clark[37] and other pioneers of the 'therapeutic community' concept have had a profound effect on the functioning of mental hospitals both here and abroad (Clark's book is a clear summary of the field). There has been a tendency to formulate the rationale in such humanistic terms as democratic participation, sharing of responsibility, equality and mutual respect rather than in psychoanalytic or group-analytic terms, ideas whose simplicity and emotional appeal were no doubt vital to the revolution in staff attitudes achieved in their name but which often made a scientific appraisal of their achievements more difficult. Patient/staff collaboration has proved fruitful not only in resolution of tensions in the ward and in discussions regarding those aspects of treatment which rest on common human issues rather than technical knowledge, but also in such decisions, formerly seen as wholly the prerogative of the staff, regarding suitability for admission or discharge. A crucial factor has clearly been the exposure and resolution of staff tensions and conflicts in the total situation.

This has frequently led, however, to naïve beliefs that equality, permissiveness and abolition of the authority structure are in themselves curative principles. Leaving aside a small but vocal professional minority who are clearly acting out their own unsolved authority problems at their patients' expense there appears to be a marked inconsistency in the thought and practice of many leaders in this field over issues of leadership and authority, whereby the therapeutic and growth-facilitating possibilities of the group are correctly emphasized but where the crucial role of the leader in making this possible are denied or at least not given the attention and study needed, if such positive situations are to be repeated by others.

The missing factor, as in other forms of group theory, seems to be the concept of *development*. Rapoport,[38] who studied Maxwell Jones's first community experiment, demonstrated the oscillations between stability and instability characteristic of any situation where growth is taking place; and Christ[39] in a critique of Maxwell Jones's views, has pointed out that excessive abdication of authority leads automatically to episodes either of rebellion or of demoralization (increasing preoccupation with self-interest and ignoring of group goals – 'I'm all right, Jack!') which have the function of provoking the more active authority structure needed.

As in small groups, more attention is needed to the forms of organization appropriate to different developmental stages. It seems likely that this resembles that appropriate to the development of children in families – at first a highly supportive relationship where the need to idealize the staff is temporarily accepted; followed by stages of passive and then active rebellion where the staff need to provide a very firm, consistent structure without being provoked; and finally a more mutual, equal, democratic structure when this degree of responsibility can be tolerated.

Unfortunately, an adequate theory of large group interaction has scarcely begun to be developed, and what is available is mostly extrapolation of individual or small group theory. Certainly everything that happens in individual psychotherapy or small groups happens also in large groups, often in clearer and more striking form, but the large group appears to possess additional therapeutic possibilities of its own which are less dependent on verbal communication.[40] Understanding of these special properties is likely to be one of the next major developments in the field of group work, and recent experience suggests that much clarification may come from the previously neglected field of religion, with its millennia of experience in management of large groups for constructive ends.

Conjoint therapy with natural groups

It is from the field of conjoint therapy, where families or couples are treated together, often by a team of therapists, that ideas are emerging which promise to illuminate and eventually to integrate the other group approaches. Though the leading techniques and schools have developed relatively separately out of different theoretical backgrounds, and though there is much in common with previous group theory and practice, certain similar novel features have regularly appeared in theories and case transcriptions. Almost without exception, family group therapists evidence much more open, spontaneous behaviour and freedom in reporting their own reactions, in the course of family interviews, than is customary in 'conventional' individual or group work. One also finds particular attention given to issues of power and dominance hierarchies in the families dealt with and the therapists characteristically see themselves as in conflict with a pathological family communication system – a struggle they must win if therapeutic change is to be possible. Three recent reviews of the subject, by Sager,[41] MacGregor[41] and Beels and Ferber,[42] have dealt particularly well with these aspects, as well as providing comprehensive surveys and bibliographies. Beels and Ferber took the trouble to observe the work of the main family therapists as well as to read their writings and classified them into three categories according to their styles of interaction. The 'conductors' – Ackerman, Satir, MacGregor, Minuchin, etc. – take a highly active, controlling role and operate according to a clear and confidently held value system regarding openness of communication, and optimal family hierarchies. They openly confront the families with any attempt to cling to collusive systems of denial which protect the comfort of some members at the expense of the growth of the family as a whole. In contrast to these, the 'reactor-analysts' – Nagy, Framo, Friedman and others of the Philadelphia school, for example – tend to have backgrounds in intensive psychoanalytic work and operate by relinquishing their protected, detached roles and exposing themselves to the family pathology, whereby they begin themselves to suffer from the family problem. Their struggle is more subtle, and made more from the position of the child or patient than the 'supra-parental' role taken by the 'conductors', but in their own way they oblige the family to become aware of its hidden destructiveness by reporting its effect upon themselves and so fighting the tendency to denial in a different way. A third group, typified by the Palo Alto group of Bateson, Jackson, Weakland, Haley, and others, and labelled 'system purists' are influenced more by sociological ideas and system theory. They have little interest in intra-personal events and out-manipulate the families by, in effect, putting them in such subtle double-binds that they are automatically confronted by the contradictions between their self-descriptions and actual behaviour.

As might be expected, family sessions conducted in these ways tend to be highly charged emotionally and at times explosive, to a degree often alarming to those used to other techniques despite the apparent safety of the family approach. There can also be astonishing rapidity of change in the family system, especially where the emphasis is more on the re-patterning of the parental role-models through the therapist's example and identification processes, rather than through transference interpretations and self-conscious insight.

The challenging directness of these conjoint family interventions has had important implications for the professionals themselves, who not only tend to share the therapeutic task by extensive use of co-therapy, by pairs and teams, but also find it possible, and indeed often helpful to the families, for disagreements among staff members to be dealt with openly in the treatment session. It will be seen that there are interesting parallels to the situation in therapeutic communities, which in fact are midway between artificial and natural groups. The influence of these radically different methods is only just beginning to be felt within the field of 'conventional' group psychotherapy even in the United States, where almost all the research has been carried out. In Britain they have until lately received little interest though their use is now growing rapidly.

The influence of 'T-groups' and encounter techniques

Until the last decade the use of 'T-groups' (training groups) developed as a separate stream from group psychotherapy, in teaching institutions where the aim was to facilitate under-standing of group processes in normal people, with the object of improving the group functioning in the task-orientated organization from which the individuals came. The staff generally had backgrounds in teaching or social psychology, and there was little interchange at first with the clinical field. The basic feature of the T-group arose more or less by accident through the members of the original experiment, which was led by K. Lewin, asking to attend the subsequent staff discussion among the leaders of the groups. The leaders, at first apprehensive at sharing their own responses and thoughts with the members as the latter did with them and each other, found that they had stumbled on an immensely powerful learning situation; this feedback principle was subsequently built into the T-groups themselves.[43]

Increasing exchange has taken place between the T-group and clinical field over the last ten years, with modification of both. On the clinical side the influence has been towards greater emphasis on openness and frankness and the confrontation of patients with their 'here and now' interaction in the group, and towards greater willingness of the therapist to express his own responses to group phenomena. On the T-group side, there has been more concern with the individual's response and in California particularly, T-groups have tended to be seen as 'therapy for normals' – ways of enhancing human potential and experience and combating the increasing alienation of the individual from his personal and social roots. The relationship between these fields has recently been reviewed.[44, 45]

Both streams have contributed, together with other influences including current dissatisfaction among the young with such established values as competitive material 'success', naïve over-valuation of science, and emphasis on intellect and knowledge at the expense of emotion and the body, to the rise of the 'encounter' group. This is a label for a variety of group activities having in common such features as communication and exchange of feeling by physical contact, activity and non-verbal interaction generally; emphasis on intensity of present experience rather than intellectual understanding or concern with past or future; and a lack of artificial barriers so that leaders are expected to set an example of openness and emotional display rather than to remain detached. Interest in certain Eastern religious ideas, particularly Zen Buddhism, has also been an important feature contributing to the abolition of artificial barriers and hierarchies.

My direct experience of this type of group is limited, but I took the opportunity, together with my wife, to participate in a day-long 'encounter' event[46] when almost the whole team at the Esalen Institute in California (one of the most reputable and responsible organizations of this type) including W. Schutz, a prominent spokesman,[47] recently visited England to demonstrate their methods. As a participant, I was convinced that there were novel principles of great power and value to be learnt from this approach and found my own conducting of conventional small therapy groups considerably enhanced, mainly through becoming able to alternate between a detached, passive role which en-courages transference phantasy, and an active, involved role which both clarifies and illuminates transference phantasy through a kind of 'figure/ground' intensification and at the same time provides a model of spontaneous and risk-taking inter-action.

How much the advantages of encounter techniques can be transferred to other methods remains to be seen, but I was pleased to find that much of the value of the Esalen experience could be reproduced in a recent large group experiment at the Institute of Group Analysis, in fact without touching or other exercises. The central issue seems to be an open, spontaneous exchange in which the leaders share without abrogating responsibility or diminishing the feeling of safety. A number of leaders appears necessary because of the fear each one feels of unfamiliar experience, obliging him to block progress unless the leader-group as a whole prevents him.

Unfortunately, the anti-establishment emphasis of the encounter movement has encouraged a vast proliferation of 'do-it-yourself' groups led by unqualified people, with increasingly wild and irresponsible experimentation. It will be a matter of regret if this uncontrolled development, which is encouraged by a curiously naïve, messianic quality in the writings of some of its leading exponents, should discredit it and limit its valuable influence.

Future trends

Even in this brief outline, certain general trends will be apparent. Though these are more obvious in the newer modes of therapy, such as conjoint treatment of couples and families or encounter groups, similar tendencies are evident in the more established group techniques as well and I believe we are dealing more with basic changes in our view of what 'normality' comprises and what treatment is about, likely eventually to affect all modes of psychotherapy, rather than mere innovations in method.

First of all, we perceive an increasing emphasis on the non-verbal relative to the verbal; living experience relative to intellectual processes and reflective thought; the wisdom of the body relative to the knowledge of the mind; the 'here and now' relative to the 'there and then'; the capacity to perceive the psychology of others directly, by simply seeing what they are, relative to intellectual deduction from historical and other data; confrontation relative to interpretation; field and system theories relative to subject/object, cause/effect explanations; 'being' relative to 'doing', and so on. All these changes in bias reflect a basic move towards a more holistic view of understanding, derived from the totality of experience, rather than trust in intellect alone.

Second, we see an increasing dissatisfaction with relationships and social systems based on artificial, false, self-deceptive or arbitrary values. Though the therapist inevitably has special responsibilities and is entitled to a natural authority commensurate with these, he is no longer permitted a privileged position as regards self-exposure and vulnerability; indeed, he is expected at the same time to set an example, to be the first among peers in straightforwardness and acceptance of valid criticism. What now matters most is what he is, not what he knows. I believe this is especially relevant to the successful working through of the problem of real envy, which is so often avoided by the therapist either distancing himself behind a professional role, or pretending to be equal, in either case hiding *himself*.

The third trend, however, is not so much a move away from classical psychoanalytic technique as increased emphasis on a particular aspect of psychoanalytic theory, namely: developmental theory. Conjoint work with families has highlighted the fact that children, as Erikson[48] has so clearly demonstrated, develop through the mastery of a succession of challenges. All psychotherapy can be seen from this point of view, as the provision of special situations where those who failed in the original attempt can have a fresh opportunity. The task of the therapist, like that of the parent, is to provide both a situation where the challenge can be encountered once again, and support, guidance and understanding towards its mastery. These challenges can be viewed as group situations of increasing complexity[49] and while there is unfortunately not space to develop this theme here a glance at the stages in group development put forward by different authors shows, despite my oversimplification and the fact that different frames of reference are being used, a meaningful pattern in relation to child development (see table opposite).

Seen from this point of view, a group might be expected to work through a sequence of stages corresponding to normal child development, in each of which different management is required by the leader. This is exactly the case in 'closed' groups, where all members begin and end together, as for example in training groups which have a definite duration. One sees such a sequence, indeed, in any type of teaching situation – first respectful, expectant listening; later criticism and unconstructive argument;

	1	2	3
Freud	Oral	Anal	Oedipal/Genital
Bion	Dependency	Fight/Flight	Pairing
Bennis	Submissiveness	Rebellion/ Independence	Interdependence/ Intimacy
Schutz	Inclusion	Control	Affection
Foulkes and Anthony	Leader-centred/Interpersonal		Group-centred/ Group Analytic
Challenge in family group terms	Mother	Father	Couple

and finally real exchange and sharing – provided the teacher can tolerate the corresponding roles required in response. The situation is more complicated in the more usual 'slow-open' therapeutic group, where a slow turnover of membership takes place and the group itself is not time-limited; in such groups the membership is at different stages of development, as in a family, but the same principles apply even though they are more difficult to perceive.

One would like to believe that all the developments in our work described are rewards for our own increasing maturity as a profession, for if the above is valid we must be subject to a developmental process as well. It may be no accident that psychotherapy began in the form of intense, dyadic, highly unequal relationships from which even relatives were excluded; that we moved on to group situations where members could share with peers or 'siblings' but which were still highly structured in relation to the therapist as a parental figure, permitting little mutual exchange; and that we are now beginning to accept, at appropriate times, the necessity for greater equality, sharing and mutual challenge, as in a healthy family where the children are old enough to teach the parents something and the parents are mature enough to listen.

Short-term therapy

Cassie Cooper

Introduction

In a sense, short-term psychotherapy has always existed. Before it was given any kind of name, doctors used it, the church taught it as a form of alleviation and exorcism, and friends used it on friends. The psychological factors inherent in human anxiety, distress and suffering were unconsciously recognized and attempts were made to cope with them long before these processes were ever classified as 'therapy'. A good listener, a person who could offer encouragement, sympathy, reassurance and suggestion was often enough to give the sufferer a number of anatomically inspired solutions to his problem. A leg up, a helping hand, a stiff upper lip, a stout heart, a shoulder to cry on, making a clean breast of things, putting on a brave face and opening your eyes to the truth were just a few of the suggestions that were made to patient and friend alike.

Historically then, these adjuncts to mental health largely followed the medical tradition whose primary aim was then, as it is still today, to remove the symptom rather than deliberate about its causation. The unconscious use of psychosomatic allegory was not recognized. It is well known that some time after the middle of the nineteenth century Freud's early work was concerned with hypnosis. In his treatment of patients with hysterical symptoms, his primary aim then was symptom removal. It took a great many years for psychoanalysis to leave its imprint on the psychiatry of its time.

Prior to psychoanalysis

Prior to the application of psychoanalytic methods then, some form of supportive treatment was the usual method of therapy. The fundamental causes of the difficulty were not probed. In fact it was termed 'unhealthy' to delve too deeply and the patient was discouraged from talking at length about his feelings since this might upset him too much and he might feel too sorry for himself. Support of a kind could be variously expressed but it generally rested on the belief of the listener that the patient could surmount his difficulties. The Church would forgive him and give him absolution, the doctor would affirm his faith in the person as an individual and admire his positive efforts and even be there to reassure and medicate him when he failed. In each case the listener was using his authority, exploiting it to give the patient an external crutch: his belief in the patient's ability to recover. Fromm has since called this a symbiotic relationship in which each person satisfies a neurotic need in the other.

Discovery of advantages of short-term analysis

Ferenczi and Rank were among the first to turn their attention to the decreasing therapeutic effectiveness of the lengthy psycho-analysis. Rank pointed out that it was easier for the patient to talk about the past because it was not what was happening in the present. He was interested in the submission to authority which is present in analysis and instituted techniques designed to challenge the patient and enable him to assert his own will. In short, he emphasized that the relationship of therapist and patient was not merely a repetition of past relationships but a new relationship which the patient was trying to treat in the old way.

Ferenczi's attempt to stress another aspect of the analyst–patient relationship is well known. He maintained that an important factor in therapy was the experiencing of a new relationship which was both accepting and loving. In the security of this atmosphere of tolerance and acceptance the analyst could be a different person from the parent in his attitude to the patient. In this new situation the patient could then become more fully aware of the frustrations of his earlier childhood and adolescent experiences.

Recent developments

More recently there have been Wolpe's early claims that neurotic symptoms could be successfully treated without recourse to the personality problems of the patient. These original theories have now been considerably modified but they have, nevertheless, aroused a new interest in the therapeutic function aimed at symptom relief. Malan's experiences in brief psychotherapeutic work have suggested that almost all of the lengthy processes which play an overwhelming part in the development of the analytical technique can, in certain cases, be counteracted and avoided. More direct interpretations of transference manifestations can be used to simplify the problems of resistance, dependence, negative transference and termination. A frank discussion with the patient on the limitations of the therapy, together with the formation of a plan for a limited therapeutic aim can be accomplished within the techniques of a therapy which can still be described as 'brief'.

Suffice to say that notwithstanding the enormous advances made during the last hundred years in the treatment and understanding of the neuroses there is a continuous evolvement of problems and needs which are pressing and still have to be solved. More recently the developmental function of psychotherapy has been stressed by Winnicott[1] who envisaged the provision of a 'facilitating environment' for patients which would allow the normal maturation processes to take place in the patient's ego development. Others have emphasized the point that the development of an individual does not take place in isolation but in the continuous process of relating to persons and objects both external and internal. Guntrip had favoured the theory that if progress in personal development is to be made during a psychotherapeutic relationship, both the transference relationship and, at the same time, reality relationship of patient and therapist are of equal importance.

It is as a partial reaction to the increasing interest which is being shown in the developmental aspects of psychotherapy, that therapists who are psychodynamically orientated or otherwise are now trying to improve their therapeutic function by looking for techniques which could lead to better and quicker results in treatment.

The role of transference

So much has been written on the role of transference in psychotherapy. It is still the chief means available for making unconscious feelings in the patient available to him. Psychoanalytic theory consists of a series of such personal discoveries and it is with each discovery that there is a favourable evolvement of the personality in the direction of health. The dynamic use of the transference as a therapeutic tool leads to a more durable personality evolvement.

Whilst in most other forms of psychotherapy the transference is used in another way. In the short-term therapy, no attempt is made to remove the irrational feelings of over-evaluation of the therapist or indeed of the irrational fear of disapproval. These feelings are instead utilized in giving force to positive playback. The holding up of a mirror. This is what you are feeling, doing, saying with me.

Three necessary conditions for therapy

Carl Rogers[2, 3] formulated three attitudinal conditions which he held as the necessary and sufficient conditions for therapy. If these three conditions were fulfilled, effective therapy could take place regardless of the technique or method the therapist was using and regardless of what orientation he may have. *Congruence* between the patient and the therapist's experience of his thoughts and his behaviour. *Empathy* with which the therapist was able to sense the meaning expressed by the client and relay this understanding and meaning back to the client, and, thirdly, *unconditional positive regard*. A warm and positive feeling for the patient and an ability to convey a sense of valuing the patient, regardless of whether his patient's feelings may be of benefit or not.

The choice of the patient

Fromm and Reichmann were not enthusiastic in their approach to short-term psychotherapy. They recognized that there are, of course, many therapeutic methods which set themselves the limited goal of curing patients' symptoms and promoting their social adjustment. Those which aimed for a limited amount of focal insight for their patients could, no doubt, justify their usage in the treatment of certain types of patients. These patients would have to be carefully selected as to diagnosis and personality.

Therapists who practised these short-term methods were warned that there was a danger that their choice of method and their selection of patient may well be determined by a personal pessimism of which they were unaware, or by the gloomy outlook which they harboured with regard to the prognoses and general potentialities of the mentally sick.

The aim of therapy

Most textbooks state that the aim of the joint endeavour in which a psychotherapist engages with his patient if he works with intensive dynamic therapy should be the following, regardless of the school to which the therapist belongs: the patient is expected to become free from mental symptoms, especially from excess anxiety and free to utilize his innate tendencies towards personal growth and maturation, unhampered by greed, envy or jealousy; he should also be free for a creative expansion of his personality and for striving for self-realization; he should be able to give and accept love and tenderness and to form durable relationships of emotional and physical intimacy.

A proper choice of therapy – psychoanalysis versus short-term therapy

If all this cannot be accomplished, once and for all, even by a full successful course of psychotherapy, is the short-term therapy a depressed attempt to come to terms with a patient who for one reason or another has to make do with skimmed milk whilst another gets the cream? In 1965, Wolberg[4] echoed this depressive approach when asking himself how our present-day formulations affected one of the major decisions confronting any therapist at the beginning of treatment: his choice between short-term versus long-term therapy or classical analysis. The question itself implied that the therapist (or the patient) was in a position to make the choice. Unfortunately, this was rarely the case. Whereas a therapist lacking proper psychoanalytic training would of necessity resort to one of the briefer forms of treatment – analytic or otherwise – the duly trained psychoanalyst would, on the other hand, be led to ignore the possibility of brief therapy in preference for long-term 'medical tax reduction' until insight was achieved (i.e. phase out over a period what could in some cases be dealt with fairly rapidly). It was hoped that practical limitations or financial considerations of this order would not tip the balance in favour of one decision or another. Unfortunately, more compelling clinical criteria to determine the therapist's course of action were difficult to formulate.

He went on to say that a judicious decision should be based on a tentative appraisal of the patient's personality, of his ego resources or ego-strength, on the evaluation of his capacity to cope with stress and on his response to interpretation. In short, he felt that the decision required a preliminary trial analysis to say nothing of making allowances for the patient's social class, solvency or income bracket.

In certain circumstances, it could be a useful strategy to assume that every patient, irrespective of diagnosis, would respond to short-term therapy unless he proved himself refractory to it. Put another way, the decision should be contingent on the patient's capacity to derive more than temporary benefits from the existential shift effected in the opening phase of the treatment (i.e. the change in life style which occurs immediately the patient decides to come for therapy).

The question is whether the shift is capable of liberating constructive forces in the individual, propelling him towards further spontaneous growth and whether it succeeds in setting up chain reactions that become self-perpetuating. Does the shift jolt the patient out of his regressive form of adaptation or to a more progressive form of adaptation? The patient's favourable response to short-term psychotherapy was by no means due to the myth-induced existential shift alone, characteristic of the opening phases of treatment, it should be based on the proper dynamic understanding of his problem. This serves as a guide for the therapist's active intervention without the need for deeper analytic interpretations which would, at any rate, go beyond the patient's comprehension.

Nevertheless, re-education in a minor key is an important feature of the brief contact. The patient's quick response to the procedure would be due to the limited goal set for him and for the relatively low intensity of his conflicts.

Every school of psychoanalysis prescribes a deliberate set of techniques and procedures which tends to glamorize its practitioners and gives them the gloss of a somewhat special professional status. This is true equally, for instance, of the psychiatrist, the psychoanalyst, the individual psychologist, the group psychotherapist and the counsellor.

The role of the therapist and changing factors
Everyone knows that the psychonalyst must be trained in the art of analysis and his function is to analyse his patient. The analyst is paid for his work by the patient and during the treatment he is placed on a couch or a chair with the analyst by his side or slightly behind him. It is not expected that the patient can analyse the therapist, or that the therapist should pay him for being a patient. Similarly, too, we have definite patterns for the conduct of the group therapist. It is not merely left to chance. A doctor can undertake certain roles in which his work is more easily distinguished from that of an optician, a dentist or a surgeon, although even here where the separation of these roles is only a matter of degree, there is no such thing as uninvolvement.

In the psychotherapies, however, it is well nigh impossible to separate the personality of the therapist from the techniques and skills which are used in the work. The personality of the therapist is the skill.

If it can be accepted that the right kind of therapy depends on the right kind of therapist then it can be seen at the outset that the short-term therapy is doomed to failure if it tries to be what it is not: a poor relation of psychoanalysis. Any technique of short-term therapy must, therefore, be based on the difference between it and long-term analysis, and particularly to a conscious opposition to the use of the word long-term and reference to the lengthening factors which are part of the classic analysis. It represents a calculated step away from the sacrosanct atmosphere of the couch and the passivity of the analyst. In most techniques of short-term therapy all these factors such as the use of the couch, the sense of leisure, the acceptance of material as it is presented, are changed.

The substitution of the chair for the couch creates an entirely different atmosphere. The patient is no longer talking to a vacant space, he is talking to the therapist, therapy then more naturally becomes part of a dialogue in which the therapist tends to take a more active part. So the short-term therapy tends to make for more active handling of the patient's material. A different aspect of this activity is the abandonment of therapeutic perfectionism, the setting up of a limited goal for the therapy which is planned from the outset of the treatment. The goal is reached by guiding the patient through selection of the material presented. This idea of the limited aim is one that is most common to most forms of short-term psychotherapy. But it must be stressed that 'although limited aims were sometimes stated in terms of therapeutic results, what was most commonly practised was a limited aim in terms of working through briefly a given aspect of psychopathology and, in effect, seeing what result would follow'.[5] In these circumstances the therapeutic result is often much more far reaching than could ever have been expected.

The extent of the time limit
The essential technique in this limited therapy is to convey to the patient that this is a short-term procedure. This can be done in a number of ways. 'I suggest that we go ahead with treatment once a week for a few months and then see what we've achieved', or 'I would like to see you for three or four times', and in both cases 'At the end of that time we can take a look at what has been happening. If it looks as though you need more therapy then you can be transferred to a longer form of treatment.' The sense of finality can be avoided by the suggestion that although the regular

interviews have come to an end, it will still be possible to return at any time for occasional sessions if the patients need further help.

At this point, it could be asked – when does therapy cease to be short-term? After six months and twenty-five interviews, short-term dynamic work would surely be impeded by growing feelings of dependence.

Rogers felt that a patient who was treated correctly should be able to take charge of his own affairs after six to fifteen contacts. If the maladjustment was not severe, and with a patient who was not deeply neurotic, two, four or six contacts were felt to be enough for the patient to find the help he needed.

Malan gives the figure of from ten to forty sessions but it is obvious that any definition of length must depend wholly on the therapist's own experience of what gives a satisfactory result.

The definition of short-term therapy: method and practice
To recapitulate, the short-term therapy differentiates from analysis in three major ways. Firstly, it has a limited aim which, secondly, the patient is made clearly to understand right from the initial interview, and thirdly the therapist keeps in his mind an aim on which his therapy is based. This aim is kept clearly in view and the therapist uses selective methods of either drawing attention to or completely neglecting the material which the patient is bringing to him. This implies an active rather than a passive role.

In the short-term treatment process, the therapist works quickly to establish rapport with the patient and some measure of equality, warmth and compassion. Obviously this early work depends for its success entirely on the successful interaction of the patient and the therapist. The therapist has, at the same time, to assess the patient's psychological condition and get an idea of what he is like and what he would like to be.

The therapist must give the patient confidence that he is the one who can help. He must resist the temptation to conduct the interview as a conversation, substituting his views for those of the patient, and resist interrupting the patient in an attempt to relieve anxiety – anxiety which will increase as therapy proceeds. He must resist the use of jargon and knowledge as a means of increasing his prestige at the expense of the client.

In helping the patient to reach a better understanding of himself in relationship with others, the therapist must discourage dependency which is harmful in brief contact, and concentrate instead on the adult parts of the patient's personality. In the limited-aim therapy with interviews given once a week or even once a fortnight, the incentive to work really hard quickly brings forward feelings of emerging achievement.

As treatment progresses, the therapist becomes aware of many problems and it is not easy to effectively select what is the most pressing anxiety. The patient is bringing the essence of his problem; his anxiety comes to the front right at the beginning, he is implying what he feels is wrong in the very first moments of the interview, if only we had the instinct to recognize it.

For example, if the initial interview with the patient is concerned with taking the life history in free association or in a more formal account, the therapist listens and encourages now and then. 'Tell me about your family.' 'Tell me what you feel is wrong.' As a minimum to be achieved, the relinquishing by the patient of these details of his social and medical history is, in itself, a valuable part of the therapy.

Many psychotherapists will have had the experience of having seen a patient only once, presumably for what could be termed a diagnostic interview, and of hearing at some later date of the way in which this one interview helped the patient concerned to resolve some of his difficulties. In spite of this, the diagnostic interview is still considered by some as an adjunct to treatment.

There is a therapeutic reaction when one is thought to be understood. The childish part of the patient can project his anxiety quite quickly to the therapist. This can be formulated and given back in a more moderate form. The patient can then take back into himself an anxiety that can be contained.

This form of insightive therapy is used in varying degrees according to the needs of the patient and the time available. If, for instance, the patient can only come for three months twice a

week, or if only for three or four interviews once a week or once
a fortnight, the therapist could plan his programme of treatment
accordingly. In brief therapy the patient must often be given
more insight than he can utilize at that moment in time, with the
hope that he eventually will be able to make some use of it. This
is an extreme example where the emphasis is on interpretation.
But at this point or at some later date, the client can choose to
return for further therapy to the same or to another therapist.
He or she is then free to choose from the ever extending range of
therapies available, which can graduate from a psychoanalytically
orientated psychotherapy to a mixture of support and advice.

With both patient and therapist aware of the limited time set
for the therapy, it is obvious that brief work of this kind must
attract more of the childishness and inadequacy than is shown in
longer-term work. Unresolved problems of infancy will be
brought out. The therapist is aware of the transference and the
feelings it invokes in himself but it is his job to use it for understanding of the patient rather than for open interpretation.
Understanding of the counter transference and transference is
implicit for interpretation which can be verbalized as 'now what
is happening here'. It is possible to make the patient realize that
his infantile feelings are overt. 'This is a part of you that hasn't
grown up.'

It is both dangerous and ineffectual at this time to interpret
unconscious material which cannot be used in later referral.
The short-term therapist is not attempting to make a deep
personality change in the character of his patient. Rather, the
therapist can only admit to himself alone: 'The person makes me
feel in a certain way.'

The presentation to the patient is of a working relationship
rather than a re-enactment of earlier childhood deprivation and
behaviour. If the relationship must have some attitudinal basis, it
can be put back to that of an uncle or aunt or close family friend.
But we are here to work.

For example, a woman client had recently been promoted to
the post of departmental supervisor in a large central telephone
exchange: a position of great responsibility since her department

received the great bulk of overseas work. She had been working as a senior telephonist for over ten years at the same exchange and there was no evidence of any previous marked difficulty in her working relationships. She had functioned adequately until her promotion when she became depressed and quite unable to cope with the demands that the job made of her.

Without a doubt one could make a profitable and exhaustive study of this patient's life history and personality problems. She was, however, referred for therapy at a time when she was in imminent danger of losing not only her hard-won promotion but her means of livelihood.

In this case, progress was rapidly made by concentrating on the presenting problem: her irrational reaction to her promotion and its responsibility. After some initial difficulty, Miss X was able to tell me that she was a practising lesbian. She had felt it necessary to keep this part of her life quite separate from her working situation. The majority of telephonists employed at the exchange were women. My client was sure that she had, up till now, successfully negated any attraction she may have felt for her fellow workers. But now that she had been put 'in control' as it were in her new role as supervisor, would this upset the delicate balance she had achieved and put her out of control in her sexual relationships?

Miss X had allowed herself to believe that she could really function as two separate people and at these two conflicting levels in her relationships with women. She was able to understand that the actual promotion had, in fact, made no difference to her sexual identity, and that she had been functioning previously as a lesbian and that this had obviously been accepted by the people around her. It did not necessarily follow that a change of work role would mean a change of sexual role or turn her into a marauder of innocent women – unless that was what she really wanted to do.

After six interviews which took place over a period of three weeks, Miss X was able to make considerable progress in the way she regarded her lesbianism. The transference was utilized, in this instance, to eliminate the irrationalities. It did not increase her dependency. She re-asserted her functioning at work and is still doing quite well.

From a spectrum of problems which reel from the psychological to the practical, the therapist must, therefore, decide which of these are not relevant to the progress of his therapy. This process can be summarized as follows:

1. Whilst retaining the original symptom presentation, relating the features of each case and classifying them into what is and what is not a problem.
2. Recognizing the limits of the therapy and discussing this with the patient.
3. Observing what has not been mentioned.
4. Reinforcing the coping elements and the propensity for self-understanding.
5. Maintaining a feeling capacity and not intellectualizing.

The initial moment of any psychotherapeutic relationship occurs when an unhappy, maladjusted, perplexed and disturbed person comes to a therapist. What happens at this original point is the primary responsibility of the therapist. How the patient comes, whether he is sent or whether he comes of his own accord are other problems which have to be recognized.

Does the short-term therapist have to assume an Emma Lazarus-like approach to his patients – a kind of 'give me your tired, your homeless, etc., etc.'. Indeed it seems to be a common assumption. An American lady therapist was described in a newspaper article: 'She recognized the potential of those whose problems often involved over-conflict with the conventional restraints of our society – the homosexual, the single woman and the schizophrenic. Consequently, she attempted the treatment of many who were rejected as hopeless by other therapists.'

Since there has been very little systematic research into the problem of selection criteria, there still remains the pressure to accept for therapy anyone who presents themselves as wishing to receive it. This is done regardless of the type of disturbance or the severity of their symptoms. Psychotherapists in general are hesitant to differentiate between those patients who would benefit from either a long or a short term of therapy. Without regard for the diagnosis, insistence is placed on daily treatment sessions and as a consequence of this many psychotherapists find themselves committed for years with a very few patients.

If it is possible for psychotherapists to free themselves from the rigid belief that anything other than a full-scale analysis must always be second best, then it is possible such lengthy processes can, in certain cases, be by-passed or avoided.

Malan gives the following as his criteria for the acceptance of short-term therapy patients:

1. They were willing and able to explore their feelings.
2. They were judged to be capable of working within a therapeutic relationship based on interpretation.
3. The therapist's ability to feel that he understands the patient's problem in dynamic terms.
4. The therapist's ability to formulate some kind of circumscribed therapeutic plan.

He goes on to say that ill and neurotic patients can often be helped and that lasting improvements in neurotic behaviour patterns can be obtained in patients who have moderately severe and long-standing illnesses. These effects can be obtained with the use of a technique which closely resembles psychoanalysis and deals with most of the same material. He adds that such a technique carries few dangers if properly used.

In recent years, interest having extended from the pathological to the normal, there have accrued a great many professional individuals who spend a considerable proportion of their time in interviewing people: clergymen, marriage guidance counsellors, probation officers, psychiatrists, psychologists, social workers, student counsellors, teachers and university tutors, and there are many more.

There are various names which may be attached to such interviewing processes, but all in all they attempt to bring about some constructive attitudinal change in the client and would hope to leave the individual with some better form of adjustment to his or her presenting problem.

All psychological methods have a common aim in attempting to understand and combat the excess anxieties of their patients.

But it is the common lot of us all, whether we are mentally healthy or disturbed, to experience at times the mild anxieties which are an inherent part of our cultural system. These mild anxieties are part and parcel of every personality pattern and are not necessarily detrimental but can be utilized in a constructive way. It is in this area that the delineation between what is normal and pathological is very ill-defined.

Conclusion

'Counselling' is the word which is in increasing usage, more particularly in educational circles, in an attempt to define the help which can be offered in relationship to such disturbances of the norm. Some forms of counselling can, therefore, be seen to have much in common with the psychotherapeutic approach to short-term therapy with a disturbed individual.

It can be said that the most intensive and successful counselling has much in common with intensive short-term psychotherapy. Carl Rogers has said that acute observation was the most desirable characteristic in a counsellor. He contended that anyone could become a counsellor if acutely observant of human beings. In this period of evolvement there is obviously a time and place for all the forms of short-term therapy that have been mentioned. It is important, however, at this point to re-emphasize that since the personality of the therapist is, in all methods, the instrument with which he works to come to an understanding of his patient, it is essential that he should have made a sincere analytic effort to understand his own character. Blind spots in the instrument could have consequences of a very serious nature.

Day therapy

Richard Meyer

In 1946 Joshua Bierer in London and D. Ewen Cameron in Montreal, independently, opened the first psychiatric day hospitals. The purpose of these was to provide a therapeutic environment during working hours for psychiatric patients who were too sick to work; who needed more treatment than could be given in occasional out-patient interviews; and who did not, in their opinion, need total residential care.

Pinel[1] initiated the humane treatment of mentally sick patients in 1793 by the removal of chains from the inmates of the Bicêtre Hospital in Paris. Tuke[2] and Conolly[3] in Great Britain and Dick in the USA were other early pioneers of humane methods of treatment in asylums. It was not, however, till 1949 that Bell, in Scotland, established the first 'open-door' mental hospital, in which patients although residing in the institution, were not locked in. Day, as opposed to residential, treatment was a considerable innovation.

There are many disadvantages in residential treatment. In extreme instances if the hospital is run in an authoritarian way and with an inadequate number of staff, patients may develop, imposed on their original illness, an 'institutional neurosis'.[4] This is characterized by extreme apathy, deterioration in personal habits, a humble posture and shuffling gait. The condition should be distinguished from such physical illnesses as organic dementia, Parkinson's disease (both due to physical changes in the brain) and thyroid deficiency. In most cases the symptoms will disappear if the patient is encouraged by nurses to become more active and is given more contact with the outside world. But even in a modern residential hospital, with an enthusiastic staff and active methods of occupational treatment and group psycho-therapy, the patient is insulated from the normal tensions of living in his family and working in the outside community, and he may well become dependent on the protected environment of the institution. This militates against improvement. The danger of dependency is much less in a day hospital.

Selection of patients

The selection of suitable patients for day treatment depends largely on the attitude of the staff and of the surrounding com-munity.

An architecturally perfect day hospital was built near a large town in Northern Europe, with the idea that it should cater for the sort of patient who was being admitted to a large, old-fashioned asylum many miles away. However, the director of the new hospital was anxious about admitting patients who might attempt suicide; he also did not want obviously schizophrenic people who might cause adverse comment from the local middle-class community. He had similar qualms about delinquents. Therefore, instead of reducing the need for beds in the asylum, the new day hospital tapped a fresh supply of local patients, mainly mildly depressed and anxious housewives who had previously been treated at home by general practitioners. Sicker patients were still sent away to the old asylum.

By contrast Bierer,[5] in a similar middle-class district in London, has successfully treated a wide range of neurotic, psychotic and sociopathic patients in a day hospital and without objection from neighbours. There still remains a small number of patients – drug addicts, some recidivist delinquents, deeply depressed or wildly manic patients – who cannot benefit – at least initially – from the open conditions of a day hospital. But vastly greater numbers of patients are suitable for such conditions than the medical profession had imagined twenty-five years ago. It is a fact that many gross signs of emotional disturbance disappear, if they are not treated by total institutionalization or punishment.

It should be emphasized that the day hospital movement started before the introduction of chlorpromazine, the first of the modern tranquillizing drugs, in 1952; though it is possible that the use of such drugs has increased the number of patients able to benefit from open conditions.

The day hospital as a therapeutic community

Day hospitals vary widely in structure. At one extreme there can be a rigidly hierarchical community in which the potential of patients helping each other is ignored and where the patients are occupied in simple repetitive tasks. This could be called an occupational centre rather than a day hospital, and such centres deal mainly with very chronic patients.

At the other extreme is the type of community originally created by Maxwell Jones[6] in a residential hospital for psychopaths. This would be 'a small unit with face-to-face gatherings of all members, social analysis of events, opening of communications, flattening of the authority pyramid and blurring of roles'. Clark[7, 8] has called this the 'therapeutic community proper' and has differentiated it from the 'therapeutic community approach' of 'increased activity, freedom and responsibility for all patients in the hospital'; a less definitely democratic structure, but one which is probably more suited to a community containing a number of psychotic patients who need more active guidance than do neurotic or psychopathic patients. Even with sociopaths in a residential setting it has been suggested that the less mature members may be confused by a permissive and democratic regime, just as much as the more mature members may rebel against one which deprives them of initiative. Crocket[9] calls the 'therapeutic community proper' a 'psychotherapeutic community' and defines it in its fullest form as 'a consciously contrived large group of people made up of patients and staff, to which both patients and staff are expected to relate for therapeutic purposes to the maximum degree possible, rather than to individual therapists'. This is less immediately gratifying to many patients and therapists than individual or small-group treatment but may ultimately help the patients more, if they are able to become mature enough to relate to the larger group.

A standard feature of the less hierarchical community is a daily meeting of staff and patients. Today common recurrent themes for discussion are rejection, violence, sexuality, dependence and independence, staff friction and relations with outside bodies.

Patients and often staff feel that they misunderstand each other's needs, or the whole community may feel rejected by outside bodies.

At first the community is concerned with 'how to stop, prevent or punish violence'. Later, 'to understanding why it occurred'.

Sexuality tends at first to be discussed in abstract terms – such as the place of sexuality in religion or in marriage; later more in relation to feelings between members of the community.

Dependence–independence conflicts may concern imminent discharge of patients or anxiety about those who, though useful to the community, seem to have become too dependent on the hospital. The staff often have ambivalent feelings towards these steady members of the group.

Staff divisions can be exploited by patients and it is important for staff to be conscious of their differences of attitude.

Public relations between the small community and community at large should not be neglected. Although complaints about outside authorities can be interpreted in terms of projection it can also be useful to invite members of those bodies to the meeting so that they can express the reality situation.

Occupational therapy

Only a small part of the day is passed in formal group or individual psychotherapy. Eating takes up another small part. Occupational therapy, which has in the popular mind become associated with the themes of 'making baskets' or 'killing time' or with direct retraining for work, in a psychiatric day hospital needs to be a skilfully devised programme catering for a wide range of emotionally disturbed patients.

Domestic chores – A small amount of domestic work has to be done by the community, for example, washing up crockery after meals. This is a perennial focus of contention but potentially an activity which can be discussed and manipulated in a therapeutic way. A pile of dirty dishes arouses the anxiety of those staff who have doubts about the value of permissive, non-directive methods of treatment. This anxiety is inflamed if important visitors, such as members of the hospital management committee, are critical. Staff also have to consider whether or not they should share in the work.

The patients' committee can experiment with practices such as a rota for this task – but quickly finds that younger – and more sociopathic members do not do their share of the work which is either not done, or done resentfully by older members, who could often be viewed as over-conscientious. Small improvements, such as more dishes being washed more often by a greater number of patients are not easily noticed. The problem can be avoided by employing paid domestics, but then other chores, such as signing a list for meals or tidying rooms after use (which like washing-up concern food and dirt) will become focal points of conflict in the community.

Drama – A secure and very structured activity is that of play reading. At the other extreme is psychodrama, which involves the acting of a patient's particular problems in relationships. Staff and other patients collaborate with the patient as members of his family, his friends and enemies. Roles can be interchanged. Psychodrama may generate much emotional disturbance which needs skilled intervention by the staff member directing the drama. In between these extremes is sociodrama.[10] The themes in sociodrama are not so intimate as those in psychodrama but they are ones obviously relevant to a majority of the community, such as being interviewed for a job, or dealing with a domineering employer. Different staff and patients can re-enact the same scene which is then discussed.

Music – Patients can listen – more or less passively – to gramophone records and the music can be discussed. More active forms of music therapy might involve groups of people clapping in contrary rhythms together, or free yelling of a vowel sound up and down the scale.[11]

Painting – Painting, too, can be used in varied ways. The therapist can require naturalistic representation of objects – teaching the patients to observe more accurately. Or he can encourage free expression. The benefit of the creative art itself may remain the main point of the activity though some therapists interpret the content of the painting and encourage other patients to comment.

Patients and staff can work together on, for example, a large collage, as a group project.

Other activities – These vary according to the experience of the therapist and facilities available. Boxing, for example, has been used as a form of therapy for disturbed adolescents. The withdrawn boy can be encouraged to be less controlled and more aggressive and the psychopath to gain more control. This clearly needs very skilled supervision.

Resistances to occupational therapy – Resistances may occur to any form of therapy. Those more specific to occupational therapy include: 1) the idea that occupation is only meaningful if paid, 2) the idea that work can only be an escape from solving interpersonal relationships, 3) over-valuation of verbal communication if topical analysis of problems is opposed to activity, 4) negative attitudes to anyone in the role of a teacher.[12]

Other alternatives to full residential treatment

Bierer, as well as introducing day hospitalization also advocated that selected patients should be treated by night or weekend hospitalization. These patients could continue to work but would be to some degree freed from home tensions during the period of treatment. This would consist of intensive group and/or occupational therapy – sometimes combined with chemical abreaction.

Valuable supportive psychotherapy can be offered in Therapeutic Social Clubs. The members of these clubs are mainly patients and ex-patients. They are supervised by psychiatric staff. The surroundings are often more congenial to a psychiatric patient than are those of 'normal' clubs. There is less need for the patient to keep up appearances and greater tolerance of morose, bizarre and aggressive behaviour.

Psychiatrists should be aware of other special club facilities which are unconnected with psychiatry but which may suit some patients better. For example there are, in large towns, clubs run for widows, divorcees, ex-prisoners, drug addicts, homosexuals and also for specific age groups such as Youth Clubs and the Eighteen Plus clubs for people between eighteen years and thirty years old.[13]

Day hospitals for disturbed children

Several day hospitals for children have been described. In her unit for autistic children at the Marlborough Day Hospital Dundas[14] directly supervises a team of selected voluntary workers so that each child has a one-to-one relationship with an adult for the five hours daily spent in the unit. Intensive social work is done with the parents. This use of suitable voluntary workers, adequately supported by professional staff, seems to be a realistic way of tackling the enormous problem of mental health.[15, 16]

Allied developments in the prison system

The harmful effects of long-term residence in a 'total institution' are equally severe in the penal system. Even if rehabilitation or psychiatric treatment is practised prisoners are deprived of the opportunity of earning adequate wages; their families need costly support by the State; they mix with criminals often more experienced than themselves; and lack of incentive to behave in a responsible manner fortifies immature behaviour. Inadequate recidivists often deliberately commit offences in order to return to the only secure environment they have known, where childish dependence is encouraged.[17]

Since 1963, Periodic Detention Work Centres have been established in New Zealand. The sentence of periodic detention entails weekend (and usually, also for one evening a week) attendance with the aim of being taught, during these leisure hours, how to make more constructive use of free time, through a full programme of activities, with emphasis placed on work both within and without the centre, particularly on community projects. The maximum period to be served is twelve months.

In Belgium, weekend imprisonments and 'semi-detention' or night imprisonment have since 1963 been available as alternatives, for selected offenders, otherwise sentenced to short-term imprisonment. The offences for which these types of intermittent custody are most frequently ordered are drunken-driving, battery, larceny and public drunkenness. Weekend detention is also practised in Holland and West Germany.

Bierer in his earliest publications noted the value of the day hospital itself as a halfway house between prison and ordinary life for certain neurotic criminals. It is preferable that a worker from the day hospital concerned should make regular contact with the prisoner before the date of his release.

Results of day treatment

Farndale in 1961[18] surveyed the day hospital movement in Great Britain. He confirmed that the cost of upkeep per patient was about one-third of the cost in a residential hospital. Only one shift of personnel was needed instead of three and only one meal instead of three. He noted, however, that there was some transfer of costs by day hospitals to other parts of the Health Service or National Economy – e.g. in the case of prescription or transport. He also noted that sometimes day hospital treatment should be seen as a more satisfactory form of out-patient treatment rather than an alternative to in-patient treatment.

In a Pilot Survey of fifteen British Day Hospitals conducted in 1969[19] the overall length of attendance was one-third for less than a month, one-half for less than two months, four-fifths for less than six months, one-eighth for over a year and only one-fortieth for over two years.

Herz *et al*[20] followed up patients for whom either day or residential treatment seemed equally feasible, who were assigned randomly for one or other treatment. They claim that there was clear evidence of the superiority of day treatment over residential treatment.

Richards[21] studied the quality of change in very disabled

patients who had attended a local authority day centre for the mentally ill. Only eleven per cent of patients were known to have worked steadily after leaving the day centre but sixty-six per cent remained in contact with psychiatric or social work agencies. She comments that this apparent failure of purpose was offset by the improved quality of life which many of those who had attended the clinic experienced.

The usefulness of day hospitals and day centres seems to have been established.[22, 23, 24] The present trend in Great Britain is for the vast mental hospitals, built outside main towns in the last century, to be replaced by some small residential and very many day units, more appropriately scattered through the country.

Psychotherapy outside
the National Health Service

Malcolm Pines

An article on psychotherapy outside the National Health Service must also consider the psychotherapy which is available within the National Health Service. A brief survey of the similarities and differences in the types of psychotherapies found in these two situations will help to make the discussion of psychotherapy outside the National Health Service more meaningful.

We can use the term psychotherapy in two ways. Firstly as a general term covering the establishment of a relationship with a patient and then using this relationship to support, to assist or to persuade the patient to alter his behaviour in the direction of what we consider to be a healthier mode of adjustment. In this general sense a great deal of psychotherapy is practised by psychiatrists, general practitioners, psychiatric social workers, nurses and many other people within the National Health Service. Using the term psychotherapy in a more specific sense, as a specialized method of treatment by psychological methods, practised by a person with a professionally recognized specialist training in that discipline, then far more psychotherapy is practised outside the National Health Service than within it.

This article addresses itself to the following points:

1. What forms of specialized psychotherapy are available inside and outside the National Health Service?
2. How are these services distributed?
3. What standards of professional training in specialized psychotherapy can be sought for by the doctor or patient concerned?
4. If fees are payable what is the cost of psychotherapy outside the National Health Service?

As well as these matters of information and of detail we shall also look at what it is that patients hope to gain from psychotherapy outside the National Health Service. Also, why do therapists elect to work outside the National Health Service?

Psychotherapy available within the National Health Service
There is no secret about the fact that specialized psychotherapy is provided by the National Health Service only in small measure. The case has been argued by some that there is no reason for the National Health Service to provide more psychotherapeutic services than it does at present, that we must await the evidence of research on the efficacy of psychotherapy. This respectable, if somewhat academic argument, is of little comfort to those patients and doctors who are confronted with the clinical needs of patients who turn to the psychiatric services of the National Health Service for help with their neuroses and personality problems and who have to be told that no treatment facilities exist.

A recent article* has attempted to survey the psychotherapeutic services provided within the National Health Service and to calculate how adequate is this service to the estimated needs of the population. The study concerned the psychotherapy services of the National Health Service in the Camberwell area of London during 1965. Services here are provided by the staff of the Maudsley Hospital, a large post-graduate teaching hospital with the largest psychotherapeutic department of any hospital in the United Kingdom, by three undergraduate teaching hospitals and by several other general hospitals with psychiatric clinics. Patients receiving psychotherapy were defined as those who, it was intended, should be seen at least weekly, for a minimum of six months, by a psychiatrist who was either a trained analyst or analytically orientated, and who devoted himself mainly to psychotherapy. In addition a survey was made of all patients receiving 'supportive treatment'. These patients were defined as those who made at least twenty out-patient contacts in the year of the study. The population served by these hospitals is approxi-

*J. K. & L. Wing. Psychotherapy and the National Health Service: an operational study. *Brit. J. Psychiatry* 1970, 116, 51–5.

mately a hundred and seventy-five thousand and it is estimated that the psychotherapy services for this population are approximately twice as intensive as those available nationally. (This is certainly a very conservative estimate.) The survey showed that in this area the National Health Service provided only fifteen hours of specialist psychotherapeutic treatment and eleven hours of supportive psychotherapy per week. By an examination of case records of patients referred for psychotherapy as compared with those who are not referred it could be seen that the number of comparable cases was such that in the author's estimate the numbers who could, or should (?), have been referred for specialized psychotherapy could easily have been increased four-fold. To cope with this increased case-load, a further full-time consultant would be needed for each hundred thousand members of the population. On a national scale this could represent four hundred and eighty new consultant posts in psychotherapy. It must be remembered at this point that there are very few consultant specialist posts in psychotherapy in the National Health Service and that these are probably confined entirely to the teaching hospitals. As we know that the National Health Service psychiatric services as they exist already fail to cope adequately with the number of patients who are referred to them, that conservative estimates agree that at least one-third of patients seen in general practice suffer from primarily emotional disturbances, that only approximately five per cent of the identifiably psychiatrically abnormal population are referred to hospital at all, then we begin to see the origin of the need and the demand for psychotherapy outside the National Health Service.

An approximate total of trained psychotherapists, that is those persons who are members of and who for the most part have completed a recognized training at a particular training institute for psychotherapy, is round about four hundred. Included here are the Institute of Psychoanalysis (Freudian) the Institute of Analytical Psychology (Jungian) the Association of Psychotherapists (Eclectic) and the Institute of Group Analysis. As many of these therapists work part-time within the National Health Service, an estimate of twenty hours per week has been made for work done in private practice. This totals seven thousand hours per week, which according to the writer's calculation, would be the required amount of time for a population of ten millions. It is not possible to estimate the numbers of patients being treated by these three hundred and fifty therapists as the range of treatment varies between five times a week analysis to groups of eight patients attending the same therapist once a week.

We shall proceed no further with this line of argument. Quality, surely not quantity, is of the essence in psychotherapy and to achieve and maintain quality, there must be adequate training. It is to the question of training, therefore, that we now turn.

We shall first consider the therapists who work outside the National Health Service. Very many of these therapists do work for part of their time within the National Health Service in roles for which their professional training qualifies them, e.g. psychiatrists, psychologists, psychiatric social workers, lay-psychotherapists. Their techniques are necessarily limited by the framework of the National Health Service and, therefore, they choose to practise other forms of psychotherapy outside the National Health Service in a setting of their own choice. The majority of these psychotherapists have been trained in one of the techniques of one of the psychodynamic schools, principally psychoanalysis and analytical psychology. Henceforth unless special reference is made to the differences between these two techniques the term psychoanalysis will be used to refer both to psychoanalysis (Freud) and analytical psychology (Jung).

It is generally accepted within the psychiatric and psychotherapeutic profession that the term 'psychoanalyst' and 'analytical psychologist' should be restricted to persons who have completed a formal training at one of the institutes recognized by the international training associations of the Freudian and Jungian schools respectively. The term 'psychotherapist' is a general term, and as such, carries with it no connotation of professional training. There is at present no scheme for recognition or accreditation of psychotherapists organized by the responsible professional bodies in this country. Such a scheme is long overdue and has been called for by Sir John Foster in his report on an

enquiry into the *Practice and Effects of Scientology* (HMSO, 1971).
Any treatment that can help can also harm. The medical profession, through long experience, holds to the tradition of
primum non nocere – above all, do not harm. This tendency to be
conservative can be misunderstood and lead to attacks on medical
practice; the sufferer is impatient to be relieved and finds the
role of patient (one who suffers) intolerable; rapid, even
miraculous, solutions are eagerly sought after. This pressure
produces its inevitable response, the appearance and espousal of
new, often dramatic, forms of treatment. Some, such as psychoanalysis and its derivatives, have survived the initial hostility
and scepticism that greeted them. In our time other therapies
based on new insights into communication processes are being
tried and tested. Many other techniques will be found wanting
and will fade into obscurity. Sir John Foster has provided us
with a lucid and succinct description of the general situation of
psychotherapy which merits great attention:

Enough is now known about the techniques of psychotherapy
to establish the following propositions, with which I think
few practising psychiatrists would disagree:
(a) given the right conjunction of therapist and patient,
psychotherapy can do much to relieve the latter's suffering;
(b) on the other hand, there are certain conditions (often
recognizable only to an expert in the field) which respond very
little, or not at all, to psychotherapy, whoever performs it;
(c) the techniques of psychotherapy are exceedingly complex
and require great skill and long experience for their successful
application;
(d) the possibilities of harm to the patient from the abuse, or
the unskilled use, of these techniques are at least as great as the
possibilities of good in the right hands.

One special aspect of psychotherapy requires mention here,
and that is the so-called 'transference' effect. From his earliest
days, Freud observed that his patients were apt to transfer to
him many of the emotions which had, for one reason or
another, remained unresolved in their childhood, so that

during the course of treatment he became the object of their most deeply seated feelings of love and hatred, of greed and generosity, of envy and gratitude, and often of sexuality. Such a situation imposes a considerable strain on the therapist, and places a great weight of responsibility upon him. More than ever today, psychotherapists regard the ultimate dissolution of the transference at the end of the treatment as the most difficult, and yet the crucial, part of their task.

Here is a classic case of something which appears to the uninitiated as a wholly harmless procedure: all that you would see in a psychotherapist's consulting room is two people – or sometimes a group of people – talking to each other. Yet the danger in anything other than the most skilled hands is great and, what is worse, the possibilities of abuse by the unscrupulous are immense. The trained and selfless practitioner is concerned only to convert the deep emotional dependence on him which his patient develops during the treatment into an ability on the patient's part to wean himself from the therapist, and to achieve the maturity, and the independent ability to make relationships by choice, which are the aim of most of us. But it is fatally easy for the unscrupulous therapist, who knows enough to create the dependence in the first place, to exploit it for years on end to his own advantage in the form of a steady income, to say nothing of the opportunities for sexual gratification. While the latter would rapidly spell the end of a medically qualified therapist's practice at the hands of the General Medical Council, that body has no jurisdiction over therapists who do not happen to be doctors.

Further, it will not have escaped attention that those who feel they need psychotherapy tend to be the very people who are most easily exploited: the weak, the insecure, the nervous, the lonely, the inadequate, and the depressed, whose desperation is often such that they are willing to do and pay anything for some improvement of their condition.

In all this, there are analogies with a number of skilled activities which have been practised for much longer. Laywers, doctors, architects and nurses, for example, all put at their clients' service, for reward, intricate skills of which the clients are ignorant and which they must largely take on trust. All of them are conscious of the dependence which their professional relationships tend to create, and of the harm which they could do if they failed to use all their skill, or exploited the dependence in a selfish fashion.

Sir John Foster in his report on an enquiry into the practice and effects of scientology has given us a timely reminder that we cannot afford to throw away any of the hard-learned lessons embodied in the professional code of conduct of the medical and allied professions. All professionals are answerable to the judgement of their peers if they fail to meet the expected standard of their profession. Psychotherapy, both individual and group, is leading to the creation of many new and as yet untried forms of psychotherapy. The opportunities for emotional gratification offered by these psychotherapists are many and various; the effect of what is offered has not yet been properly studied and if it is effective will no doubt prove harmful to some though helpful to others.

Psychoanalytic training and psychoanalytic treatment takes place entirely outside the National Health Service. That handful of patients who are treated at the London Clinic of Psychoanalysis under the auspices of the National Health Service are so small in numbers that their significance is virtually confined to giving support to the claim that psychoanalytic treatment is available under the National Health Service, a useful token to display when the health authorities are asked why psychoanalytic treatment is not provided!

Training in psychoanalysis is long, arduous, expensive and has been, until very recently, completely unsubsidized by public money. Most trainees have to combine a full-time job, as well as what becomes virtually another half-time job for several years whilst undergoing training, usually at a stage in their careers when they do not receive large salaries. The National Health Service benefits by their skills as psychotherapists and even sometimes imposes a condition that psychoanalytic training is required of the occupant of a particular post. Despite this lack of official assistance many trainees have cause to be grateful for the unofficial co-operation of their colleagues and seniors in the institutions where they are employed which enables them to carry on their work and their training at the same time. This co-operation is offered because in many cases the colleagues of these trainees recognize that the special skills they are acquiring will be of use to the services that they together in their hospitals or clinics are trying to provide.

It must also be remembered that until very recently a specialized intensive training in psychotherapy has not been provided by any National Health Service institution. A few post-graduate teaching hospitals, led by the Maudsley, now recognize their obligation to train psychiatrists more intensively in psychotherapeutic methods. However, none yet provides what the adherents of the psychodynamic schools are in complete agreement about, a personal experience of psychotherapy by the psychotherapist. This is an essential part of his training and has never been provided within the National Health Service. I refer to the training analysis and other modifications of this classic model.

It is worthwhile here to look back at the history of the development of psychotherapy in this country over the past forty years in order to understand the present situation.

Psychoanalysis and dynamic psychotherapy gained a foothold during the inter-war years in the setting of private practice and private training institutes. With very few exceptions the mental hospitals and the teaching hospitals opposed the psychoanalytic viewpoint and few psychoanalysts were employed either as teachers or as practitioners of psychotherapy. To complete the picture most psychotherapists considered that their special skills were appropriate only to the setting of private practice. There they could work, as individuals, in the manner of their own choice, meeting in their own societies and in the appropriate specialist sections of the medical and psychiatric societies. Outside this setting of individual psychotherapy carried out in private practice, two institutions were founded in which psychotherapy was studied, fostered and practised. These were the Tavistock

Clinic for out-patient psychotherapy and the Cassell Hospital for in-patient psychotherapy. Both of these privately founded institutes are now part of the National Health Service.

During the Second World War psychiatrists from the mental hospitals and teaching hospitals and psychotherapists working in private practice were brought together in psychiatric teams of the armed forces. After initial suspicions and hesitations both groups found that they could learn from each other. The concepts that underlie the organization and structure of the modern mental hospital are derived from these war-time experiences. In particular the techniques of group psychotherapy which had begun to be practised in the 1930s were greatly expanded and refined, notably at Northfield Military Hospital. The works of Foulkes, Bion, Rickman, Main and others attest to the rich harvest of these years. After the war there was a great increase in the number of psychiatrists who wished to train as psychotherapists. The only available training was that provided at the analytic institutes so there was a considerable increase in the number of trained psychotherapists. Unlike their colleagues of the inter-war years many of these psychiatrists did not wish to confine their work to the setting of private practice and, therefore, sought part-time or full-time employment in the National Health Service. The majority, however, wished to retain the right to practise psycho-analysis which has never been an acceptable technique within National Health Service psychiatry, and understandably so, as the amount of time involved in the treatment of any one patient is completely uneconomic for a state service. The influence of those analytically trained psychiatrists who remained within the National Health Service has gradually helped to bring about a great change in the climate of opinion within our psychiatric hospitals and teaching schools. Psychodynamic ideas are much more widely accepted and the average psychiatrist in training has much more chance now of becoming familiar with at least an outline of psychodynamic theories and practice.

We may see in the future that this changed climate of opinion will alter the geographical distribution of trained psychotherapists. A survey of the membership of the Institute of Psychoanalysis and the Institute of Analytical Psychology shows that less than a score out of a total membership of some three hundred of these two institutes practise outside the metropolitan and home counties areas. Thus some two-thirds of the population of the United Kingdom have no access to this type of specialized psychotherapy. Only two of the major centres outside London have ever had a substantial body of psychoanalysts practising and working together there. During the 1939–45 war years, Michael Balint lived in Manchester and a small training scheme was started there under his guidance. This ceased after he left Manchester leaving two psychoanalysts resident and practising there. In more recent years several psychoanalysts came from Glasgow to London to obtain their training and then returned to Glasgow. Unfortunately this group has now broken up and most of its members have moved to other centres in the United Kingdom and overseas.

Although I shall now proceed to discuss in greater detail the availability of psychoanalysis, it should not be assumed that I am suggesting that psychoanalytic treatment should be the only or even the most desirable form of psychotherapy to be more widely distributed. The situation is simply that there is no other professionally controlled method of training in psychotherapy of a specialized kind other than that provided by psychoanalytic and similar training institutes. There is a great need for a large number of trained psychotherapists who can apply techniques other than the psychoanalytic ones. Just as one American President once stated what his country needed was a good five cents cigar, so it seems that what this country needs is a large number of therapists trained to carry out many different modes of psychotherapy.

Psychoanalysis and analytic psychology
The some three hundred members of these two institutes practise in and around London. Although fifty per cent of the younger members of the Institute of Psychoanalysis hold full-time or part-time appointments within the National Health Service, the others, confining their activities entirely to private practice, nearly all manage to treat some patients psychoanalytically. The realities of the situation are such that most analysts treat patients

by less intensive modes of therapy than psychoanalysis though they do not like to admit that this is the case. Full psychoanalytic treatment involves the patient attending four or five times a week and problems of time and finance ensure that the population able to afford this type of treatment is always small. The range of fees charged nowadays (1973) is between four and ten pounds per session and, therefore, the cost per year of psychoanalytic treatment can range from between eight hundred to two thousand pounds. The patient should be clear before embarking on psychoanalytic treatment that the course of treatment is unlikely to last less than two years. Analytic psychologists often see their patients less often, perhaps two to three times a week, though recently there has been a move to increase the intensity of the treatment so that the technical situation now resembles more closely that of psychoanalysis. Referral to a psychoanalyst is usually made through a general practitioner or through another psychiatrist. Where the analyst is not medically qualified (lay) a medically qualified analyst is required to take medical responsibility whilst the patient is in treatment and this may entail a separate consultation with that analyst. It is often the case that the patient or the medical referer does not know of an analyst to whom to refer the case. The Institute of Psychoanalysis in London if approached in this matter is able to give the enquirer a choice of two senior analysts with whom they may have a consultation to assess the suitability of analysis and to find the proper channels of referral. These analysts are chosen from a rota of senior analysts who have no financial interest in taking on such patients and are therefore able to give an objective assessment of the situation. Analysts themselves often have a lot of difficulty in placing patients with other analysts if they are unable to take them on for treatment themselves. The channels for referral within psychotherapists are informal, poorly defined and need greatly to be improved.

What of the many patients seen by analytically trained therapists who are unable to afford formal psychoanalysis or may not be suitable for this method of treatment? I cannot go into detail here about the indications and contra-indications for psychoanalysis but it must be emphasized that it is no universal panacea for all psychic ailments.

Modified analytical psychotherapy usually involves one or two attendances per week, the techniques are usually derived from the psychoanalytic model but there is little doubt that the situation here is unsatisfactory. It is difficult for psychoanalysts openly to acknowledge to each other that they are involved in other forms of psychotherapy and they have no meeting place at which their problems and the search for new techniques can be discussed. A greater flexibility in attitude of mind and a willingness to experiment with new techniques is needed and there are signs that it is now appearing. It is unlikely that this will be done within the psychoanalytic institutes and the logical alternative would be the creation of a new institute for the study of psychotherapy.

It is not possible to describe and to evaluate the practice and competence of individual psychotherapists in this article. What follows is a description of clinics and organizations either staffed by psychotherapists of recognized competence or where supervision of the work of less highly trained staff is the responsibility of the recognized psychotherapists. Some clinics that carry out training in psychotherapy offer treatment facilities to the public so as to enable trainees to gain experience under supervision. All the organizations mentioned here are operated under the auspices of charitable trusts and are non-profit-making.

London Clinic of Psychoanalysis
(The Clinic of the British Institute of Psychoanalysis)
A limited number of patients (ninety at present) are accepted for full psychoanalytic treatment at reduced fees. The cost to the patient may range from fifty pence per session to ten pounds per week. Persons able to pay more than this amount are expected to make arrangements for private treatment. A special scheme exists that enables professional workers in fields allied to psychiatry and psychoanalysis to obtain psychoanalytic treatment at a cost of one pound per session. This scheme is designed to familiarize other professionals in the mental health field with techniques and aims of psychoanalysis.

Only a small number of those applying for treatment to the clinic can be taken on and the criteria for selection are stringent. Application for treatment should be made to the Director of the Clinic, 63 New Cavendish Street, London W1.

The Society of Analytical Psychology
30 Devonshire Place, W1
The C. G. Jung clinic offers full analysis to a limited number of patients. The number under treatment at present are fifty-three and has remained about the same in recent years. The majority of patients pay between fifty new pence and two pounds per session and twenty patients are seen three or four times a week. The aim is to provide full analysis for people who cannot afford the full fees.

The Langham Clinic for Psychotherapy
26 Belsize Square, NW3
This clinic was established about fifteen years ago. It became a charity in its own right in December 1969 with the object of providing psychotherapeutic treatment, and also of carrying out teaching and research in this subject. It was recently moved to a temporary address at 26 Belsize Square, NW3, and is in the process of a fund-raising campaign to enable a new building to be erected so that the services of the clinic can be expanded. All the staff are part-time, most of them trained analysts, members of the British Analytic Society or the Society of Analytical Psychology and medically qualified and trained in psychiatry. The treatment here is individual involving two or more attendances per week and the clinic also provides group psychotherapy. About a hundred patients are at present in treatment, and receive either individual or group psychotherapy. Most patients seen individually have two sessions a week and the range of fee is between two pounds and fifty new pence and five pounds and fifty new pence; the consultation fee is five pounds. Some group psychotherapy is also provided on the basis of groups meeting once a week in the evening at a fee of one pound and fifty new pence. At present the clinic does not provide child psychotherapy.

The London Centre for Psychotherapy

48 Montagu Mansions, W1 (formerly the Well Walk Centre for Psychotherapy)

The centre is affiliated to The British Association of Psychotherapists, registered as a charitable trust. The Association was founded in 1946 and has slowly and gradually expanded to a present membership of seventy-one and organizes training in individual and group psychotherapy. The Centre sets out to provide skilled psychotherapy for patients of moderate means. During 1970–71, one hundred and thirty-one patients were referred to the clinic and those taken on for treatment may either be seen individually on the basis of two to four sessions per week or taken into therapeutic groups which meet once or twice a week. Most of the staff have received their training at the Association of Psychotherapists' training scheme which is strongly influenced by both the Freudian and Jungian approaches.

The Davidson Clinic*

18 Hartington Place, Edinburgh, EH10 4LE

This clinic was established in 1941 and provides analytical psychotherapy. There is a staff of six, one medical and five lay, and patients are seen either once or twice a week. Patients are expected to pay according to their means and if patients can afford to pay more than three pounds a week they are not eligible to become clinic patients but are referred to a therapist with whom they can arrange private fees. The scale of charges based on weekly income is adjusted for married men so as to bring them into line with single persons. The maximum total net family income per week under which a patient is eligible for treatment at the clinic is at present approximately twenty-two pounds.

In the year ending November 1970 between sixty-five and seventy-five patients were seen twice weekly and sixty-two new patients were seen during the year. The clinic has a branch in Glasgow which operates on a smaller scale than does the one in Edinburgh.

*Since this book went to press, the Davidson clinic (Edinburgh) has closed down through financial difficulties, although the Glasgow branch is still operating.

Psychosexual disorders

Very many people need help with psychosexual problems. Frigidity, impotence, non-consummation, sexual deviations, all contribute to personal unhappiness and to marital and family tension. All too often the patient lacks the confidence to disclose the difficulties directly to the general practitioner and all too often receives little help when he or she does. Agencies where patients may present their problems more readily and which are making efforts to meet their needs include those founded specifically for Family Planning work.

Family Planning Association – Special 'Marital Problem sessions' are provided where patients who need counselling or psychotherapy for sexual difficulties are seen. Patients do not have to be married to be eligible! The FPA has its own training scheme for enabling doctors, mostly general practitioners, to develop the special skills in psychotherapy needed for this work.

One hundred and seventy of the one thousand, four hundred doctors who staff the FPA clinics have received some special training and in 1970 one thousand, five hundred and thirty-six marital problem sessions were held and three thousand, eight hundred and three patients were seen. The cost for the patient is three pounds for the initial sessions and two pounds for subsequent; as with other similar schemes, it has to be heavily subsidized by the organization. Skilled individual help is always expensive and is becoming ever more so. The FPA is looking for ways to extend its service and to contact the very many persons in need of such psychosexual counselling who do not approach the clinics. At present the contact has to be made either by the general practitioner referring the patient to the local clinic or by the patient coming himself. The network of the FPA clinics is widespread and represents the possible beginning of a nation-wide service for psychotherapy of psychosexual disorders.

The Institute of Marital Studies, Tavistock Centre
Belsize Lane, NW3 5BA
This unique institution has worked with some two thousand,

five hundred couples in the past twenty years. Several of the permanent staff of eleven are psychoanalysts or analytical psychologists and the value of the work of the Institute is widely recognized. Much research into problems of marriage and marital conflict has been done. During 1970 six thousand hours of casework was provided for the couple attending for treatment; one hundred and sixty-three referrals involving three hundred and twenty-six clients were made.

The Institute receives support from the Home Office and other bodies but has recently had to reduce its training activities for lack of finance.

Patients are charged four pounds each for the initial consultation and subsequently three pounds each. This is below the actual cost and where appropriate the fee is waived or lowered.

Psychotherapy for adolescents
Many universities now recognize that students often need psychotherapy or counselling. Though these are schemes outside the National Health Service no further reference will be made to them here. Outside the universities, however, there are very few services.

Outstanding is the Brent Consultation Centre (Johnston House, 51 Winchester Avenue, NW6), which has pioneered treatment and research into adolescent consultation problems in this country. The service is advertised in a variety of ways, such as in local youth clubs and local newspapers. The Centre tries to encourage self-referral and to discourage the usual channels of referral for psychotherapy, believing that the adolescent who is self-referred is easier to help than one who has been sent.

The Brent Consultation Centre is a free, walk-in consultation service for adolescents. It is under the auspices of the London Borough of Brent Education Department. Adolescents can see a member of the interviewing staff to discuss problems and, if considered necessary, once-weekly, short-term treatment is available. This short-term treatment is, however, available only to those adolescents who live, work or attend school, college or other institutions in the Borough of Brent. Other adolescents who are in need of treatment are referred to the appropriate services.

All members of the Centre staff are psychoanalysts or child psychotherapists. In addition to work with adolescents, the Centre organizes seminars for teachers, social workers, psychiatrists, and police.

The Centre's interviewing hours are Monday and Thursday evenings from 7.30 p.m. to 10.00 p.m., and Tuesday afternoons from 4.30 p.m. to 6.00 p.m. The Centre's offices are open each weekday from 9.00 a.m. to 6.00 p.m. when inquiries can be made.

The Centre for the Study of Adolescence is a research organization associated with the Brent Consultation Centre whose main function is the study of psychopathology in adolescence. Through this Centre, it is possible to study, through intensive treatment, up to twenty adolescents. At present the studies undertaken at the Centre include i) suicide attempts and self-mutilation, ii) promiscuity in adolescent girls, and iii) sudden academic or work failure. Treatment through the Study Centre consists of analytic treatment or intensive psychotherapy. This treatment is free. Adolescents from any part of London can be considered to be included in the studies of the Centre. The Centre for the Study of Adolescence is registered as a charity. Its funds for research come, at present, from private sources.

The Centre for the Analytic Study of Student Problems
(a registered charity) 27 Shepherds Close, N6

This recently-formed organization consists of a number of psychonalysts and analytical psychologists who give two hours a week of unpaid time to the Centre. It is hoped that sufficient funds will be accumulated to provide for a permanent centre and to organize treatment and research on a larger scale. The service at present consists of group therapy or individual psychotherapy; discussion groups for university staff and contact and collaboration with counsellors, chaplains and tutors.

London Youth Advisory Centre
(sponsored by the Community Development Trust)
31 Nottingham Place, Marylebone Road, W1
Staff: four part-time doctors trained in psychosexual counselling.
One psychotherapist and part-time psychiatric social workers.
Offers psychotherapy and casework with an emphasis on immediate contact and crisis intervention. The fee for the initial consultation may be up to two pounds and subsequent sessions cost one to two pounds.

Brook Advisory Centre for Young People
55 Dawes Street, SE17
This voluntary body, to which many young people come for contraceptive advice, provides a psychosexual counselling service at its London centre. Here a medically qualified psychotherapist provides two sessions a week at which six clients can be seen individually at a cost of one pound each per session.

Messenger House Trust
17 Malcom Road, SW19
This unusual venture is the personal creation of a psychoanalyst and child psychiatrist, Dr Josephine Lomax-Simpson. She began by attempting to treat psychopathic, attention-seeking girls by providing residential accommodation in a home which she shared with them. The aim is to provide 'a realistic standard of living at a realistic fee with realistic supervision and treatment'. Dr Lomax-Simpson aims at a form of psychotherapy where her psychoanalytic insight enables her to interpret unconscious material both in an individual and a group setting, but considers that it is equally important that the people concerned should live with the knowledge of their true circumstances. Influenced by amongst others the work of the late D. W. Winnicott, she attempts to provide an environment that can become a 'holding situation' from which more normal maturation may occur. She has dealt with about a hundred persons, most of them illegitimate, many below average intelligence.

Religion and psychotherapy

The churches have long been aware of the need for psychotherapy for many of those who bring their problems to them. In some centres priests are being trained in modern psychodynamic psychology by methods which involve the priest in having to understand his own personality and problems in the light of the concepts that he will have to apply to his parishioners. The concept of 'pastoral care' includes understanding and assisting the normal reactions to stress and grief that is part of our daily lot and that follows on pain, disappointment, death. 'Pastoral counselling' goes further in the direction of specialized psychotherapy in that account is now taken of unconscious motivation and of the conflicts and abnormal reactions that arise in disturbed individuals as the result of these unconscious forces.

Clinics are being set up with trained psychotherapists and counsellors on the staff. Though subsidized by religious charities they are non-denominational in their approach.

Westminster Pastoral Foundation

The Central Hall, SW1

The Foundation has a very active in-service training for clergy and youth leaders. Treatment is offered in the form of counselling in personal, marital and family problems under the supervision of a consultant psychiatrist. Most clients are seen weekly, either individually or in groups and at present a hundred are in treatment by the staff of twenty-seven part-time counsellors who between them provide seventy hours a week. Payment for individual sessions is a matter for individual assessment; the fee for group attendance is fifty new pence per session at present.

Lincoln Memorial Clinic for Psychotherapy Ltd

(The Christian Psychotherapy Foundation)

The Lincoln Towers, 77 Westminster Bridge Road, SE1

The clinic provides 'analytical psychotherapy' by a staff of registered medical practitioners or analytically trained psychotherapists whose work is supervised by a consultant medical psychotherapist. A medical referral is required before the patient is seen. Patients are accepted for individual or group psychotherapy and the individual fees, which may be reduced in special circumstances, are in the region of three pounds per session.

Group psychotherapy

The pressing need for more psychotherapists has led to a great surge of interest in group psychotherapy. The work of Foulkes and of Bion have been the most influential amongst medical psychotherapists in this country and has led to a healthy marriage of individual psychoanalytic skills with those skills that come from interest and experience of group methods which derive partly from interactional (social) psychology. Group psychotherapy is available at some of the clinics already mentioned and, in addition, at a large private practice centre in London. Fees vary from eight pounds to fifteen pounds per month for weekly sessions. Training in group-analytic psychotherapy is now offered by the Institute of Group Analysis.

Many other forms of group 'treatment' situations are now being offered to the public. The Encounter group movement has flourished in the USA and is now establishing itself in this country. Although the movement has characterized itself as 'group therapy for normal persons' there is no doubt that many persons attending these groups do so for reasons similar to those who attend professional psychiatrists and psychotherapists. Unlike the latter body of workers the Encounter group work as a whole has no professional standards to ensure that the treatment offered is competent and safe. At present anyone can make his services available to the public, who cannot discriminate between the sincere and skilled and the unscrupulous and dangerous. The Task Force report of the American Psychiatric Association, *Encounter groups and psychiatry* (April 1970) gives a balanced and comprehensive survey of the American scene. It warns that 'in the hands of some leaders, the group experience can be dangerous for some participants. The more powerful the emotions evoked, the less clinically perspicacious and responsible the leader, the more psychologically troubled the group member, then the greater the risk of adverse outcome.'

'Alternative' psychotherapy

Many young people in need of psychiatric help will not consent to have dealings with the National Health Service or established organizations functioning in the private sector. They view them with suspicion and scepticism as manifestations of a society whose values they reject. They may accept help from those people who they regard as sharing their own values, that of the 'alternative society'. Organizations such as Release, BIT, Street-aid, have been created to meet the needs of this population, many of whom are socially inadequate, drug-dependent or neurotic. Release (113 Westbourne Grove, W9) is the largest 'underground' organization in Britain and provides counselling for its clients on the whole range of problems that are brought to them. Beyond this a modest beginning has been made in offering psychotherapy in the form of group therapy with the aid of sympathetic trained junior psychiatrists.

More ambitious schemes are those established by the Philadelphia Association (7 Antrim Mansions, Antrim Road, NW3) and The Arbours Housing Association Ltd (50 Coulthorpe Road, NW3). The Philadelphia Association devotes itself particularly to an approach to the problems of schizophrenia which is based on the work of R. D. Laing. Within this theoretical framework there is no place for the conventional psychiatric hospital nor for individual based forms of therapy. A community, Kingsley Hall, was founded where these theories were applied. Between 1964 and 1968, one hundred and eighty-eight people have lived in Kingsley Hall (closed in 1970) and other households organized by the Philadelphia Association. Many had previously been classified as patients and had lived in mental hospitals.

The Arbours Housing Association runs two communities, each accommodating eight to ten persons. A 'network' of helpers outside these communities has been established so as to extend the aid available beyond these confines.

Within both these organizations there are psychiatrists, psychologists, social workers and nurses, though the philosophy underlying their activities decrees that defined professional roles are often unnecessary and even harmful in the treatment of mental illness.

Some of the theories and techniques of these organizations are thought-provoking and challenging and it is to be hoped that their present isolation will give place to a closer co-operation with other professional workers in the same field.

Conclusion

Psychotherapy in the private sector will continue to set standards that the public sector will be encouraged to emulate. Within the private sector more careful regulation of standards of training and practice are called for and will be provided, thereby protecting the public from exploitation and ill-informed though sincere practice.

Training in dynamic aspects of psychotherapy

Malcolm Pines

Rising living standards in poor countries often precede and may eventually lead to revolution; similar conditions in more advanced, western societies lead to a demand for psychotherapy; the hungry mind replaces the empty belly; the emotional sickness shows.

Satisfied basic physical needs expose basic emotional needs and disturbances. Each society determines to what extent it is prepared to devote health resources to the study and treatment of such disorders. In our own society the decision has been negative; the State does not foster the need for training or for research into psychotherapy, which, therefore, develops in the private sector. Some tolerance is displayed for those individuals and organizations whose contributions are outstanding and undeniable. The work of Balint, Bion, Foulkes, and Main was facilitated by the Cassel Hospital, the Maudsley Hospital, and the Tavistock Clinic. But there is still little general advance in the state of psychotherapeutic work within the National Health Service over that existing a decade ago. This article will survey training in medical psychotherapy both within and without the National Health Service, at undergraduate and post-graduate levels; specialist post-graduate training in psychotherapy and the privately organized institutions catering for doctors and members of other professions. (Training in psychotherapy for case workers has not been discussed as a separate issue.)

It is remarkable how many of the post-war innovations in psychotherapy training in this country are connected with the work of Michael Balint.[1] Throughout his long and distinguished psychoanalytic career, he sowed the seeds of fruitful research. He formed the nucleus of a psychoanalytic training centre in Manchester; began the Tavistock general practitioner seminars; a short-term psychotherapy workshop staffed by psychoanalysts from the Cassel Hospital and Tavistock Clinic was the source of David Malan's monograph on brief psychotherapy; he started the Family Planning Association seminars in the treatment of psychosexual problems; he finally moved on to undergraduate teaching at University College Hospital. His work on the training seminar – 'the Balint Seminar' – has had a world-wide impact. The Balint Society, formed after his death, by some of those general practitioners who had been most closely associated with his work, hopes to be able to launch a new scheme for general practitioner training in psychotherapy at a level appropriate to the general practitioner.

The lesson that Michael Balint constantly emphasized was the need to identify and to respect the setting in which the psychotherapeutic work is being carried out; the general practitioner carries out his psychotherapy in his surgery, in the setting of a long-term relationship with his patient to whom he is always available. The patient can present his illness to the general practitioner in various guises and whether the illness becomes 'organized' as a psychoneurotic illness which then can openly be recognized as such by both doctor and patient, depends to a considerable extent on the 'apostolic' role of the doctor whose notions about illness influence, mainly unconsciously, his response to what the patient offers of himself in the opening of the patient/ doctor relationship.[2] The fact that the general practitioner has encounters with the patient, both in his family and social network, gives him a different view and vantage-point in his therapy to that of the hospital doctor or psychoanalyst, whose contacts are contractually stated and limited. Thus, in discussing training in psychotherapy we must be aware of the setting in which the treatment is to be carried out – surgery, clinic, consulting room, hospital, in-patient or out-patient. The doctor/patient relationship exists within the framework of the setting and the doctor's training should be appropriate to that. We expect the specialist psychotherapist to have had a different training to that of the general practitioner but not that the general practitioner should be untrained, rather that he should be trained to work appropriately to his role and setting.

We will sketch out the training possibilities available to doctors at the different stages of their career, undergraduate and post-graduate, in general psychiatry and specialized psychotherapy.

Undergraduate training

The Todd Report; The Royal Commission on Medical Education, 1965–68, Command Paper 3569, emphasized the need for more teaching in psychiatry and psychotherapeutic aspects of psychiatry and medicine as a whole. The existing medical curriculum of most medical schools allows little time for psychiatry, and that is mostly devoted to the study of organized disease entities. Though the undergraduate certainly needs to recognize the major psychoses and to grasp the general outlines of psychiatric treatment, he is poorly prepared for the discomfiture of general practice and hospital medicine where he will meet people, not disease entities. Only when medical schools teach 'whole person medicine' throughout the undergraduate training, will the student graduate with a basic understanding of interpersonal relationships in medicine and possessing some confidence in his basic technique.

The best observed experiment in training medical students in psychotherapy was that made at the University of Chicago by Heine *et al.*[3] The defined aims of their experiment were to enable students to:

1. Increase their own sensitivity to the patients' attitudes and feelings.
2. To see more clearly the significance of the doctor's role in the interpersonal relationship with the patient.
3. To develop some awareness of his characteristic way of relating to patients.
4. To learn corrective rather than disjunctive responses to patients' demands, expectations and emotional turmoil.

5. To learn to recognize situations where the student interacts with comfort, as well as with anxiety.

These aims were attained through allowing and encouraging undergraduates to treat out-patients psychotherapeutically under good conditions of appropriate selection of patients and adequate supervision. Such a scheme requires a large amount of staff time, and pre-supposes the existence of proper training skills in the supervisory staff, together with a consensus amongst them of the general theoretical background to psychotherapy. No medical school in the United Kingdom, to my knowledge, is yet in the position to implement such a scheme though some students, notably at University College Hospital, do have the opportunity to treat patients under supervision.

The presence of psychoanalytically trained psychiatrists on the staff of a teaching hospital does indicate that increased attention is being given to the teaching of psychotherapy in the undergraduate curriculum. Eight London undergraduate teaching hospitals now have psychoanalysts on their staff, though the amount of time and the degree of influence on the teaching programme that they possess varies greatly, with University College Hospital and King's College Hospital being standard bearers at present. About twenty psychoanalysts are engaged in part-time work at the London undergraduate teaching hospitals and thirteen psychoanalysts are to be found on the staff of eight of the provincial centres (Birmingham, Newcastle, Leeds, Sheffield, Edinburgh, Aberdeen), of whom three are at Edinburgh. Leeds was the first medical school to appoint a psychotherapist as a Professor of Psychiatry (Dr H. V. Dicks), and Aberdeen openly declares its personal knowledge of, and interest in psychoanalysis.

We must conclude that the training the medical student receives in psychotherapy is at present quite inadequate to their future careers, although in most cases their general training in psychiatry is vastly better than it was a generation ago.[4] Adequate training would enable the student to begin to feel at ease in the interview situation with a wide range of disturbed people; to begin to understand some of the complexities of the doctor/patient relationship as it appears in hospital and general practice;

to understand the nature of human nature (including his own), and the powerful drives towards both sickness and health omnipresent throughout the life-cycle; hopefully, to prevent a future withdrawal to a distant cold mechanistic attitude to emotional disorders or the opposite, over-intensive absorption by them.

Post-graduate training

The Royal College of Psychiatry has issued guidelines for the training of general psychiatrists in psychotherapy. These state that 'some degree of skill in psychotherapy is an essential part of equipment of every psychiatrist. Opportunities for learning should include individual and group psychotherapy; supervision of the trainee whilst caring for a few selected patients for a long time, with an emphasis on the study of doctor/patient relationships and their meanings.'[5] A system of accreditation of hospitals offering general psychiatric training is under way which again emphasizes that training in that degree of psychotherapeutic skill which is essential for all psychiatrists is important.

We are still a long way from satisfying the conditions put forward in these guidelines and there is little cause for optimism as yet. These recommendations cannot possibly be realized until more psychotherapeutically trained psychiatrists are available, and posts created for them. A basic confusion arises from the fact that the Royal College of Psychiatry and the National Health Service, though recognizing the importance of training in psychotherapy, do not yet provide the means for such training. Psychiatrists receive a training in psychotherapy mainly outside the National Health Service, in a setting that does not resemble that found within it. Psychoanalytic training does not qualify a psychotherapist either to practise or to train other psychiatrists in psychotherapy adapted to the need of the National Health Service.

Some of the more adequate schemes available within the National Health Service for training of psychiatrists in psycho-therapy will be described in the following section.

Specialized training programmes in psychotherapy for psychiatrists who have completed their basic training

a) *London* – For many years the best known programme available for psychiatrists in the National Health Service has been that organized by the Tavistock Clinic and known as an Introductory Course to Psychotherapy. Basically this has been a two-year programme involving weekly evening attendances. The programme is composed of a mixture of lectures, supervision sessions, and observations of treatment situations (mainly group), behind the one-way screen, followed by discussion between the therapist and the students. This course has been well attended and draws mainly on trainees in the North West Metropolitan Region and has been their main opportunity to become acquainted with the psychodynamic viewpoint.

Inevitably there has been a sharp and often painful contrast between the institutional values and attitudes encountered at the Tavistock Clinic and at their own parent hospital. Though we know that growth and maturity is often derived from the experience of conflict and conflict resolution and that training schemes are bound to generate such conflicts, and that we need to be prepared to aid resolutions, this aspect of training programmes is not often recognized by administrators, who have not themselves personally experienced such problems. Such factors may interfere with the learning process.

The Tavistock Clinic offers an intensive training in psychotherapy to its own junior staff who are almost always in concurrent psychoanalytic training. Unique to this country is the short-term psychotherapy Workshop originated by Balint and now carried on by David Malan. This Workshop has acquired international recognition for the value of its work.[6]

The Tavistock Clinic is planning an advanced course of training for psychiatrists who wish to attain the status of consultant psychotherapist within the National Health Service. This will probably take the form of a four-year attachment to the clinic, with the opportunity for personal analysis and systematic training in intensive, analytically orientated psychotherapy. This training will differ significantly from psychoanalytic training proper which is a training intended only for the psychoanalytic setting, almost entirely to be found in private practice. The new teaching scheme will train consultant psychotherapists for the National Health Service who should be able to plan, to train, to advise, and to supervise other psychiatrists within the setting of the National Health Service. The need for such training is now generally accepted and the new scheme has an important part to play in National Health Service psychiatry.

The Cassel Hospital (Director, Dr T. F. Main, Ham Common, Richmond, Surrey), has long been a centre of training in hospital psychotherapy in this country. All trainees are expected to undertake personal psychoanalytic training thereby leaving the consultant staff free to concentrate on studying and teaching techniques appropriate to the hospital setting. The experience obtained in the four years' average length of training covers psychotherapy with adults, with families and adolescents, both in an in-patient and out-patient setting.

The Cassel Hospital is now planning to offer weekly half-day seminars in psychotherapy for psychiatrists who have completed their Diploma in Psychological Medicine or Royal College of Psychiatry training and who now wish to learn more about psychotherapy and a Director of Post-Graduate Training has been appointed.

Many opportunities for training lie in the path of Maudsley registrars who have the opportunity of an attachment for nine months to the out-patient psychotherapy unit where ample supervision from the four consultant psychotherapists and four senior tutors in psychotherapy is available.[7] As well as registrars, clinical assistants from home and overseas can be allocated to the department. Theory is taught at lectures and seminars by the clinical staff, by the tutors and by an eminent teacher of psychoanalysis, Dr J. Sandler, Senior Lecturer in the Institute of Psychiatry who has his own team of assistants and research workers. The orientation is psychoanalytical and the emphasis is mostly on individual and small group methods of psychotherapy. The out-patient psychotherapy programme was launched by S. H. Foulkes, well known for his basic and influential writings on psychoanalytic psychotherapy.[8] The Maudsley is also strong on teaching psychotherapy based on learning theory.

Of the other London teaching hospitals, King's College Hospital, the London Hospital, the Middlesex, St George's and University College Hospitals have the strongest psychotherapeutic training programmes.

Adequate post-graduate training in psychotherapy for all psychiatrists would suppose: a reasonable grasp of modern psychodynamic theories (basically the structural model of psychoanalysis); the ability to apply this knowledge in diagnosis and prognosis of mental illness; the ability to plan treatment appropriate to the available resources (personal skills and those of other members of a therapeutic team, referral to specialized treatment resources); supervised experience in short- and long-term therapy of individuals and groups (including marital and family groups).

Training in psychotherapy for registrars at mental hospitals

Registrars' training is directed mainly towards passing the DPM and membership of the Royal College of Psychiatry. Few mental hospitals outside the Metropolitan areas have consultant psychotherapists, or psychotherapeutically trained psychiatrists on their staff. Though efforts are being made to organize tutorials and seminars on a regional basis and regional tutors have been appointed to co-ordinate and to improve training facilities,[9] the resources for training in psychotherapy are still very limited. The most advanced scheme that I have been able to identify is that organized by the Wessex Regional School of Psychiatry in co-operation with the mental hospitals of its area. The three-year training scheme which involves a day-release course for registrars, gives considerable emphasis to the study of the doctor/patient relationship, systematic psychopathology, supervision of individual psychotherapy, theoretical and clinical training in group psychotherapy. Some of the group work is done in conjunction with the Southampton University Department of Social Psychology and opportunities exist for registrars to observe and to engage in sensitivity training group situations. It is of interest that training facilities are offered also to trainee general practitioners in the same area. This scheme, developed under the direction of Dr Steven MacKeith (retd), seems to create a precedent which could well be followed by other regions.

The educational success of such a scheme must depend on the quality of the teaching, the time available for the students to really study and to be free from work commitments, and on the general climate of acceptance of the psychodynamic approach in the parent institution from which they come. This Wessex scheme is based on a day release course and enables trainees from hospitals within a radius of forty miles to meet together in numbers of up to twenty, which justifies a major educational investment. An especially interesting feature is the opportunity to participate in the group work course of the Department of Social Psychology of the University of Southampton where there is a flourishing practice in 'T-group' work enabling the participants to gain first-hand experience of themselves in the group situation and hopefully to gain in sensitivity and empathy, and to deepen self-understanding.

b) *Teaching hospitals outside London* – The strongest teaching programme inevitably is to be found at centres where psychotherapists are themselves to be found. As the distribution of psychoanalytically trained psychiatrists outside London is so sparse, there are few centres able to provide systematic training in psychotherapy for post-graduates. The main exceptions are Edinburgh and Aberdeen. All psychiatrists in training in the Edinburgh area can now take part in a 3-year psychotherapy training scheme. One hour a week is officially allocated for seminars and the timetable is coordinated so that all can attend. Another Scottish innovation is that two residential weekends a year on psychotherapy are arranged by the Scottish division of the Psychotherapy section of the Royal College of Psychiatrists.

The Department of Mental Health of the University of Aberdeen, has the distinction of being the first, and so far the only university openly to recognize that 'what the British psychiatric scene signally fails to provide, especially outside the London area, is training in psychotherapy for doctors not necessarily wishing to

FIRST DRAFT

LEARNING THE PSYCHODYNAMIC PSYCHIATRY OF ADULT MENTAL ILLNESS

Year of training	General teaching about the individual patient	Special experience with individual patients	General group teaching and experience	Special group experience and teaching
FIRST YEAR	The doctor/patient relationship. The interview as a dynamic process. Non-directive counselling. (Own Consultant and WRSP Course)		Outline of *basic* phenomena of Group, small and medium-sized. Regular attendance at Ward 'House Meetings'.	Southampton University EMD (or other) Basic Group Work Course.
SECOND YEAR	Outline of 'Systematic' Psychopathology, considered in terms of the individual patient. (WRSP Course) Voluntary Seminars on Psychotherapy. (Psychotherapy Tutor)	Closely supervised Individual Psychotherapy of one or two selected patients.	Regular attendance at Ward 'House Meetings'. Voluntary regular 'sitting-in' at therapeutic group.	(Second chance of) Southampton University EMD Basic Group Work Course.
THIRD YEAR		Individual Psychotherapy of a few selected patients under less intensive supervision.	Regular attendance at Ward 'House Meetings'. Running of own Therapeutic Group (as assistant leader or with regular supervision).	If desired, Southampton University EMD Advanced Group Work Course.

WRSP = Wessex Regional School of Psychiatry.   *EMD* = Extra-mural Department.

Stephen MacKeith

become full-time psychotherapists, but wishing to add some skill and understanding in psychotherapy to their therapeutic armamentarium as general, all-round psychiatrists.'

'Parallel to this clinical deficiency there is an academic deficiency in studies into the deepest and most important human feelings. University departments of psychiatry and psychology have for the most part concerned themselves primarily with the study of the more objective aspects of human behaviour which are more readily explained and modified in terms of traditional scientific hypotheses. The study of dynamic, internal processes and of human relationships generally has been largely ignored.' The very significant contributions of British medical psychologists to the understanding of human personality have, with a few exceptions, been made by workers outside the academic setting. One such worker, W. D. Fairbairn, remarked in 1939 on the 'widespread tendency in university circles to exclude psychoanalytic theory from the field of academic study. This tendency is not common everywhere; in general it is sufficiently marked to make it little exaggeration to say, so far from being a *prescribed* subject in the psychological curriculum, psychoanalytic theory is actually a *proscribed* subject.' This situation seems, unfortunately, to be almost as true as when it was made 35 years ago.

For the past eight years a course leading to a diploma in psychotherapy has been offered and so far twenty-nine trainees have completed this. The fee for the course is seventy-five pounds and some scholarships are available from time to time. Finance for full-time students is obviously a problem though help has been generously given by the Leverhulme Trust and the Rowntree Social Services Trust.

Candidates must be medical graduates in possession of the DPM or equivalent. The length of the course is a whole year full-time or not less than twenty months' part-time study. At least two hundred and forty sessions of formal psychotherapy with patients and eight hundred hours of supervision are required; a hundred and twenty hours of practical instruction include demonstrations of group and individual psychotherapy; eighty hours of systematic teaching, protocols of treated patients, and a dissertation on an aspect of psychotherapy are required for completion of the diploma course.

The theoretical syllabus begins with Freudian psychology, object relationship theory (a speciality of the Scottish psychiatric scene related to the influence of R. D. Fairbairn), and assessment of psychotherapy, moves on in the second term to community and social psychiatry, child and adolescent psychotherapy, forensic psychiatry, the psychotherapy and sociology of mental illness and existentialist psychotherapy.

It was recognized by the organizers that the work will mobilize training anxieties and that if these are not dealt with the trainees will be unlikely to be able to help patients with difficulties in the same areas. Experience shows that the most important anxieties are those clustered round separation, helplessness, and depression, guarded against previously by the doctors' efforts to be omnipotent and omniscient, and by preoccupation with success. Efforts to help trainees with these problems centre on discussion of their feelings in different settings. Personal psychotherapy is not part of the course.

The Aberdeen course deserves close attention and study for it raises fundamental questions. Does one year of full-time study and experience suffice to train a psychiatrist to the level of a consultant psychotherapist, or does it bring him to the level that we should expect from all consultant psychiatrists in the National Health Service and, therefore, the equivalent of the Royal College of Psychiatry examination or the M.Phil. Diploma of the Institute of Psychiatry of the University of London? Does the process of maturing into a competent specialist psychotherapist take a number of years and is it, therefore, a matter of gradual growth in a setting favourable to slow growth and experience, or can the learning experience be accelerated by concentration; does removal of the trainee from his home, his environment, and hospital affect the learning process; how does the process of arrival and departure and the need to establish the new network of professional and social relationships affect the trainee; what problems arise as a result of the pre-determined length of the course in the treatment of patients and education of the psychiatrist; what are the problems facing the trainee in his re-adjustment to his own environment after completion of training; does the training lead to further interest and development of psychotherapeutic skills and equip the trainee for the responsibilities he may be expected to assume? The experience of the training and supervising staff should be of great value to those in other university departments that may propose to offer systematic training courses.

My own impression of the Aberdeen experiment is that it offers a model to such departments in universities and teaching hospitals of the level to which they should aspire in the training of *their own staff*. A consultant psychiatrist nowadays should be literate, articulate and competent with a range of knowledge of psychotherapeutic techniques comparable to his grasp of other psychiatric techniques. However, the training of a psychiatrist to a highly specialized consultant level in psychotherapy will take longer and will have to include an adequate personal experience in psychotherapy, either in the individual or group setting. A career in psychotherapy is so emotionally stressful and demanding that personal difficulties are constantly encountered. The need for the training analysis was discovered early in the history of psychoanalysis and is likely to be re-discovered regularly as courses of psychotherapy are organized. The signal difference between the training schemes described so far and those to be considered next lies in the provision of the training analysis. All the *training schemes* in the next section are organized in the private sector, outside the National Health Service and universities.

Psychoanalytic (Freudian) training is the most carefully studied form of psychotherapeutic training, and has provided the model for most other forms of training in 'depth-psychology'. The International Psychoanalytic Association hold regular and frequent conferences on training where the varied experiences of Institutes in North and South America and Europe are shared.

The training in the United Kingdom adheres closely to the classic methods, using both the apprenticeship and scholastic models. Psychoanalytic training confers a high degree of specialized professional skill on the candidate, i.e the use of psychoanalytic theory and technique.

It has already been mentioned that most teachers of psychotherapy in the National Health Service are psychoanalytically trained psychiatrists, who perforce have to adapt their basic psychoanalytic training to a very different setting. Opportunities for joint study of problems and solutions in this field are still very limited and should be greatly increased.

Institute of Psychoanalysis
63 New Cavendish Street, London, W1

The training here is on traditional psychoanalytic lines. Rigorous criteria of selection are operated and the successful applicant is then faced with several (at least four) years of personal analysis five times a week, and at least three, usually four, years of twice-weekly evening seminars and lectures. In the later stages of training, at least two clinic patients have to be treated under supervision on a five times a week basis, often in addition to the normal working day of the candidate. This, therefore, limits selection of trainees to those who either live in or near London, and to those persons from overseas who are able to transfer residence to London for the period of their training.

Although some assistance from training funds is now available, with loans for British students only of up to nine hundred pounds, training remains an expensive and arduous procedure. Training fees for candidates are lower than those charged to the general public but nowadays are at a minimum of four pounds a session. The charges for seminars and lectures are moderate. Supervision fees are charged, often at the same rate as for personal analysis. Grants to accepted candidates are sometimes made from certain private funds. Forty-seven students are in training at present.

The years of high controversy and differences between the Freudian and Kleinian schools of analysis are largely matters of the past. A considerable effort has been made to organize an integrated curriculum acceptable to both sides. The institute has gradually become more flexible and open to feedback from students' comments and the curriculum itself has become more flexible and takes more account of recent developments in psychoanalysis than was the case ten years ago.

Training in child analysis usually follows, but may sometimes be concurrent with adult training. Three cases are treated under supervision, one of each in the age ranges of pre-latency, latency and adolescence.

Society of Analytical Psychology
30 Devonshire Place, London, W1
Again, carefully selected candidates undertake a personal analysis of at least three, and usually four, or five times a week. Four hundred sessions are normally required before a candidate can be considered for the training course. (Candidates should not normally be over the age of fifty at the time of application.) Personal analysis continues usually for at least the period of training, the minimum duration of which is two years.

Two clinic patients are treated under supervision, the patients being seen four or five times weekly. Theoretical training takes place in twice-weekly evening seminars over two years.

The cost of personal analysis is upwards of five guineas a session, that of supervisory sessions is normally four guineas. Under certain conditions the Society is able to guarantee a few bank loans for supervision fees up to two hundred pounds per annum may be available from the Society's training funds. Some fifteen candidates are in training at present.

Adlerian psychotherapy
Although well established in Europe and the USA, at present there is no full training in Adlerian methods available in this country. The Adlerian Society of Great Britain holds seminars and lectures; details from the Secretary, Adlerian Society of Great Britain, 11 Osborne House, 414 Wimbledon Park Road, London, SW19.

British Association of Psychotherapists

48 Montagu Mansions, London, W1

This Association was founded in 1946 and at present (1971), has a total of eighty members. It offers a training programme in psychotherapy which though it is intended to be distinct from a training in psychoanalysis, is psychoanalytically orientated. There are two training streams, Freudian and Jungian. At the present, twenty-three candidates are training in the Freudian scheme and five in the Jungian. Personal analysis is an essential part of the training scheme and lasts a minimum of three and a half years at a frequency of at least three sessions per week. The theoretical part of the course consists of three years of lectures and seminars and there is an optional two-year course in group therapy for candidates who have completed their training in individual psychotherapy.

The Association of Psychotherapists has a number of qualified psychoanalysts and psychoanalytical psychotherapists on its teaching staff. The other staff members are eclectic psychotherapists, many of whom have a long experience of psychotherapy in different settings. Although the Association of Psychotherapists has not yet gained equal recognition with the Institute of Psychoanalysis or the Institute of Analytical Psychology, it is hoped that it will eventually do so on the basis of continuous improvement in the standard of training offered.

Scottish Institute of Human Relations

This recent foundation is the creation of those psychoanalysts living in Scotland, several of whom hold university posts. They offer a 3-year training in psychotherapy that includes personal analysis, seminars and supervision of trainee cases. Persons eligible for training are psychiatrists, psychologists, social workers and nurses. Psychiatrists who have received this training should, it is hoped, be regarded as equipped for posts as Consultant Psychotherapists with the NHS. Personal analysis has to be paid for at current rates but seminars may be paid for by employing authorities. Training in group and family therapy will be added to the course later. (Enquiries to The Secretary, Miss Ann Gray, 35 Morningside Park, Edinburgh EH10 5HD.

Training in group psychotherapy

Group psychotherapy has attracted a great deal of interest and support in recent years. Systematic training in group psychotherapy has, however, not been available. Certain centres, such as the Tavistock Clinic, influenced by the theories of Bion, Sutherland and Ezriel, and the Maudsley Hospital, influenced principally by the theories of Foulkes, have trained a considerable number of registrars, who have in turn been responsible for the building up of group psychotherapeutic facilities throughout the country. Systematic training for doctors, psychologists, and social workers, who are increasingly being involved in group methods of work, has not, however, been available until recently.

Institute of Group Analysis
88 Montagu Mansions, London, W1H 1LF

For the past six years the Institute of Group Analysis has offered an Introductory Course in Group Work. As conducted at present this involves attendance on a half day a week for three terms of ten weeks on a one-year course. The first two terms are divided into a lecture period and a small group period. Though this is not intended directly as a therapeutic experience, it is inevitable that the persons exposed to an unstructured small group obtain a good deal of feedback and insight into their own personal characteristics as evinced in the group situation. The small group experience lasts throughout the three terms of the year, but during the third term the lectures are replaced by a large group experience where all students and staff meet together for ten sessions. The aim here is to try to investigate and become more clear about the phenomena that arise in large group situations. This experience is particularly useful for persons working in therapeutic community situations.

Membership of the course has consisted of psychiatrists, psychologists, social workers, sociologists, probation officers, social scientists and other persons in the helping and allied professions, concerned with group processes. Current fees are eighty pounds and information is available from the Institute of Group Analysis (The Hon. Training Secretary), 88 Montagu Mansions, London, W1H 1LF.

Advanced seminars are available to selected persons who have completed the Introductory Group Course. Topics covered include family and marital work, further theoretical studies and supervision of on-going groups.

A recent innovation has been the introduction of a Qualifying Course in group-analytic psychotherapy. A small number of carefully selected candidates are chosen for a three-year course. This involves attendance at a twice a week therapeutic group, and attendance at theoretical seminars and supervision seminars. Attendance at the groups is paid for at the same rate as that which patients coming for treatment are expected to pay, that is twenty-five pounds a month, three hundred pounds a year, and the charges for lectures and seminars are eighty pounds. On completion of the course the candidate is admitted to Associate Membership of the Institute of Group Analysis. This training is intended as an equivalent in the field of group psychotherapy to the training in psychoanalysis.

Other trainings in group psychotherapy

The Institute of Psychotherapists runs its own internal training scheme for persons who have completed the Association's own training scheme in individual psychotherapy.

The British Association of Social Psychiatry has announced a forthcoming course 'Human Malfunction, Maladjustment and Community Health'. This course consists of lectures followed by training group sessions. The Directors of Studies are Dr Joshua Bierer and Dr Walter Schindler. The fee for the course is a hundred and fifty pounds per annum; enquiries to the British Association of Social Psychiatry, 18 Park Avenue, London, NW11.

General practitioner training in psychotherapy

This is to all extent and purpose identical with the seminar training programme initiated by Balint at the Tavistock Clinic

that has already been mentioned.[10] The programme continues
though the numbers attending in recent years have dropped. A
recent comprehensive review of the training scheme is provided
by Marinker, *Journal of Royal College of General Practitioners*,
1970, 19, 79.[11]

I am certain, however, that if opportunities existed for such
seminars at other centres outside London, this would be a most
welcome and needed addition to the vocational training of the
general practitioner. The National Association for Mental Health
organizes weekend courses for general practitioners in 'family
psychiatry for family doctors' (Director, Dr M. Pines) which
attracts attendances from distant parts of the country and the

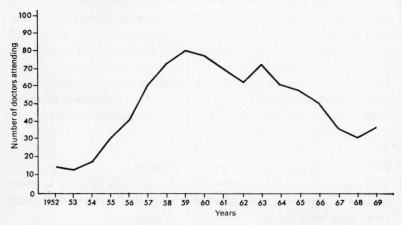

Figure 1. Doctors taking part in the training scheme at the
Tavistock Clinic. (*Graph from the article.*)

constant theme is the need to have such facilities available locally.
A hospital psychiatrist who can only offer hospital-based treatment to the general practitioner's patients is of little help to
him in understanding the problems of a large number of his
emotionally disturbed patients.

The Wessex scheme, already mentioned, devotes a good deal
of time to the study of the doctor/patient relationship in general
practice; the Tavistock Clinic and the Cassel Hospital are at

present reviewing their schemes for general practitioner training; the newly formed Balint Society may be able to initiate its own seminar schemes; all are welcome, all are too few.

Training in psychosexual disorders

An interesting example of how a training network can spread widely throughout the country is provided by the Family Planning Association scheme directed by Dr T. F. Main (Cassel Hospital). Doctors are trained in these techniques by the seminar method and after completion of their own training are able to act as leaders of similar seminars in the provinces. They retain their links with the training scheme by attending special leaders' seminars. Plymouth, Bristol, Cardiff, Birmingham, and other towns are, or have been, drawn into the training network. One seminar, conducted by Dr T. F. Main at the Cassel Hospital, for seminar leaders thereby services the training of something like a hundred and forty doctors who are studying the psychotherapy of psychosexual disorders. This scheme shows how given energy and skills (admittedly out of the ordinary), a network of training seminars can be set up, though as Marinker points out,[11] there are significant differences between the work task of the general practitioner seminar and that of the FPA clinic doctor. A doctor can become familiar more quickly and certainly with the range of psychosexual problems as they present in the clinic than he can in the vast range of problems presented to the general practitioner in his surgery.

At the same time, the FPA is actively considering whether other schemes of training for doctors and co-workers in a therapeutic team can be found which will reduce the amount of time that has been found necessary to train the clinic doctor to the high level of skill required for dealing with the more complicated disorders that present in the clinic. It is hoped that some simpler way of training can be found that will enable larger numbers of clinic staff to deal with the large number of less complex problems that also present at the clinic.

Several interesting publications by general practitioners attest to the value of this training.[12]

Family psychiatry

In recent years it is becoming increasingly appreciated that often treatment of the isolated patient will be less productive than treatment of the family unit. At the very least an understanding of family dynamics may enable treatment of the individual to be set into its correct perspective. Opportunities for training in family psychiatry are still limited. The former Tavistock Clinic's Children's Department has for some years concentrated on this type of approach and registrars and other junior staff who are in in-service training at the Tavistock Clinic naturally receive a training in these methods.

Dr J. G. Howells has developed a provincial centre for treatment and training in family psychiatry at Ipswich. The Institute of Family Psychiatry (23 Henley Road, Ipswich, Suffolk), offers the following courses:

1. Annual introductory seminars in family psychiatry for training psychiatrists, lasting five days.
2. Annual introductory courses in family psychiatry for medical practitioners (special regard being paid to the interests of the general practitioner, the Medical Officer of Health, the School Medical Officer, and the Maternity and Child Welfare Officer). This course is for five days.
3. Annual refresher course for the nursing profession, lasting five days.
4. General course in family psychiatry (extending over two terms, eleven weeks in the Autumn and ten weeks in the Spring), designed for professional workers wishing to receive an introduction to family psychiatry.

The Institute of Group Analysis (88 Montagu Mansions, London, W1) also offers training seminars, conducted by Dr A. C. R. Skynner, in family psychiatry.

Course in family and marital therapy

The recognition that many emotional problems originate from or within the setting of marriage and family life is a major shift in the psychotherapist's approach to his patients. This viewpoint, which dovetails neatly with the group analyst's concept of illness arising and needing to be treated in a network of people, has led to the practice of family and marital therapy by therapists trained in the group analytic approach. In 1973 a training course was started which runs for one year, involves attendance for an afternoon a week for three terms of ten weeks. Lectures and discussions are followed by small groups that utilize role playing and simulated family situations amongst other techniques.

The fees are £96. The Course Director is: Dr A. C. R. Skynner, The Trust for Group Analysis, 1 Bickenhall Mansions, London WiH 3LF.

Training of non-medical child psychotherapists

The training of these workers has reached a remarkable degree of organizational efficiency and agreement. Four institutions are recognized by the Association of Child Psychotherapists (non-medical), as providing an approved training.

These centres are:

1. The Hampstead Child Therapy Course and Clinic, 21 Maresfield Gardens, London, NW3 5SH. Director – Miss Anna Freud.
2. The Institute of Child Psychology, 6 Pembridge Villas, London, NW11. Physician in Charge – Dr Margaret Lowenfeld.
3. The Tavistock Centre (The School of Family Psychiatry and Community Mental Health), Belsize Lane, London, NW3. Organizing Tutor – Mrs Martha Harris, BA.
4. The Society of Analytical Psychology, 30 Devonshire Place, London, W1.

The first training courses in non-medical child psychotherapy were organized by Dr Margaret Lowenfeld in 1933, followed by Miss Anna Freud's Hampstead Child Therapy Course in 1947 and the training course at the Tavistock Clinic was instituted in 1949. In 1951, the Association of Child Psychotherapists (non-medical) was organized and amongst its functions it undertakes that of approving properly constituted training courses, governing selection of candidates for training, and keeping a register of persons whom the Association has recognized as being properly qualified to practise. At present, the Association numbers a hundred and twenty. The Association lays down these qualifications which are considered necessary before an applicant can be accepted for training:

1. A suitable personality for the course.
2. (a) An honours degree in psychology or its recognized equivalent, or
   (b) A university degree not covered in (a) in subjects which include a basic training in psychology or the scientific study of human relations and which the training council shall approve, or
   (c) A university degree and either a post-graduate diploma or higher degree in psychology approved by the training council or a diploma or higher degree in social work, or such further training in the psychological field as the training council shall approve.

Persons who have proved outstanding in allied fields, such as education or the social services, not falling within any of the above categories, may be accepted for training on the recommendation of the training council and the agreement of the executive committee and the medical advisory council of the Association of Child Psychotherapists. Each student is required to undergo a personal analysis with an analyst approved by the training council. *Reference: Bulletin British Psychological Society,* (1970) 23, 303–7. Author – Jess Guthrie, Child Guidance Training Centre, Tavistock Centre, London.

Once again we see that the same situation exists in the training of child psychotherapists as exists in that of adult psychotherapists, that is, the training facilities outside London do not exist.

Training in other forms of psychotherapy

Is it preferable to have too few rather than too many training schemes? In the USA and in some other European countries, trainings are offered in different schools of psychoanalysis: Existential Analysis, Transactional Analysis (Berne), Neo-Freudian Analysis (Horney, Fromm), Sullivanian Analysis (The W. A. White Institute, Washington); Rogerian counselling has found wide acceptance in the USA; Psychodrama (Moreno), is coming of age and developing a systematic communicable training that may yet find roots in this country which so far has proved stony soil.

The shortage of competent psychotherapists is such that well trained persons from all these fields could find acceptance here, especially if they are prepared to work outside London. In the absence of properly trained professionals, we may find a flourishing of ill-trained persons who may partly retard the growth and acceptance of psychotherapy as a much-needed and responsible profession.

Child psychotherapy

The Hampstead Child Therapy Course and Clinic was founded by Miss Anna Freud, who is its Director. It is entirely outside the National Health Service and is supported by privately raised funds which mostly come from the USA. The Clinic has an international reputation for its training of child psychotherapists and for the research activities of its staff. The professional staff are all either psychoanalytically trained or else graduates of the Hampstead Child Therapy Course.

The Clinic is the largest psychotherapeutic clinic in this country outside the National Health Service. In 1970 the professional staff consisted of:

Sixteen part-time psychoanalysts and psychiatrists.
Four residents in psychoanalytic psychiatry.
Two part-time psychologists.
Two part-time social workers.
Ten full-time qualified child therapists.
Thirteen part-time qualified child therapists.

Seventy-four children were referred for consultation; seventy-five children were in analysis (five sessions weekly), nineteen children were in non-intensive treatment, being seen once or twice a week. A number of parents were either in analysis or being seen less frequently. The Clinic also operates preventative and educational services for children such as a nursery school for normal children and a special one for blind children.

Fees – The cost of treatment is related to the financial circumstances of the family. The fees are always kept low (up to a maximum of one pound per session) and the well-to-do are encouraged to seek private treatment.

References

Psychotherapy in the past, present and future
1. ELLENBERGER, HENRY F. *The discovery of the unconscious: the history and evolution of dynamic psychiatry.* Harmondsworth: Allen Lane, The Penguin Press, 1970.

Psychotherapy with the pre-school child
1. FREUD, S. *Fragments of an analysis of a case of hysteria.* Standard Edition, vol. 7, 1905.
2. FREUD, S. *Analysis of a phobia in a five-year old boy.* Standard Edition, vol. 10, 1909.
3. FREUD, A. *The psychoanalytic treatment of children.* London: Imago, 1946.
4. KLEIN M. *The psychoanalysis of children.* London: Hogarth, 1932.
5. KLEIN, M. The psychoanalytic play technique: its history and significance. In *New directions in psychoanalysis.* London: Tavistock, 1955.
6. HARRIS, M. The child psychotherapist and the patient's family. *Journal of Child Psychotherapy,* 2, 2, 1968.
7. HARRIS, M. and CARR, H. Therapeutic consultations. *Journal of Child Psychotherapy,* 1, 4, 1966.
8. SEGAL, H. *Introduction to the work of Melanie Klein.* London: Heinemann, 1964.
9. KLEIN, M. *Our adult world and other essays.* London: Heinemann, 1963.
10. WINNICOTT, D. W. *Playing and reality.* London: Tavistock, 1971.
11. STRACHEY, J. The nature of the therapeutic action in psychoanalysis. *Int. J. Psychoanal,* 15, 1934.
12. KLEIN, M. The origins of transference. *Int. J. Psychoanal,* 33, 1935.

Psychotherapy for the school-aged child – A Margaret Lowenfeld approach

1. LOWENFELD, M. *Play in childhood*. London: Victor Gollancz, 1935. Reprinted 1966 by Cedric Chivers Ltd.
2. GRIFFITHS, R. *Imagination in early childhood*. London: Kegan Paul, 1935.
3. LOWENFELD, M. A new approach to the problems of psychoneurosis in childhood. *Brit. J. Med. Psychol,* part 3, 1931.
4. LOWENFELD, M. The world pictures of children: a method of recording and studying. *Brit. J. Med. Psychol.* XVIII, part 1, 1939.
5. LOWENFELD, M. Psychogenic factors in chronic disease in childhood. *Medical Women's Federation Newsletter,* 1934.
6. STOTT, D. H. An empirical approach to motivation based on the behaviour of a young child. *Journal of Child Psychol. & Psychiat.,* 1961.

Other references

1. International Congress of Psychotherapy, 1954. The structure of transference. *Acta psychotherapeutica.* Supplementum 3, 1955.
2. LOWENFELD, M., TRAILL, M., ROWLES, H. *The non-verbal thinking of children and its place in psychotherapy.* Institute of Child Psychology pamphlet.
3. TRAILL, M. An account of Lowenfeld technique in a child guidance clinic with a survey of therapeutic play techniques to USA. *Journal of Mental Science* XCI, 382, 1945.

Psychotherapy with adolescents

1. HOBSON, R. F. Imagination and amplification in psychotherapy. *Journal of Analytical Psychology,* 16, 1, 95, 1971.
2. JASPERS, K. *The nature of psychotherapy.* Manchester: Manchester University Press, 26, 1963.
3. HOBSON, R. F. *An approach to group analysis in current trends in analytical psychology.* London: Tavistock, 288, 1961.
4. JASPERS, K., *op. cit.,* 27.
5. VARMA, V. P. A psychological study of home, job, friendship and personal problems in late adolescence. Unpublished PhD. thesis, University of London, 1968.
6. ROGERS, D., *The psychology of adolescence.* New York. Appleton-Century-Crofts, 1962.
7. Ibid.
8. HURLOCK, E. B., *Child Development.* New York: McGraw, 1955.
9. WALL, W. D. and VARMA, V. P. *Advances in educational psychology* 1. London: University of London Press Ltd, 1972.

10. PRINGLE, M. L., KELLMER and VARMA, V. P. *Advances in educational psychology* 2. London: University of London Press (In press).
11. JASPERS, K., *op. cit.*, 9.

Psychotherapy with adults
1. RYCROFT, C. *A critical dictionary of psychoanalysis*. London: Nelson, 1968.
2. WING, J. K. and WING, L. Psychotherapy and the National Health Service: an operational study. *British Journal of Psychiatry*, 116, 51–5, 1970.
3. MALAN, D. H. *A study of brief psychotherapy*. London: Tavistock, 1963.

Freud and psychotherapy
1. I have borrowed this argument from the works of Carl Jung, who, surprisingly enough, paid more lip-service to the phenomenon of the 'opposites' than those psychoanalysts who emphasize the importance in mental life of what they call 'ambivalence'. A like comment can be applied to the views of the 'flat earthers' and other observers who take their perceptual assessments as conclusive evidence of their scientific status.

    What is more suprising is the amount of kudos and the reputation for fair-minded virtuosity the eclectic acquires through the simple expedient of sitting on the fence, or, should there be no fence, of turning his back on the yet unsolved problems of medical psychology. Indeed, pursuing this train of thought one is tempted to believe that the title-head assigned to this chapter might well be reversed: that the crucial issue is not so much 'What is Freudian therapy' but 'What, where, how and why is a Freudian a Freudian?'
2. Strictly speaking this can best be achieved by working one's way through Freud's *Collected papers*, preferably in the original German. Those who are not in a position to follow this course should at least read his *Introductory lectures* (1916). His *magnum opus* (*The Interpretation of Dreams, 1900*), although scriptural, is perhaps too advanced for the beginner.

    Fortunately, there are many excellent expositions of its content, in particular those of Ernest Jones, who incidentally in his biography of Freud gives one of the clearest accounts of the progress and content of Freud's more advanced theories. In this connection it is interesting to note that the concepts most vital to psychoanalysis date from about 1900 to 1937. Since Freud's death an enormous literature has made its appearance which for theoretical understanding and clinical application is immensely inferior in quality and accuracy. But no matter; a revolutionary discovery remains revolutionary despite the lapse of time.

3. Should he happen to be a lay aspirant he must produce evidence of training in allied scientific disciplines, in particular a thorough grounding in dynamic anthropology. Officially this condition applies only to those countries where lay qualifications are recognized as a *pis aller*. But, unofficially speaking, every analyst should be a competent anthropologist.

4. Nevertheless even in these more perfectionist and interminable days it is still possible for an unanalysed person to be greeted (in Britain) as a pioneer in modern psychoanalysis.

5. I have often thought that the most idiomatic answer to the taunts of the 'indoctrinationist' critics was anticipated by the diagnostic comment of the ogre in *Jack and the Beanstalk*. In the *argot* of modern psychological controversy this would run 'Fee-fi-foo-fum, I scent the logomachy of an English behaviourist' seeking to defend his vaguely apprehended hostility to the term 'psychology'. How on earth does he think, so like some conventional psychoanalysts, that his teachings are sacrosanct? Chinese or Double Dutch?

6. Needless to say such reviews would involve direct examination, as meticulous as the original diagnostic consultation.

7. It is not difficult to imagine the confusion that would arise if physical examination of brain disorders were confined to, let us say, the inspection of the face or the great toe.

Contributions of Melanie Klein to psychoanalytic technique
1. ABRAHAM, K. The influence of oral erotism on character. Formation in *Selected papers of Karl Abraham*. London: Hogarth Press, 1927.
2. KLEIN, M. The development of a child. In *Contributions to psychoanalysis*. London: Hogarth Press, 1921.
3. KLEIN, M. *Our adult world and its roots in infancy*. Tavistock Pamphlet, 2, 1960.
4. KLEIN, M. On the theory of anxiety and guilt. In *Developments in Psychoanalysis*. London: Hogarth Press, 1948.
5. KLEIN, M. *Envy and gratitude: a study of unconscious sources*. London: Tavistock, 1957.
6. SEGAL, H. *Introduction to the work of Melanie Klein*, London: Heinemann, 1964.

7. ROSENFELD. *Psychotic states: a psychoanalytical approach.* London: Hogarth Press, 1965.

8. SALZBERGER-WITTENBERG, I. *Psychoanalytic insight and relationships: a Kleinian approach.* London: Routledge and Kegan Paul, 1970.

9. KLEIN, M. The Oedipus Complex in the light of early anxieties. In *Contributions to psychoanalysis.* London: Hogarth Press, 378, 1945.

10. KLEIN, M., *The psychoanalysis of children.* London: Hogarth Press, 1932.

11. MIDDLEMORE. *The nursing couple.* London: Hamish Hamilton, 1941.

12. MELTZER, D. *The psychoanalytical process.* London: Heinemann, 1967.

Behavioural therapy

1. ULLMANN, L. P. and KRASNER, L. (Eds). *Case studies in behavior modification.* New York: Holt, Rinehart and Winston, 1965.

2. YATES, A. J. *Behavior Therapy.* New York: Wiley, 1970.

3. EYSENCK, H. J. and RACHMAN, S. *The causes and cures of neurosis.* London: Routledge and Kegan Paul, 1965.

4. MEYER, V. and CHESSER, E. S. *Behaviour therapy in clinical psychiatry.* Harmondsworth: Allan Lane, The Penguin Press, 1970.

5. EYSENCK, H. J., *Fact and fiction in psychology.* Harmondsworth, Penguin, 1965.

6. BANDURA, A. *Principles of behaviour modification.* New York: Holt, Rinehart, Winston, 1969.

7. EYSENCK, H. J. (Ed). *Experiments in behaviour therapy.* Oxford: Pergamon Press, 1964.

8. EYSENCK, H. J. The effects of psychotherapy. *J. Cons. Psychol,* 16, 319–24, 1952.

9. RACHMAN, S. *The effects of psychotherapy.* Oxford: Pergamon Press, 1972.

10. LEVITT, E. E. Results of psychotherapy with children: an evaluation. *J. Consult. Psychol.,* 21, 189–96, 1957.

11. LEVITT, E. E. Psychotherapy with children: a further evaluation. *Behav. Res. Ther.,* 1, 45–51, 1963.

12. LEVITT, E. E. Research on psychotherapy with children. A. E. Bergin, and S. L. Garfield (Eds). *Handbook of psychotherapy and behaviour change: an empirical analysis.* New York: John Wiley, 1971.

13. BEECH, H. R. *Changing man's behaviour.* Harmondsworth: Allen Lane, Penguin Press, 1969.

14. RACHMAN, S. *Phobias: their nature and control.* Springfield, Illinois: Charles C. Thomas, 1968.

15. WOLPE, J. *Psychotherapy by reciprocal inhibition.* Stanford, Calif.: Stanford University Press, 1958.

16. MARKS, I. M. and GELDER, M. G. Transvestism and fetishism: clinical and psychological changes during faradic aversion. *British Journal of Psychiatry*, 113, 711–29, 1967.

17. RACHMAN, S. and TEASDALE, J. *Aversion and behaviour disorders: an analysis.* London: Routledge, 1969.

18. MARKS, I., *Management of sexual disorders*, in H. LEITENBERG (Ed.), *Handbook in behavior modification*, New York: Appleton-Century-Crofts, 1974.

19. FELDMAN, M. P. Aversion therapy for sexual deviations: a critical review. *Psychol. Bull.*, 65, 65–9, 1966.

20. AYLLON. T. and AZRIN, N. H. *The token economy: a motivational system for therapy and rehabilitation.* New York: Appleton-Century-Crofts, 1968.

21. RACHMAN, S., HODGSON, R. and MARZILLIER, J. Treatment of an obsessional-compulsive disorder by modelling. *Behav. Res. Ther.*, 8, 385–92, 1970.

22. YULE, W. and BERGER, M. Behaviour modification principles and speech delay, in M. Rutter and J. A. M. Martin (Eds). *The child with delayed speech.* London: Heinemann Medical and Spastics International Medical Publications, 1972.

23. RACHMAN, S. Learning theory and child psychology: therapeutic possibilities. *J. Child Psychol. Psychiat.*, 3, 149–63, 1962.

24. PATTERSON, G. R. and GULLION, M. E. *Living with children: new methods for parents and teachers.* Champaign, Illinois: Research Press, 1968.

25. RUSSO, S. Adaptations in behaviour therapy with children. *Behav. Res. Ther.*, 2, 43–7, 1964.

26. WHALER, R. G., WINKEL, G. H., PETERSON, R. F. and MORRISON, D. C. Mothers as behaviour therapists for their own children. *Behav. Res., Ther.*, 3, 113–24, 1965.

27. BERGER, M. An introduction to behaviour modification techniques in the classroom. Paper presented to a conference on 'The modification of behaviour' at Trinity College, Dublin, Eire, September, 1969. (To appear in the conference proceedings.)

28. BECKER, W. C., MADSEN, C. H., ARNOLD, C. R. and THOMAS, D. R. The contingent use of teacher attention and praise in reducing classroom behaviour problems. *J. Spec. Education*, 1, 287–307, 1967.

29. LOVITT, T. Behaviour modification: The current scene. *Excep. Children*, 37, 85–91, 1970.

30. RUTTER, M., TIZARD, J. and WHITMORE, K. (Eds). *Education, Health and Behaviour.* London: Longmans, 1970.

31. LARSEN, L. A. and BRICKER, W. A. A manual for parents and

teachers of severely and moderately retarded children. George Peabody College: IMRID papers and reports, 5, 22, 1968.

32. O'CONNOR, R. D. Modification of social withdrawal through symbolic modelling. *J. Appl. Behav. Anal.*, 2, 15–22, 1969.

33. LOVIBOND, S. H. *Conditioning and enuresis.* Oxford: Pergamon Press, 1964.

34. TURNER, R. K. and YOUNG, G. C. C.N.S. stimulant drugs and conditioning treatment of noctural enuresis: a long term follow-up study. *Behav. Res. Ther.*, 4, 225–8, 1966.

Jungian psychotherapy

1. JUNG, CARL. *Collected works.* London: Routledge and Kegan Paul, page 102, vol. 16, 1954.
2. *Collected works.* vol. 16, page 10.
3. *Ibid.*
4. *Op. cit.* page 5.
5. *Op. cit.* page 3.
6. *Op. cit.* page 19.
7. *Op. cit.* page 123.
8. *Op. cit.* page 124.
9. *Op. cit.* pages 101–2.
10. JUNG, EMMA, and VON FRANZ, MARIE-LOUISE. *The grail legend.* London: Hodder and Stoughton, pages 133–4, 1971.
11. *The grail legend, op. cit.,* pages 98–9.
12. *Collected works.* vol. 16, page 135.
13. *Op. cit.* page 136.
14. *Op. cit.* page 71.
15. *Ibid.*
16. *Op. cit.* page 74.
17. *Op. cit.* page 75.
18. *Op. cit.* pages 320–1.

The diagrams on p. 151 are reproduced from J. JACOBI, *The Psychology of Jung.* London: Routledge and Kegan Paul, 1969.

Adlerian therapy

1. BEATTIE, NEIL R. *The position of the child in the family and its significance.* National Society of Children's Nurseries, London, 1971.
2. ADLER, ALFRED. *Der Sinn des Lebens.* Vienna: Dr Rolf Passer, 1933.
3. ADLER, ALFRED. *Studie über die Minderwertigkeit von Organen und ihre seelische Kompensation.* (1 ed.) Vienna: Urban and Schwarzenberg, 1907.

4. ADLER, ALFRED. *Study of organ inferiority and its psychical compensation a contribution to clinical medicine.* New York: Nervous and Mental Publ. Co., 1917.

5. PICKFORD, R. W. Colour vision defective art students. In W. D. Wall and V. P. Varma (Eds). *Advances in educational psychology.* London: University of London Press, 1972.

6. WISEMAN, STEPHEN. Environmental handicap and the teacher. In W. D. Wall and V. P. Varma (Eds). *Advances in educational psychology.* 1. London: University of London Press, 1972.

7. VERNON, P. E. *Intelligence and attainment tests.* London: University of London Press, 1968.

8. VERNON, P. E. *Intelligence and cultural environment.* London: Methuen, 1969.

9. WALL, W. D. *Child of our times.* National Children's Home, Convocation Lectures, vol. 4 Highbury, Bath Chivers, 1966.

10. HOFF, H. and RINGEL. A modern psychosomatic view of the theory of organ inferiority by Alfred Adler. *Advances in psychosomatic medicine.* Basel, New York: I. S. Karger, 1960.

11. SPIEL, OSKAR. Foreword to *Alfred Adler Der Mann und sein Werk Triumph uber den Minderwertigkeitskomplex* by Hertha Orgler. Vienna, Munich: Urban and Schwarzenberg, 1956, 2nd 1972.

12. FRANKL, VIKTOR. The spiritual dimension in existential analysis and logotherapy. *Journal of Individual Psychology,* 15, 1959.

13. FRANKL, VIKTOR. *Theorie und Therapie der Neurosen.* München Basel: Ernst Reinhardt, 1970.

14. ADLER, ALEXANDRA. Present-day Adlerian psychiatric practice. *Journal of Individual Psychology,* 27, 2. Vermont: University of Vermont, 1971.

15. SONSTEGARD, MANFORD. Personal communication. Report, December 1971. Morgantown, USA: Clinical Study Division, West Virginia University.

16. SHOOBS, NAHUM E. (Ed). *Directory of the International Association of Individual Psychology,* 145 Hook St, Brooklyn, New York, 11201, 1971.

17. MEIERS, J. Historian of The American Society of Adlerian Psychology, 601, West, 115th St, New York 10025.

18. ORGLER, HERTHA. *Alfred Adler: The man and his work triumph over the inferiority complex.* London: Sidgwick and Jackson, 1973.

Drug therapy

1. PFEIFFER, C. and MURPHRE, H. B. *Drill's pharmacology in medicine.* New York: McGraw Hill (3rd Edn), ch. 22, 1965.

2. CAFFEY, E. M. *et al.* Drug treatment in psychiatry. *International Journal of Psychiatry*, 9, 428, 1970.

3. KALINOWSKY, L. B. and HILLIUS, H. *Pharmacological, convulsive and other somatic treatments in psychiatry.* (3rd Edn), Grune and Stratton, 1969.

4. SHEPHERD, M. *et al.* Clinical psychopharmacology. *Modern Medicine*, 1968.

5. MCGRATH, S. D. *et al.* The use of reserpine in psychiatry. *Journal of Irish Medical Association*, 39.1, 1956.

6. COLE, J. O. Phenothiazine treatment in acute schizophrenia. *Archives of General Psychiatry*, 10, 246–61, 1964.

7. REES, L. International symposium on Pimozide (Orap). *Clinical Trials Journal.* 8 Supp. 11, 77, 1971.

8. BARO, F. *et al.* Maintenance therapy of chronic psychotic patients with a weekly oral dose of R16,341. *Journal of Clinical Pharmacology*, 10, 330, 1970.

9. LOWTHER, J. The effects of Fluphenazine Enanthate on chronic and relapsing schizophrenia. *British Journal of Psychiatry*, 115, 691–2, 1969.

10. RENTON, C. A. *et al.* A follow-up study of schizophrenic patients in Edinburgh. *Acta Psychiatrica Scandinavica*, 39, 548, 1963.

11. GREENBLATT, D. J. and SHADER, R. I. Mebrobamate, a study of irrational drug use. *American Journal of Psychiatry*, 127, 1297, 1971.

12. DUNLOP, D. Adverse reactions to drugs. *Journal of the Royal College of Surgeons in Ireland*, 5, 88–98, 1970.

13. GIBBONS, J. L. Coppen and Walk (Eds). *Recent developments in affective disorders.* RMPA. Headley Brothers, 1968.

14. EYSENCK, H. J. Classification of depressive illness. *British Journal of Psychiatry*, 117, 241–50, 1970.

15. KILOH, L. G. and BRANDON, D. Habituation and addiction to Amphetamine. *British Medical Journal*, 1, 1225–7, 1962.

16. CONNELL, P. H. *Amphetamine psychosis.* London: Chapman Hall, 1958.

17. MILLICHAP, J. GORDON. Drugs in the management of the hyperkinetic and perceptually handicapped children. *Journal of American Medical Association*, 206, 1527, 1968.

18. PARE, C. M. B. *Recent developments in affective disorders.* RMPA. Headley Brothers, 1968.

19. KUHN, R. Uber die behundlung depressiver zustande mit einem iminodinzlderivat. (22–355). *Schwitz Med. Whchr*, 87.1135.40, 1957.

20. MEDICAL RESEARCH COUNCIL. Clinical trial of the treatment of depressive illness. *British Medical Journal*, 1, 881, 1965.

L*

21. WECHSLER, H. *et al.* Research evaluating antidepressant medications on hospitalized mental patients: a survey of published reports during a five-year period. *Journal Nervous Mental Diseases,* 141, 231, 1965.

22. BENNETT, I. F. Is there a superior antidepressant? In S. Garatini and M. N. G. Dukes (Eds). *Antidepressant drugs,* Exercepta Media Foundation, p. 375, 1967.

23. WEST, E. D. and DALLY, P. J. Effects of Iproniazid in depressive syndromes, *Bristol Medical Journal,* 1, 1491, 1959.

24. KLINE, N. S. *Modern problems in pharmacopsychiatry,* 3. New York: S. Karger, 1969.

25. FROMMER, E. A. Physical methods of treatment in psychiatry. Sargant *et al.* London: Churchill, 1972.

26. WINSTON, F. Combined antidepressant therapy. *British Journal of Psychiatry,* 118, 301, 1971.

27. ANGST, J. Antidepressiver Effekt und Genitsche Faktoren. *Arznei-mittel-Forsch,* 14, 496, 1964.

28. PARE, C. M. B. *et al.* Differentation of two genetically specific types of depression by response to antidepressant drugs. *Lancet,* 11, 1340, 1962.

29. SCHOU, M. *Depressive states in childhood and adolescence.* Stockholm: Almquvist and Wiksell, 1971.

30. COPPEN, A. *et al.* Prophylactic Lithium in affective disorders, a controlled trial. *Lancet,* 11, 275–9, 1971.

31. FISH, B. *Annual progress in child psychiatry and child development.* New York: Brunner, 1969.

32. STACK, JOHN J. *Depressive states in childhood and adolescence.* Stockholm: Almquvist and Wiksell, 1971.

33. *British Medical Journal.* Research in psychiatry. p. 61–2, 1972.

34. KRECH, D. *The anatomy of memory.* Palo Alto, California: Science and Behaviour Books Inc., 1965.

35. CADE, J. F. J. Lithium salts in the treatment of psychotic excitement, *Med. J. Austr.,* 2, 349–52, 1949.

Social therapy

1. AUSTIN, L. N. Trends in differential treatment in social casework. *Journal of Social Casework,* June 1948, 203–11. Quoted by F. Hollis in *Casework: a psychosocial therapy.* New York: Random House, 1964.

2. SARGENT, W. *Proceeding of the conference on post-graduate psychiatric education.* G. F. M. Russell and H. J. Walton (Eds). Kent: Headley Brothers, 1970.

3. BENNET, D. Social therapy and drug treatment in schizophrenics. H. L. Freeman and J. Farndale (Eds). *New Aspects of the Mental Health Service*. Oxford: Pergamon Press, 1967.
4. HUNTER, T. D. Hierarchy or arena? The administrative implication of a sociotherapeutic regime. H. L. Freeman and J. Farndale (Eds). *New Aspects of the Mental Service*. Oxford: Pergamon Press, 1967.
5. JONES, M. The current place of therapeutic communities in psychiatric practices. H. L. Freeman and J. Farndale (Eds). *New Aspects of the Mental Health Service*. Oxford: Pergamon Press, 1967.
6. RUESH, J. Social psychiatry an overview. *Social Psychiatry*. London: Routledge, Kegan and Paul, vol. 1, 1970.
7. TITMUS, R. M. *Essays on the Welfare State*. London: Allen and Unwin, 1958.
8. ETZIONI, A. *Modern organizations*. New Jersey: Prentice Hall, 1964.
9. HMSO. *National Health Service Hospital Advisory Service Annual Report for 1969–70*. Published 1971.

Religious therapy

1. See JUNG, C. J. *Answer to Job, Collected works*, Vol. 11. London: Routledge and Kegan Paul, 1969. Page 360, para 555. And also COX, D. *Jung and St Paul*. London: Longmans, 1959.
2. FREUD, S. *The future of an illusion*. International Psychoanalytic Library no. 15, 1927.
3. JUNG, K. *Modern man in search of a soul*. London: Routledge, 1932.
4. WHITE, V. *God and the Unconscious*. London: Harvill, 1952.
5. JAMES, WILLIAM. The varieties of religious experience. Gifford Lectures: Edinburgh, 1901–2.
6. ROBINSON, J. A. T. (Bishop of Woolwich). *Honest to God*. SRC paperback, 1963.
7. FREUD, S. Autobiography. London: Hogarth Press, 1959, p. 70.
8. MOWRER, O. *The crisis in psychiatry and religion*. New Jersey: Insight Books, Van Nostrand, 1961.
9. FREUD, S. *An autobiographical study*. Standard Ed. London: Hogarth Press, 1959, p. 70.
10. FREUD, S. *Future of an illusion*. Rev. Ed. London: Hogarth Press, 1962, p. 43.
11. *Op. cit.*, p. 33.
12. ACTION OF MENTAL HEALTH. Final Report of the Joint Commission on Mental Illness and Health, 1961.
13. RUMKE, H. C. *The psychology of unbelief*. London: Rockliff, 1952.
14. WHITE, V. *Soul and Psyche*. London: Collins and Harvill, 1960.

15. BRACELAND, J. (Ed). *Faith, reason and modern psychiatry.* New York: Kenedy and Sons, 1955.

Further References

1. ACADEMY OF RELIGION AND MENTAL HEALTH. *Journal of Religion and Health* (Ongoing).
2. ACADEMY OF RELIGION AND MENTAL HEALTH. *Research in religion and mental health,* 1963.
3. FARNSWORTH, L. and BRACELAND, J. Ed. *Psychiatry, the clergy and pastoral counselling.* Collegeville, Minnesota: St John's University Press, 1969.
4. GODIN, A. *The pastor as counsellor.* New York: Holt, Rinehart and Winston, 1965.
5. GROUP FOR THE ADVANCEMENT OF PSYCHIATRY. *The psychic function in illness and mental health,* 1968.
6. HOSTIE, R. *Pastoral counselling.* London: Sheed and Ward, 1966.
7. O'DOHERTY, E. F. *Religion and personality problems.* New York: Alba House, 1964.
8. O'DOHERTY, E. F. and MCGRATH, D. *The priest and mental health.* New York: Alba House, 1963.

Educational therapy

1. MORRIS, J. M. *Reading in the primary school.* London: Newnes, 1959.
2. MORRIS, J. M. *Standards and progress in reading.* Slough: National Foundation for Educational Research, 1966.
3. NEWTON, M. A neuropsychological investigation into dyslexia; CRITCHLEY, M. A neurological approach; VERNON, P. D., Specific developmental dyslexia in FRANKLIN, A. W. and NAIDOO, S. (Eds). *Assessment of teaching of dyslexic children.* Invalid Children's Aid Association, 1970.
4. FROSTIG, M. *Developmental test of visual perception.* Palo Alto, Calif.: Consulting Psychologists Press, 1963.
5. FROSTIG, M. Pictures and patterns. *The Frostig program for the development of visual perception.* Chicago: Follett, 1967.
6. TANSLEY, A. E. *Reading and remedial teaching.* London: Routledge and Kegan Paul, 1967.
7. FRANKLIN, A. W. and NAIDOO, S. *Op. cit.*
8. NAIDOO, S. *Specific dyslexia.* London: Pitman, 1972.
9. STOTT, D. H. *Manual for the programmed reading kit.* Holmes-McDougall Ltd., 1962.
10. MOXON, C. A. V. *A remedial teaching method.* London: Methuen, 1962.

11. DOWNING, JOHN. *An educational theory for i.t.a.* New University, 1969.

12. DAVIS, M. Unpublished treatment notes, 1961.

13. DANIEL, J. C. and DIACK, H. *Progress in reading in the infant school.* Nottingham: The University, Institute of Education, 1960.

Further References

1. CASPARI, I. E. Anxiety about learning in school children. In V. P. Varma (Ed). *Anxiety in school children.* London: Pitman Medical forthcoming.

2. SCHONELL, F. E. *Backwardness in the basic subjects.* London and Edinburgh: Oliver and Boyd, 1948.

3. SCHONNELL, F. E. *Diagnostic and attainment testing.* London and Edinburgh: Oliver and Boyd, 1950.

Group therapy

1. BION, W. *Experiences in groups.* London: Tavistock, 1961.

2. YALOM, I. W. *The theory and practice of group psychotherapy.* London: Basic Books, 1970.

3. EZRIEL, H. A psychoanalytic approach to group treatment. *Brit. J. Med. Psychol.*, 23, 59, 1950.

4. FOULKES, S. H. *Introduction to group analytic psychotherapy.* London: Heinemann, 1948.

5. FOULKES, S. H. *Therapeutic group analysis.* London: Allen and Unwin, 1964.

6. FOULKES, S. H. and ANTHONY, E. J. *Group psychotherapy: the psychoanalytic approach.* Harmondsworth: Penguin Books, 1965.

7. YALOM, I. W. *Op. cit.*

8. MORENO, J. L. *Who shall survive?* New York: Beacon House, 1953.

9. LEBOVICI, S. Psychodrama as applied to adolescents. *J. Child. Psychol. Psychiat.*, 1, 298, 1961.

10. SCHUTZEMBERGER, A. A. *Précis de psychodrame.* Paris: Ed. Universitaires, 1966.

11. SLAVSON, S. R. *An introduction to group therapy.* New York: Commonwealth Fund and Harvard Univ. Press, 1943.

12. SLAVSON, S. R. *Analytic group psychotherapy with children, adolescents and adults.* New York: Columbia, 1950.

13. SLAVSON, S. R. *Child centered group guidance of parents.* New York: Int. Univ. Press., 1958.

14. WOLF, A. and SCHWARZ, E. *Psychoanalysis in groups.* New York: Grune and Stratton, 1962.

15. WHITAKER, D. S. and LIEBERMAN, M. A. *Psychotherapy through the group process.* New York: Atherton Press, 1964.

16. DURKIN, H. *The group in depth.* New York: Int. Univ. Press, 1964.

17. SCHUTZ, W. *Firo: a three dimensional theory of interpersonal behavior.* New York: Rinehart, 1958.

18. SCHUTZ, W. *Joy: expanding human awareness.* New York: Grove Press, 1967.

19. YALOM, I. W. *Op. cit.*

20. GINNOTT, H. *Group psychotherapy with children.* New York: McGraw Hill, 1961.

21. FOULKES, S. H. and ANTHONY, E. J. *Group psychotherapy: the psychoanalytic approach.* Harmondsworth: Penguin Books, 1965.

22. FRANK, M. G. and ZILBACH, J. Current trends in group therapy with children. *Int. J. Group Psychother.*, 18, 447, 1968.

23. SKYNNER, A. C. R. Group therapy with adolescents. *Annual Review of the Residential Child Care Association*, 8, 16, 1970–71.

24. EVANS, J. Inpatient analytic group therapy of neurotic and delinquent adolescents. *Psychosom.*, 13, 265, 1965.

25. KRAFT, I. A. An overview of group therapy with adolescents. *Int. J. Group Psychother.*, 18, 461, 1968.

26. DURKIN, H. Mothers. In S. R. Slavson (Ed). *The fields of group psychotherapy.* New York: Int. Univ. Press, 1956.

27. SLAVSON, S. R. *Child centered group guidance of parents.* New York: Int. Univ. Press, 1958.

28. THOMPSON, S. and KAHN, J. H. *The group process as a helping technique.* Oxford: Pergamon, 1970.

29. SKYNNER, A. C. R. Group methods in treating anxiety in children, in V. P. Varma (Ed). *Anxiety in school children.* London: Pitman. In press.

30. SCHEIDLINGER, S. Group psychotherapy in the sixties. *Am. J. Psychother.*, 22, 1970, 1968.

31. ANTHONY, E. J. Reflections on twenty-five years of group psychotherapy. *Int. J. Group Psychother.*, 18, 277, 1968.

32. PINES, M. Problems of choice in psychotherapy – individual or group. Lecture to Royal Medico-Psychological Association (unpublished), 1970.

33. MAIN, T. F. The hospital as a therapeutic institution. *Bull. Men. Clin.*, 10, 66, 1946.

34. JONES, M. *Social psychiatry.* London: Tavistock, 1952.

35. JONES, M. *Social psychiatry in practice.* Harmondsworth: Penguin Books, 1968.

36. MARTIN, D. V. *Adventure in psychiatry.* London: Cessirer, 1962.

37. CLARK, D. H. *Administrative therapy.* London, Tavistock, 1964.

38. RAPOPORT, R. N. *Community as doctor.* London: Tavistock, 1960.

39. CHRIST, J. Discussion. In M. Jones. A passing glance at the therapeutic community in 1964. *Int. J. Group Psychother.*, 15, 5, 1965.

40. Since this chapter was written a book entitled *The large group: therapy and dynamics*, edited by L. Kreeger and containing a chapter by R. C. Skynner, is in press and will be published in Autumn 1974.

41. SAGER, C. An overview of family therapy. *Int. J. Group Psychotherapy*, 18, 302, 1968. MACGREGOR, R. Group and family therapy: moving into the present and letting go of the past. *Int. J. Group Psychother.*, 20, 495, 1970.

42. BEELS, C. C. and FERBER, A. Family therapy: a view. *Family Process*, 8, 280, 1969.

43. BRADFORD, L. P., GIBB, J. R. and BEUNE, K. D. (Eds). *T-group theory and laboratory method*. New York: Wiley, 1964.

44. LUBIN, B. and EDDY, W. B. The laboratory training model: rationale, method and some thoughts for the future. *Int. J. Group Psychother.*, 20, 305, 1970.

45. PARLOFF, M. B. Group therapy and the small group field: an encounter. *Int. J. Group Psychother.*, 20, 267, 1970.

46. SKYNNER, A. C. R. An encounter with Esalen. *Group Analysis*, 3, 180, 1970.

47. SCHUTZ, W. *Joy, expanding human awareness*. New York: Grove Press, 1967.

48. ERIKSON, E. H. *Childhood and society*. New York: Norton, 1950. Harmondsworth, U.K.: Penguin Books, 1965.

49. SKYNNER, A. C. R. A group-analytic approach to conjoint family therapy. *J. Child. Psychol. Psychiat.*, 10, 81, 1969.

Short-term therapy

1. WINNICOTT, D. W. *The child, the family and the outside world*. Harmondsworth: Penguin Books, 1964.

2. ROGERS, C. R. *Client-centered therapy*. New York: Houghton, Mifflin Co., 1951.

3. ROGERS, C. R. *Psychotherapy and personality change*. Chicago: University of Chicago Press, 1954.

4. WOLBERG, L. *Short-term psychotherapy*. New York: Grune and Stratton (Distributed by Heinemann Medical Books Ltd), 1965.

5. MALAN, D. H. *A study of brief psychotherapy*. London: Social Science Paperbacks, 1963.

Further References

1. BELLAK, L. and SMALL, L. *Emergency psychotherapy and brief psychotherapy.* New York: Grune and Stratton (Distributed by Heinemann Medical Books Ltd.), 1965.
2. COURTENAY, M. *Sexual discord in marriage.* London: Tavistock, 1968.
3. DEWALD, P. A. *Psychotherapy – a dynamic approach.* London: Allen and Unwin, 1964.
4. ELLIS, A. *Reason and emotion in psychotherapy.* New York: Lyle Stuart, 1962.
5. FREUD, S. *The question of lay analysis.* London: Hogarth Press, 1927.
6. HALMOS, P. *The faith of the counsellors.* London: Constable, 1965.
7. PHILLIPS, E. V. and WEINER, D. W. *Short-term psychotherapy and structural change.* New York: McGraw, 1966.
8. SINGER, E. *Key concepts in psychotherapy.* London: Basic Books, 1970.
9. TRUAX, C. B. and CARKHUFF, R. R. *Toward effective counseling and psychotherapy.* Chicago: Aldine, 1967.

Day therapy

1. PINEL, P. *A treatise on insanity.* New York: Hathner Publishing Co., 1806. (Reprinted 1962.)
2. TUKE, S. *Description of the retreat, York.* York: Alexander, 1813.
3. CONOLLY, J. *The treatment of the insane without mechanical restraints.* London: Smith Elder and Co., 1856.
4. BARTON, R. *Institutional neuroses.* Bristol: J. Wright and Sons, 1959.
5. BIERER, J. and EVANS, R. I. *Innovations in social psychiatry.* London: Avenue Publishing Co., 1969.
6. JONES, M. *Social psychiatry in practice.* Harmondsworth: Penguin Books, 1968.
7. CLARK, D. H. and MYERS, K. Themes in a therapeutic community. *Brit. J. Psychiatry,* 117, 389–95, 1970.
8. CLARK, D. H. *Administrative therapy.* London: Tavistock, 1964.
9. CROCKET, R. Authority and permissiveness in the psychotherapeutic community. *Amer. J. Psychother.,* XX, 4, 669–76, 1966.
10. PENNIALL, S. Socio-drama. *Occ. Ther.,* 30, II, 17–21, 1967.
11. PENNIALL, S. Basic music groups for the unmusical occupational therapist. *Occ. Ther.,* 31, 6, 19–22, 1968.
12. MEYER, R. Resistances to occupational therapy. *Occ. Ther.,* 32, 10, 39–42, 1969.
13. MEYER, R., HONIG, P. and LONG, E. A youth club for psychiatric outpatients. *J. Child Psychol. Psychiat.,* 277–85, 1961.
14. DUNDAS, M. H. One to one relationship in the treatment of autistic children. *Acta Paedopsychiat,* 35, 242–5, 1968.

15. CONNELL, P. H. A day hospital for disturbed children. *J. Ment. Sci.*, 107, 969, 1961.
16. FROMMER, E. A. A day hospital for disturbed children. *Lancet*, 377–9, 1967.
17. HMSO. *Non-custodial and semi-custodial penalties.* Report of the Advisory Council on the Penal System. London: Home Office, 1970.
18. FARNDALE, J. *The day hospital in Great Britain.* London: Pergamon Press, 1961.
19. HMSO. *A pilot survey of patients attending day hospitals.* London: Statistical Report Series No. 7, 1969.
20. HERZ, M. I., ENDICOTT, J. and SPITZEN, R. Day hospital versus inpatient hospitalization: a controlled study. *Amer. J. Psychiat.*, 127, 10, 1371–82, 1971.
21. RICHARDS, H. A local authority day centre for the mentally ill. *Lancet*, 7703, I, 793–4, 1971.
22. CAMERON, D. E. The day hospital. In A. E. Bennett (Ed.), *The practice of psychiatry in general hospitals.* Los Angeles: Univ. of California Press, 1956.
23. CRAFT, M. An evaluation of depressive illness in a day hospital. *Lancet*, ii, 149–51, 1958.
24. SMITH, S. and CROSS, E. G. Review of 1,000 patients treated in a psychiatric day hospital. *Int. J. Soc. Psychiatr.*, 2, 292–8, 1957.

Psychotherapy outside the National Health Service

1. BION, W. R. *Experience in groups.* London: Tavistock, 1961.
2. FOULKES, S. H. *Therapeutic group analysis.* London: George Allen and Unwin, 1964.
3. FOULKES, S. H. and ANTHONY, E. J. *Group psychotherapy: the psychoanalytic approach.* Harmondsworth: Penguin Books, 1965.
4. MAIN, T. F. The ailment. *Brit. J. Med. Psychol.*, 30, 3, 121–45, 1957.
5. MAIN, T. F. The hospital as a therapeutic institution. *Bulletin of Menninger Clinic*, 10, 66–70, 1964.

Acknowledgement of written help:
I am grateful for the co-operation of many colleagues who have provided me with information as to the work conducted by their organizations. They have often provided me with much more information than can be included in this article and some which did not fit into the terms of reference has had to be left out altogether.

Training in dynamic aspects of psychotherapy

1. BALINT, MICHAEL and ENID. *Psychotherapeutic techniques in medicine.* London: Tavistock, 1961.

2. BALINT, MICHAEL. *The doctor, his patient, and the illness.* London: Pitman Medical, 1964.

3. HEINE, R., *et al. The student physician as psychotherapist.* Chicago: University of Chicago, 1962.

4. BRITISH MEDICAL STUDENTS' ASSOCIATION. Report on teaching of psychiatry and psychological medicine in British medical schools, 1959.

5. Guidelines for the training of general psychiatrists in psychotherapy. *British Journal of Psychiatry,* 119, 555–9, 1971.

6. MALAN, D. H. *A study of brief psychotherapy.* London: Tavistock, 1963.

7. WOLFF, H. H. Methods of teaching psychotherapy in the training of psychiatrics. *British Journal of Psychiatry,* Special Publication, 5, 1970.

8. FOULKES, S. H. and ANTHONY, E. J. *Group psychotherapy: the psychoanalytic approach.* Penguin Books, 1957.

9. *Clinical tutors in psychiatry.* Watt and Barraclough (Eds), 1970.

10. BALINT, M., *et al. A study of doctors.* London: Tavistock, 1966; *The doctor, his patient and the illness.* London: Pitman Medical, 1964.

11. ROYAL COLLEGE OF GENERAL PRACTITIONERS. *Report on education in psychology and psychiatry.* September, 1967.

12. FRIEDMAN, L. J. *Virgin wives.* London: Tavistock, 1970.
    COURTNEY, M. *Sexual discord in marriage.* London: Tavistock, 1970.
    TUNNADINE, L. P. D. *Contraception and sexual life.* London: Tavistock, 1970.

List of contributors

DR WILLIAM H. ALLCHIN
Consultant Psychiatrist and Psychotherapist, Leigh House Adolescent
Unit; Southampton Child and Family Guidance Clinic.

MISS IRENE E. CASPARI
Principal Psychologist and Organizing Tutor, The Tavistock Clinic,
London.

MRS H. IRENE CHAMPERNOWNE, B.SC., PH.D.
Jungian Analyst, Psychotherapist. Also Child Guidance Clinic,
Cheltenham. Member BPS and SAP.

MRS CASSIE COOPER, B.SC.(PSY.)
Clinical Psychologist and Kleinian Psychotherapist; Marriage
Guidance Counsellor; Student Counsellor, Harrow College of Tech-
nology and Art.

DR EDWARD GLOVER, M.D., LLD. (*Late*)
Hon. Fellow, British Psychological Society; Hon. Member, American
Psychoanalytic Association and of the Swiss Psychoanalytical Society;
Co-founder of the Institute for the Study and Treatment of Delin-
quency and of the former Psychopathic Clinic (now the Portman
Clinic), London.
*Books published: War, sadism and pacifism; The dangers of being human;
Psychoanalysis; The psychology of fear and courage; David Eder: memoirs of
a modern pioneer; Freud or Jung; The technique of psychoanalysis; On the
early development of mind; The roots of crime; The birth of the ego.*

MISS M. ATHOL HUGHES, M.A., PH.D.
Member, British Psychoanalytical Society and the Institute of Psychoanalysis.

DR LIONEL C. KREEGER, M.B., B.S., M.R.C.P., M.R.C.PSYCH., D.P.M.
Associate Member, British Psychoanalytic Society; Member, Group-

Analytic Society; Consultant Psychiatrist, Paddington Clinic and Day Hospital, London.
Books in preparation: An introduction to group treatments (co-author P. de Mare), Butterworths; *The large group: therapy and dynamics* (Ed), Constable.

DR S. DESMOND MCGRATH, F.R.C.P.I., F.R.C.PSYCH., D.P.M.
Medical Director, St John of God Hospital; Lecturer in Psychiatry, University College, Dublin; Consultant Psychiatrist, St Laurence's (Richmond) Hospital, Dublin, Eire.

PROF. JOHN J. MCKENNA, M.A., M.ED., PH.D., F.B.PS.S.
Professor of Psychology, Royal College of Surgeons in Ireland; Lecturer in Psychology, University College, Dublin; Director of Psychology, St John of God Brothers' Child Guidance Service, Dublin, Eire.

DR RICHARD MEYER, M.B., M.R.C.P., D.P.M.
Consultant Psychiatrist, Marlborough Day Hospital; Visiting Psychotherapist, Holloway Prison, London.

GEORGE MOUNTNEY
Lecturer, School of Social Work, Leicester.

THE REV. PROF. EAMONN F. O'DOHERTY, PH.D.(CANTAB.)
Fellow, British Psychological Society; Catholic priest; Professor of Logic and Psychology, University College, Dublin, Eire.
Books published: The priest and mental health (co-author D. J. McGrath); *Religion and personality problems; Vocation, formation, consecration and vows. The religious formation of the elementary schoolchild.* Alba House, N.Y.

MRS HERTHA ORGLER
Adlerian Psychotherapist and Lecturer, co-worker and friend of Alfred Adler.
Books published: Alfred Adler, the man and his work. Sidgwick and Jackson.

DR MALCOM PINES, F.R.C.P., F.R.C.PSYCH., D.P.M.
Associate Member, Institute of Psychoanalysis; Senior Lecturer in Psychotherapy, St George's Hospital; Senior Tutor in Psychotherapy, Institute of Psychiatry; President of Institute of Group-Analysis, London.

MISS DINA ROSENBLUTH, B.A.(HONS.)
Psychoanalyst and Child Psychotherapist. Formerly Tutor at the Child Psychotherapy Course, Tavistock Clinic, London.

DR A. C. ROBIN SKYNNER, M.B., M.R.C.PSYCH., D.P.M.
Senior Tutor in Psychotherapy, Institute of Psychiatry; Honorary Associate Consultant, The Bethlem Royal Hospital and the Maudsley Hospital, London; Honorary Secretary to the Council, Institute of Group Analysis, London.

DR JOHN J. STACK, M.D., F.R.C.PSYCH., D.P.M., D.C.H.
Medical Director, St John of God Brothers' Child Guidance Services, Dublin; Lecturer in Child Psychiatry, University College, Dublin; Consultant Child Psychiatrist: Our Lady's Hospital for Sick Children, Crumlin, Dublin, and at St Joseph's Children's Hospital, Temple Street, Dublin.

MISS PHYLLIS M. TRAILL, M.A.(CANTAB.)
Senior Child Psychotherapist, Institute of Child Psychology, London.

MR WILLIAM YULE, M.A., DIP. PSYCHOL.
Lecturer in Psychology, University of London, Institute of Psychiatry; Staff Psychologist, Children's Department, The Bethlem Royal and Maudsley Hospital, London.

Editor
VED P. VARMA, M.A., LL.B., PH.D., P.G.C.E., F.R.E.CO.S., G.M.B.P.S.
Consultant Psychologist, formerly Educational Psychologist, Child Guidance Service, London Borough of Brent.
Books published: Advances in Educational Psychology I (co-editor, W. D. Wall), *Advances in Educational Psychology II* (co-editor M. L. Kellmer Pringle), *Stresses in children* (Ed), University of London Press.

Index

n = number of reference given at the end of the book.